Tableau 10 Bootcamp

Intensive training for data visualization and dashboarding

Joshua N. Milligan
Donabel Santos

BIRMINGHAM - MUMBAI

Tableau 10 Bootcamp

First published: September 2017

Production reference: 1220917

Published by Packt Publishing Ltd.
Livery Place
35 Livery Street
Birmingham
B3 2PB, UK.
ISBN 978-1-78728-513-2

www.packtpub.com

Credits

Authors
Joshua N. Milligan
Donabel Santos

Commissioning Editor
Veena Pagare

Acquisition Editor
Divya Poojari

Content Development Editor
Trusha Shriyan

Technical Editor
Naveenkumar Jain

Copy Editor
Safis Editing

Project Coordinator
Kinjal Bari

Proofreader
Safis Editing

Indexer
Mariammal Chettiyar

Graphics
Kirk D'Penha

Production Coordinator
Shraddha Falebhai

About the Authors

Joshua N. Milligan has been with Teknion Data Solutions since 2004 and currently serves as a principal consultant. With a strong background in software development and custom .NET solutions, he brings a blend of analytical and creative thinking to BI solutions, data visualization, and data storytelling.

His years of consulting have given him hands on experience in all aspects of the BI development cycle from data modeling, ETL, enterprise deployment, data visualization, and dashboard design. He has worked with clients in numerous industries including financial, energy, healthcare, marketing, government, and services.

Joshua has been named by Tableau as a Tableau Zen Master every year since 2014. This places Joshua in a group of individuals recognized by Tableau as not only masters of the tool but also who have a deep desire to teach and help others. As a Tableau Ambassador, trainer, mentor, and leader in the online Tableau community, Joshua is passionate about helping others gain insights from their data.

He frequently broadcasts webinars to educate and inform the Tableau community and the world at large about the wonders of Tableau and is a much sought after featured speaker at Tableau conferences, user groups, and various technology and industry functions. He thrives on helping others.

Joshua is the author of the first edition of Learning Tableau, which quickly became one of the highest acclaimed Tableau books for users at all levels. He was a technical reviewer of the *Tableau Data Visualization Cookbook, Creating Data Stories with Tableau Public*, and his work has been featured multiple times on Tableau Public's Viz of the Day and Tableau's website. He also shares frequent Tableau tips, tricks, and advice along with a variety of dashboards on his fun and creative blog site, VizPainter. You can follow Joshua on Twitter at `@VizPainter`.

Donabel Santos is a self-confessed data geek. She loves working with data, writing queries, and developing reports on her SQL Server databases, and exploring and visualizing data with Tableau.

She is the principal and senior business intelligence architect at QueryWorks Solutions, a Tableau Learning and Alliance partner in Vancouver, BC, Canada, providing consulting and training services. She has spent years in consulting and has developed a variety of solutions for clients in different verticals—finance, manufacturing, healthcare, legal, higher education, and local government.

Donabel is a multi-year Microsoft Data Platform MVP (previously known as SQL Server MVP) and has extensive experience in the SQL server in different areas, such as development, administration, data warehouse, reporting (SSRS), tuning, troubleshooting, XML, CLR, and integration with ERPs and CRMs using PowerShell, C#, SSIS, and Power BI.

One of Donabel's passions is teaching and sharing her love for data. She is a Tableau Certified Professional and a Tableau accredited trainer, delivering Tableau public and on-site client training. She is also the lead instructor for a number of courses at British Columbia Institute of Technology (BCIT), including Applied Database Administration and Design (ADAD) and Applied Data Analytics (ADA) programs. She teaches SQL server administration, development, integration (SSIS), data warehouse foundations, and visual analytics with Tableau.

Donabel has also authored three other books with Packt: *SQL Server 2012 with PowerShell V3 Cookbook*, *PowerShell for SQL Server Essentials*, and *SQL Server 2014 with PowerShell V5 Cookbook*. She also contributed a chapter to PowerShell Deep Dives by Manning Publications..

www.PacktPub.com

For support files and downloads related to your book, please visit `www.PacktPub.com`. Did you know that Packt offers eBook versions of every book published, with PDF and ePub files available? You can upgrade to the eBook version at `www.PacktPub.com` and as a print book customer, you are entitled to a discount on the eBook copy. Get in touch with us at `service@packtpub.com` for more details. At `www.PacktPub.com`, you can also read a collection of free technical articles, sign up for a range of free newsletters and receive exclusive discounts and offers on Packt books and eBooks.

`https://www.packtpub.com/mapt`

Get the most in-demand software skills with Mapt. Mapt gives you full access to all Packt books and video courses, as well as industry-leading tools to help you plan your personal development and advance your career.

Why subscribe?

- Fully searchable across every book published by Packt
- Copy and paste, print, and bookmark content
- On demand and accessible via a web browser

Customer Feedback

Thanks for purchasing this Packt book. At Packt, quality is at the heart of our editorial process. To help us improve, please leave us an honest review on this book's Amazon page at `https://www.amazon.com/dp/1787285138`.

If you'd like to join our team of regular reviewers, you can e-mail us at `customerreviews@packtpub.com`. We award our regular reviewers with free eBooks and videos in exchange for their valuable feedback. Help us be relentless in improving our products!

Table of Contents

Preface

Tableau is a software package that helps explore, visualize, analyze and make sense of data. It helps us see different kinds of data in a different light. Tableau makes it easy to connect to different kinds of data sets and understand it more, and "see" what kinds of stories we can unearth. It doesn't matter if it's business data, social data, maybe your fitness tracker data or playlist, it is fascinating to see and learn something about our business, our health, our own social network, our world in general.

Tableau's uniqueness comes from Tableau's paradigm. Tableau is different from traditional BI products that force you to select a chart type and then match data to various components of the chart. You won't be confronted with wizards or pre-built dashboards that give you some insight at first but fail to deliver additional insight when you need it.

Instead, Tableau allows for hands-on interaction with data, it's easy to get into a flow of asking questions, uncovering new insights, raising new questions and answers, and finally designing a data story to share with others.

And, Tableau is fun! It allows for creativity and gives freedom to explore, understand, design, and share. Tableau doesn't lock you into a single path to a solution. Tableau designers feel like artists with data as paint and Tableau a blank canvas.

What this book covers

Chapter 1, *Creating Your First Visualization and Dashboard*, will introduce you to the basic concepts of data visualization and see multiple examples of individual visualizations that are ultimately put together in an interactive dashboard.

Chapter 2, *Interactivity*, presents different ways to incorporate interactivity within Tableau charts. Interactivity can keep whoever is consuming your charts to be more be engaged, and encourage them to ask questions, answer questions, and ask more questions without breaking the flow of analysis.

Chapter 3, *Moving from Foundational to More Advanced Visualizations*, expands upon the basic concepts of data visualization to show how to extend standard visualization types.

Chapter 4, *Dashboards and Story Points*, covers how to combine different charts together in dashboards to provide a consolidated view of the data. Story points are also introduced to provide a more effective way to present information catered to specific audiences and message.

Chapter 5, *Data Preparation*, includes ways to help clean, transform or combine data sets to prepare them for data analysis in Tableau. This chapter discusses different data preparation strategies including using the Data Interpreter, pivot, schema.ini as well as comparing operations such as union, join and blend

Chapter 6, *Using Row-Level, Aggregate, and Level of DetailCalculations*, introduces the concepts of calculated fields, the practical use of calculations, and walks through the foundational concepts for creating row level, aggregate, and level of detail calculations.

Chapter 7, *Table Calculations*, breaks down the basics of scope, direction, partitioning, and addressing to help you understand and use them to solve practical problems.

Chapter 8, *Formatting Visualizations to Look Great and Work Well*, Formatting can make a standard visualization look great, have appeal, and communicate well. This chapter introduces and explains the concepts around formatting in Tableau.

Chapter 9, *Advanced Visualizations, Techniques, Tips, and Tricks*,expands your horizons by introducing non-standard visualization types along with numerous advanced techniques while giving practical advice and tips.

Chapter 10, *Sharing Your Data Story*, explores numerous ways of sharing your stories with others because once you've built your visualizations and dashboards; you'll want to share them.

What you need for this book

You will need to install Tableau Desktop V10 to follow the recipes in this book. Tableau Desktop can be downloaded from www.tableau.com. The trial version of Tableau offers a fully functional version for 14 days.

If you are an educator or student using Tableau for your course, please check out **Tableau for Teaching** (TFT). You can find more information from http://www.tableau.com/academic/teaching. This is a great program for educators who want to integrate visual analytics in their courses.

If you are a journalist, Tableau Desktop is free for you:
`https://public.tableau.com/en-us/s/blog/2013/06/journalists-now-tableau-desktop-free-you`.

You can also use Tableau Public, a free version of the software, to complete many of the recipes. Tableau Public has some limitations, however, which may prevent you from following some of the steps. You can find the comparison and limitations of the different Tableau Desktop versions here: `https://public.tableau.com/en-us/s/download`

While this book covers Tableau V10, many of the concepts and steps still apply to other versions, barring some minor changes in steps or interface.

Conventions

In this book, you will find a number of styles of text that distinguish between different kinds of information. Here are some examples of these styles, and an explanation of their meaning.

Code words in text, database table names, folder names, filenames, file extensions, pathnames, dummy URLs, and user input are shown as follows: "We'll create a calculated field named `Floor` to determine if an apartment is upstairs or downstairs."

A block of code is set as follows:

```
IF [Apartment] >= 1 AND [Apartment] <= 3
  THEN "Downstairs"
ELSEIF [Apartment] > 3 AND [Apartment] <= 6
  THEN "Upstairs"
ELSE "Unknown"
END
```

New terms and **important words** are shown in bold. Words that you see in the Tableau interface, such as those in menus, dialog boxes or field names, appear in the text like this: "Drag and drop the **Customer** field to the **Rows** shelf."

 Warnings or important notes appear in a box like this.

Tips and tricks appear like this.

Reader feedback

Feedback from our readers is always welcome. Let us know what you think about this book—what you liked or may have disliked. Reader feedback is important for us to develop titles that you really get the most out of.

To send us general feedback, simply send an e-mail to `feedback@packtpub.com`, and mention the book title via the subject of your message.

If there is a topic that you have expertise in and you are interested in either writing or contributing to a book, see our author guide on`https://www.packtpub.com/books/info/packt/authors`.

Customer support

Now that you are the proud owner of a Packt book, we have a number of things to help you to get the most from your purchase.

Downloading the example code

You can download the example code files for all Packt books you have purchased from your account at `http://www.packtpub.com`. If you purchased this book elsewhere, you can visit `http://www.packtpub.com/support` and register to have the files e-mailed directly to you.

You can download the code files by following these steps:

1. Log in or register to our website using your e-mail address and password.
2. Hover the mouse pointer on the **SUPPORT** tab at the top.
3. Click on **Code Downloads & Errata**.
4. Enter the name of the book in the **Search** box.
5. Select the book for which you're looking to download the code files.
6. Choose from the drop-down menu where you purchased this book from.
7. Click on **Code Download**.

Once the file is downloaded, please make sure that you unzip or extract the folder using the latest version of:

- WinRAR / 7-Zip for Windows
- Zipeg / iZip / UnRarX for Mac
- 7-Zip / PeaZip for Linux

The code bundle for the book is also hosted on GitHub at `https://github.com/PacktPublishing/Tableau-10-Bootcamp`. We also have other code bundles from our rich catalog of books and videos available at `https://github.com/PacktPublishing/`. Check them out!

If you are using **Tableau Public**, you'll need to locate the workbooks that have been published to Tableau Public. These may be found at the following link: `http://goo.gl/wJzfDO`.

Downloading the color images of this book

We also provide you a PDF file that has color images of the screenshots/diagrams used in this book. The color images will help you better understand the changes in the output. You can download this file from:`http://www.packtpub.com/sites/default/files/downloads/Tableau10Bootcamp_ColorImages.pdf`.

Errata

Although we have taken every care to ensure the accuracy of our content, mistakes do happen. If you find a mistake in one of our books—maybe a mistake in the text or the code—we would be grateful if you would report this to us. By doing so, you can save other readers from frustration and help us improve subsequent versions of this book. If you find any errata, please report them by visiting `http://www.packtpub.com/submit-errata`, selecting your book, clicking on the errata submission form link, and entering the details of your errata. Once your errata are verified, your submission will be accepted and the errata will be uploaded on our website, or added to any list of existing errata, under the Errata section of that title. Any existing errata can be viewed by selecting your title from `http://www.packtpub.com/support`.

Piracy

Piracy of copyright material on the Internet is an ongoing problem across all media. At Packt, we take the protection of our copyright and licenses very seriously. If you come across any illegal copies of our works, in any form, on the Internet, please provide us with the location address or website name immediately so that we can pursue a remedy.

Please contact us at `copyright@packtpub.com` with a link to the suspected pirated material.

We appreciate your help in protecting our authors, and our ability to bring you valuable content.

Questions

You can contact us at `questions@packtpub.com` if you are having a problem with any aspect of the book, and we will do our best to address it.

1
Creating Your First Visualization and Dashboard

Tableau is an amazing platform for achieving incredible data discovery, analysis, and storytelling. You can see, understand, and make decisions based on your data, using VizQL—a visual query language that is designed for a natural and seamless flow of thought and work. You do not need to learn VizQL; it's all done behind the scenes without forcing you to write tedious SQL scripts or MDX code, or painstakingly work through numerous wizards to select a chart type and then link everything to data.

Instead, you will be interacting with your data in a visual environment where everything that you drag and drop will be translated into the necessary queries and then displayed visually. You'll be working in real time, so you will see results immediately, get answers as fast as you can ask questions, and be able to iterate through dozens of ways to visualize the data to find a key insight or tell a piece of the story.

Tableau allows you to accomplish numerous tasks, including the following:

- **Data connection, integration, and preparation**: Tableau allows you to connect to data from sources and, if necessary, create a structure that is ready to use. Most of the time, this is as easy as pointing Tableau to a database or opening a file, but Tableau gives you the tools to bring together even complex and messy data from multiple sources.
- **Data exploration**: You can explore a dataset very easily using Tableau in order to understand what data you have visually.
- **Data visualization**: This is the heart of Tableau. You can iterate through the countless ways of visualizing the data to ask and answer questions, raise new questions, and gain new insights.

- **Data analysis**: Tableau has an ever growing set of analytical functions that allow you to dive deep into understanding complex relationships, patterns, and correlations in the data.
- **Data storytelling**: Tableau allows you to build fully interactive dashboards and stories with your visualizations and insights so that you can share the data story with others.

We'll take a look at each of these tasks in the subsequent chapters. In this chapter, we will introduce the foundational principles of Tableau and focus on data visualization. We'll accomplish this through a series of examples that will introduce the basics of connecting to data, exploring and analyzing the data visually, and finally putting it all together in a fully interactive dashboard. These concepts will be developed far more extensively in the subsequent chapters. However, don't skip this chapter as it introduces key terminologies and foundational concepts, including the following:

- Connecting to data
- Foundations for building visualization
- Visualizing the data
- Creating bar charts
- Creating line charts
- Creating geographic visualizations
- Using Show Me
- Bringing everything together in a dashboard

Connecting to data

Tableau connects to data stored in a wide variety of files and databases. These include flat files, such as Excel and text files; relational databases, such as SQL Server and Oracle; cloud based data sources, such as Google Analytics and Amazon Redshift; and OLAP data sources, such as Microsoft Analysis Services. With very few exceptions, the process of building visualizations and performing analysis will be the same no matter what data source you use.

For now, we'll connect to a text file, specifically, a Comma-separated Values file (.csv). The data itself is a variation of the sample data provided with Tableau for Superstore—a fictional retail chain that sells various products to customers across the United States. It's preferable to use the supplied data file instead of the Tableau sample data as the variations will lead to differences in visualizations.

chapter 01 workbooks, included with the code files bundle, already have connections to the file; however, for this example, we'll walk through the steps of creating a connection in a new workbook:

1. Open Tableau to see the home screen with a list of connection options on the left-hand side, thumbnail previews of recently edited workbooks in the center, links to various resources on the right-hand side, and sample workbooks at the bottom.
2. Under **Connect** and **To a file**, click on**Text File**.
3. In the **Open** dialogue box, navigate to the \Learning Tableau\Chapter 01\ directory and select the Superstore.csv file.
4. You will now see the data connection screen, which allows you to visually create connections to data sources. Notice that Tableau has already added and given a preview of the file for the connection:

5. For this connection, no other configuration is required; so, to start visualizing the data, simply click on the **Sheet 1** tab at the bottom! You should now see the main work area within Tableau, which looks similar to the following screenshot:

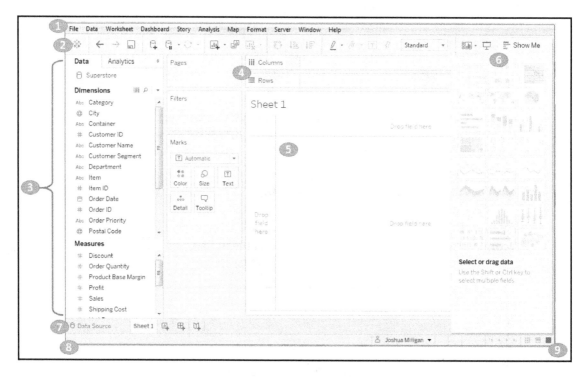

We'll refer to the elements of the interface throughout the book using specific terminology, so take a moment to get familiar with the terms used for the various components numbered in the preceding image:

- The menu contains various menu items for performing a wide range of functions.
- The toolbar allows for common functions, such as undo, redo, save, and add a data source.
- The sidebar contains tabs for **Data** and **Analytics**. When the **Data** tab is active, we'll refer to the sidebar as the data pane. When the **Analytics** tab is active, we'll refer to the sidebar as the analytics pane. We'll go into details regarding this later in this chapter, but for now, note that the data pane shows the data source at the top, contains a list of fields from the data source and is divided into dimensions and measures.

- Various shelves, such as **Columns**, **Rows**, **Pages**, and **Filters**, serve as areas to drag and drop fields from the data pane. The **Marks** card contains additional shelves, such as **Color**, **Size**, **Text**, **Detail**, and **Tooltip**. Tableau will visualize data based on the fields you drop on the shelves.

> Data fields in the data pane are available to be added to the view. Fields that have been dropped on a shelf are called in the viewer active fields because they play an active role in the way Tableau draws the visualization.

- The canvas or view is where Tableau draws data visualization. You may also drop fields directly onto the view. In Tableau 10, you'll observe the seamless title at the top of the canvas. By default, it will display the name of the sheet, but it can be either edited or hidden.
- **Show Me** is a feature that allows you to quickly iterate through various types of visualizations based on data fields of interest. We'll look at **Show Me** toward the end of the chapter.
- The tabs at the bottom of the window give you the option for editing the data source as well as navigating between and adding any number of sheets, dashboards, or stories—these are described as follows. Many times, generically, a tab (whether it is a sheet, dashboard, or story) is referred to as a sheet:

    - **A sheet**: A sheet is a single data visualization (such as a bar chart or line graph). Since sheet is also a generic term for any tab, we'll often refer to a sheet as a view because it is a single view of the data.
    - **A dashboard**: A dashboard is a presentation of any number of related views and other elements (such as text or images) arranged together as a cohesive whole to communicate a message to an audience. Dashboards are often interactive.
    - **A story**: A story is a collection of dashboards or single views arranged to communicate a narrative from the data. Stories can also be interactive.

> A Tableau workbook is the collection of data sources, sheets, dashboards, and stories. All of this is saved as a single Tableau workbook file (.twb or .twbx). We'll look at the differences in file types and explore details of what else is saved as a part of a workbook in later chapters.

- As you work, the status bar will display important information and details about the view and selections.

- Various controls allow you to navigate between sheets, dashboards, and stories as well as view the tabs as a filmstrip or switch to a **Sheet Sorter** showing an interactive thumbnail of all sheets in the workbook.

Now that you have worked through connecting to the data, we'll explore some examples that lay the foundation for data visualization and then move on to building some foundational visualization types. To prepare for this, do the following:

- From the menu, select **File | Exit**.
- When prompted to save changes, select **No**.
- From the \Learning Tableau\Chapter 01 directory, open theChapter 01 Starter.twbxfile. This file contains a connection to the **Superstore** data file and is designed to help you walk through the examples in this chapter.

 The files for each chapter include a **Starter** workbook that allows you to work through the examples given in this book. If at any time, you'd like to see the completed examples, open the **Complete** workbook for the chapter.

With a connection to the data, you are now ready to visualize and analyze the data. As you start doing so, you will take on the role of an analyst at the retail chain. You'll ask questions to the data, build visualizations to answer those questions, and ultimately design a dashboard to share the results. Let's start by laying down some foundations to understand how Tableau visualizes data.

Foundations for building visualizations

When you first connect to a data source, such as the Superstore file, Tableau will display the data connection and the fields in the data pane on the left sidebar. Fields can be dragged from the data pane into the canvas area or onto various shelves, such as **Rows**, **Columns**, **Color**, or **Size**. The placement of the fields will result in different encodings of the data based on the type of field.

Measures and dimensions

The fields from the data source are visible in the data pane and are divided into measures and dimensions. The difference between measures and dimensions is a fundamental concept to understand when using Tableau:

- **Measures**: Measures are values that are aggregated. That is, they can be summed, averaged, counted, or have a minimum or maximum.
- **Dimensions**: Dimensions are values that determine the level of detail at which measures are aggregated. You can think of them as slicing the measures or creating groups into which the measures fit. The combination of dimensions used in the view defines a view's basic level of detail.

Let's consider a view (which you can view in the `Chapter 01 Starter`workbook on the **Measures and Dimensions** sheet) created using the **Region** and **Sales**fieldsfrom the **Superstore** connection, as follows:

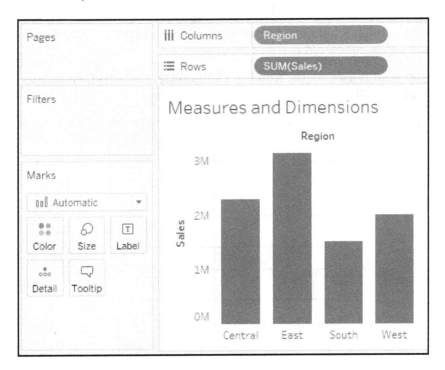

The **Sales** field is used as a measure in this view. Specifically, it is being aggregated as a sum. When you use a field as a measure in the view, the type aggregation (example `SUM`, `MIN`, `MAX`, `AVG`) will be shown in the active field. In the preceding example, the active field on **Rows** clearly indicates the sum aggregation of Sales: **SUM(Sales)**.

The **Region** field is a dimension with one of the four values for each record of data: **Central**, **East**, **South**, or **West**. When the field is used as a dimension in the view, it slices the measure. So, instead of an overall sum of sales, the preceding view shows the sum of sales for each region.

Discrete and continuous

Another important distinction to make with fields is whether a field is being used as discrete or continuous. Whether a field is discrete or continuous, determines how Tableau visualizes it based on where it is used in the view. Tableau will give you a visual indication of the default for a field (the color of the icon in the data pane) and how it is being used in the view (the color of the active field on a shelf). Discrete fields, such as **Region** in the previous example, are blue, and continuous fields, such as **Sales**, are green.

Discrete fields

Discrete (blue) fields have values that are shown as distinct and separate from each other. Discrete values can be reordered and still make sense.

When a discrete field is used on the **Rows** or **Columns** shelves, the field defines headers. Here the discrete field **Region** defines the**Columns** headers:

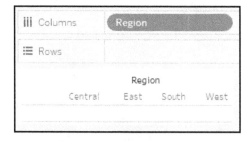

Here, it defines the**Row** headers:

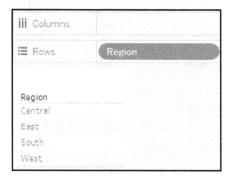

When used for color, a discrete field defines a discrete color palette in which each color aligns with a distinct value for the field:

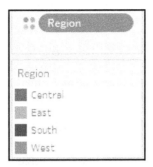

Continuous fields

Continuous (green) fields have values which flow from first to last. Numeric and date fields are often used as continuous fields in the view. The values of these fields have an order changing which would make little sense.

When used on **Rows** or **Columns**, a continuous field defines an axis:

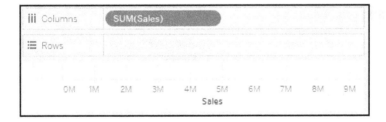

When used for color, a continuous field defines a gradient:

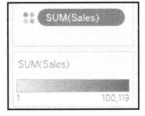

Noting that continuous and discrete are different concepts from measure and dimensionis very important. While most dimensions are discrete by default and most measures are continuous by default, it is possible to use any measure as a discrete field and some dimensions as continuous fields.

 To change the defaults of a field, right-click on the field in the data pane and select **Convert to Discrete** or **Convert to Continuous.**
To change how a field is used in the view, right-click on the field in the view and select it to be either **Discrete** or **Continuous**.

In general, you can decide whether a field is continuous or discrete, using Tableau: how to display the data (header or axis, single colors or gradient) and measure or determine dimensions, using Tableau; and decide how to organize the data (aggregate it or slice/group it).

As you work through the examples in this chapter, pay attention to the fields you are using to create the visualizations, and check whether they are dimensions or measures and whether they are discrete or continuous. Experiment with changing fields in the view from continuous to discrete and vice versa to gain an understanding of the difference in the visualization.

Visualizing data

A new connection to a data source is an invitation to explore. At times, you may come to the data with very well-defined questions and a strong sense of what you expect to find. At other times, you will come to the data with general questions and very little idea of what you will find. The data visualization capabilities of Tableau empower you to rapidly and iteratively explore the data, ask new questions, and make new discoveries.

The following visualization examples cover a few of the most foundational visualization types. Keep in mind that as you work through the examples, the goal is not simply to learn how to create a specific chart; rather, the examples are designed to help you think through the process of asking questions of the data and getting answers through iterations of visualization. Tableau is designed to make that process intuitive, rapid, and transparent. It is far more important to understand how and why to use Tableau to create a bar chart and then adjust your visualization to gain new insights as you ask new questions than memorizing steps to create a bar chart.

Creating bar charts

Bar charts visually represent data in a way that makes comparisons of a value across different categories easy. The length of the bar is the primary means by which you will visually understand the data. You may also incorporate color, size, stacking, and order to communicate additional attributes and values.

Creating bar charts in Tableau is very easy. Simply drag and drop the measure you want to see on either the **Rows** or **Columns** shelf and the dimension that defines the categories onto the opposing **Rows** or **Columns** shelf.

As an analyst for Superstore, you are ready to begin a discovery process focused on sales (especially the dollar value of sales). As you follow the examples, work your way through the sheets in the `Chapter 01 Starter.twbx` workbook. The `Chapter 01 Complete.twbx` workbook also contains the complete example so that you can compare your results at any time:

1. Navigate to the **Sales by Department** sheet (view).
2. Drag and drop the **Sales** field from **Measures** in the data pane to the **Columns** shelf. You now have a bar chart with a single bar representing the sum of sales for all the data in the data source.
3. Drag and drop the **Department** field from **Dimensions** in the data pane to the **Rows** shelf. This slices the data to give you three bars, representing the sum of sales for each department:

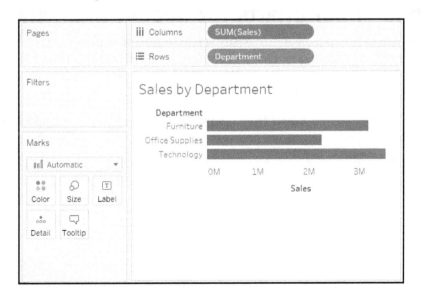

You now have a horizontal bar chart which makes the comparison of sales between the departments easy. Notice how the mark type in the drop-down menu on the **Marks** card is set to **Automatic**, and it indicates that Tableau has determined that bars are the best visualization, given the fields you have placed in the view. As a discrete dimension, the **Department** field defines row headers for each department in the data. As a continuous measure, the **Sales** field defines an axis with the length of the bar extending from 0 to the value of the sum of sales for each department.

Typically, Tableau draws a mark (bar, shape, circle, square, and so on) for every intersection of dimensional values in the view. In this simple case, Tableau is drawing a single bar mark for each dimensional value (Furniture, Office Supplies, and Technology) of the Department. The type of mark is indicated and can be changed in the drop-down menu on the **Marks** card. The number of marks drawn in the view can be observed on the lower-left status bar.

Tableau draws different marks in different ways. For example, bars are drawn from 0 (or the end of the previous bar, if stacked) along the axis. Circles and other shapes are drawn at locations defined by the value(s) of the field defining the axis. Take a moment to experiment with selecting different mark types from the drop down on the **Marks** card. Having an understanding of how Tableau draws different mark types will help you master the tool.

Iterations of bar charts for deeper analysis

Using the preceding bar chart, you can easily see that the **Technology** department has more total sales than either **Furniture** or **Office Supplies**, and **Office Supplies** has lesser total sales compared to any other department. What if you want to further understand sales amounts for departments across various regions?

1. Navigate to the **Bar Chart (two levels)** sheet, where you will find an initial view identical to the one you created previously.

2. Drag the **Region** field from **Dimensions** in the data pane to the **Rows** shelf and drop it to the left of the **Department** field already in the view, as follows:

You still have a horizontal bar chart. But now, you've introduced **Region** as another dimension, which changes the level of detail in the view and further slices the aggregate of the sum of **Sales**. By placing **Region** before **Department**, you will be able to easily compare sales for each department within a given region.

Now you are starting to make some discoveries. For example, the **Technology** department has the most sales in every region, except in the **East** where **Furniture** had higher sales. **Office Supplies** never has the highest sales in any region.

Let's take a look at an alternative view, using the same fields arranged differently:

1. Navigate to the **Bar Chart (stacked)** sheet, where you will find an initial view identical to the one you created previously.

2. Drag the **Region** field from the **Rows** shelf and drop it on the **Color** shelf:

Instead of a side-by-side bar chart, you now have a stacked bar chart. Notice how each segment of the bar is color-coded according to the **Region** field. Additionally, a color legend has been added to the workspace. You haven't changed the level of detail in the view, so sales is still summed for every combination of region and department.

The **Level of Detail** is a key concept when working with Tableau. In the most basic visualizations, the combination of values of all the dimensions in the view defines the lowest level of detail for that view. All measures will be aggregated or sliced by the lowest level of detail. In the case of the most basic views, the number of marks (indicated in the lower-left corner of the status bar) corresponds to the number of intersections of dimensional values.

If **Department** is the only field used as a dimension, you will have a view at the department level of detail and all measures in the view will be aggregated as per the department.

If **Region** is the only field used as a dimension, you will have a view at the region level of detail and all measures in the view will be aggregated as per the region.

If you use both **Department** and **Region** as dimensions in the view, you will have a view at the level of department and region. All measures will be aggregated as per the unique combination of department and region.

Stacked bars are useful when you want to understand part-to-whole relationships. It is now fairly easy to see what portion of the total sales of each department is made in each region. However, it is very difficult to compare sales for most of the regions across departments. For example, can you easily tell which department had the highest sales in the **East** region? It is difficult because, with the exception of **West**, every segment of the bar has a different starting place.

Now, let's take some time to experiment with the bar chart to see what variations you can create:

1. Navigate to the **Bar Chart (experimentation)** sheet.
2. Try dragging the **Region** field from **Color** to the other shelves on the **Marks** card, such as **Size**, **Label**, and **Detail**. Observe that in each case, the bars remain stacked but are redrawn based on the visual encoding defined by the **Region** field.
3. Use the **Swap** button on the toolbar to swap fields on **Rows** and **Columns**. This allows you to very easily change from a horizontal bar chart to a vertical bar chart (and vice versa).

4. Drag and drop **Sales** from the **Measures** section of the data pane on top of the **Region** field on the **Marks** card to replace it. Drag the **Sales** field to **Color** if necessary and notice how the color legend is a gradient for the continuous field.
5. Further, experiment by dragging and dropping other fields on to various shelves. Note the behavior of Tableau for each action you take.
6. From the **File** menu, select **Save**.

At the time of writing this book, Tableau does not have an auto-save feature. You will want to get in the habit of saving the workbook early and then pressing *Ctrl+S* or selecting **Save** from the **File** menu often to avoid losing your work.

Line charts

Line charts connect the related marks in a visualization to show movement or relationship between connected marks. The position of the marks and the lines that connect them are the primary means of communicating the data. Additionally, you can use size and color to visually communicate additional information.

The most common kind of line chart is a time series chart. Time series charts show the movement of values over time. They are very easy to create in Tableau and require only a date and a measure.

Now, continue your analysis of Superstore sales using the Chapter 01 Starterworkbook that you saved earlier. The following are the steps to get the output of theSales over Time graph:

1. Navigate to the **Sales over time** sheet.
2. Drag the **Sales** field from **Measures** to **Rows**to give you a single, vertical bar representing the sum of all the sales in the data source.
3. To turn this into a time series, you must introduce a date. Drag the **Order Date** field from **Dimensions** in the data pane on the left and drop it on **Columns**. Tableau has a built-in date hierarchy and the default level of year has given you a line chart connecting four years. Notice that you can clearly see an increase in sales year after year:

4. Use the drop-down menu of the **YEAR(Order Date)** field on **Columns** (or right-click on the field) and switch the date field to**Quarter**. You may observe that **Quarter** is listed twice in the drop-down menu. We'll explore the various options for date parts, values, and hierarchies in the *Visualizing dates and times* section of Chapter 3, *Moving from Foundational to More Advanced Visualizations*. For now, select the second option:

Notice the cyclic pattern that is quite evident when looking at the sales by quarter:

Iterations offline charts for deeper analysis

Right now, you are looking at the overall sales over time. Let's do some analysis at a slightly deeper level:

1. Navigate to the **Sales over time (overlapping lines)** sheet, where you will find a view identical to the one you just created.
2. Drag the **Region** field from **Dimensions** to **Color**. Now, you have a line per region with each line being a different color and a legend indicating which color is used for which region. As with the bars, adding a dimension to color splits the marks. However, unlike the bars where the segments were stacked, the lines are not stacked. Instead, the lines are drawn at the exact value for the sum of sales for each region and quarter. This allows for easy and accurate comparison. It is interesting to note that the cyclic pattern can be observed for each region, as shown:

With only four regions, it's fairly easy to keep the lines separate. What about dimensions that have more than four or five distinct values? For this, perform the following:

1. Navigate to the **Sales over time (multiple rows)** sheet, where you will find a view identical to the one you just created.

2. Drag the **Category** field from **Dimensions** and drop it directly on top of the **Region** field currently on the **Marks** card. This replaces the **Region** field with **Category**. You now have 17 overlapping lines. Often you'll want to avoid more than 2 to 4 overlapping lines. However, clicking on an item in the color legend will highlight the associated line in the view. Highlighting can be a good way to pick out a single item and compare it with all others.

3. Drag the **Category** field from **Color** on the **Marks** card and drop it on **Rows**. You now have a line chart for each category. Now, you have a way to compare each product over time without overwhelming the overlap function. You can still compare trends and patterns over time. This is the start of a spark-lines visualization.

Creating geographic visualizations

Tableau makes creating geographic visualizations very easy. The built-in geographic database recognizes geographic roles for fields, such as country, state, city, or zip code. Even if your data does not contain latitude and longitude values, you can simply use geographic fields to plot locations on a map. If your data contains latitude and longitude fields, you may use those instead of the generated values.

 Although most databases do not strictly define geographic roles for fields, Tableau will automatically assign geographic roles to the fields based on the field name and a sampling of values in the data. You can assign or re-assign geographic roles to any field by right-clicking on the field in the data pane and using the geographic role option. This is also a good way of seeing what built-in geographic roles are available.

In the following examples, we'll consider some of the foundational concepts of geographic visualizing.

Geographic visualization is incredibly valuable when you need to understand where things happen and if there are any spatial relationships within the data. Tableau offers two basic forms of geographic visualization:

- Filled maps
- Symbol maps

Filled maps

Filled maps, as the name implies, makes use of filled areas, such as country, state, county, or zip code, to show the location. The color which fills the area can be used to encode values of measures or dimensions.

What if you want to understand sales for Superstore and see if there are any patterns geographically? Let's take a look at how you can do this:

1. Navigate to the **Sales by State** sheet.
2. Double-click on the **State** field in the data pane. Tableau automatically creates a geographic visualization using the **Latitude (generated)**, **Longitude (generated)**, and **State** fields.

3. Drag the **Sales** field from the data pane and drop it on the **Color** shelf on the **Marks** card. Based on the fields and shelves you've used, Tableau has switched the automatic mark type to filled maps:

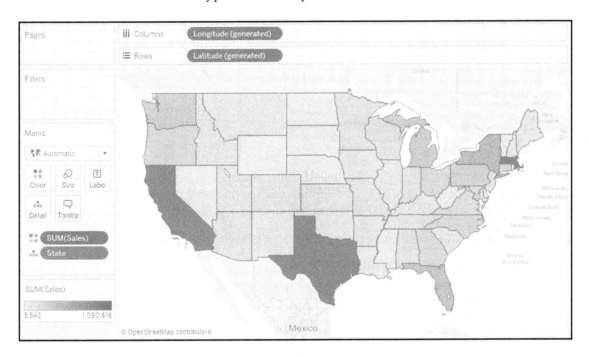

The filled map fills each state with a single color to indicate the relative sum of sales for each state. The color legend, now visible in the view, gives the range of values and indicates that the state with the least sales had a total of $3,543 and the state with the most sales had a total of $1,090,616.

When you look at the number of marks displayed on the status bar on the lower-left side, you'll see that it is 49. Careful examination reveals that the marks consist of the lower 48 states, and Washington DC, Hawaii, and Alaska are not shown. Tableau will only draw a geographic mark, such as a filled state, if it exists in the data and is not excluded by a filter.

Note that the map does display Canada, Mexico, and other locations not included in the data. These are part of a background image retrieved from an online map service. The state marks are then drawn on top of the background image.

Filled maps can work well in interactive dashboards and have quite a bit of aesthetic value. However, certain kinds of analyses are very difficult with filled maps. Unlike other visualization types where size can be used to communicate facets of data, the size of a filled geographic region only relates to the geographic size and can make comparisons difficult. For example, which state has the highest sales? You might be tempted to say Texas or California because they appear larger, but would you have guessed Massachusetts? Some locations may be small enough that they won't even show up compared with larger areas. Use filled maps with caution and consider pairing them with other visualizations on dashboards for clear communication.

Symbol maps

Another standard type of geographic visualization available in Tableau is a symbol map. Marks on this map are shapes or symbols placed at specific geographic locations. Size, color, and shape may also be used to encode additional dimensions and measures.

Let's continue with our analysis of Superstore sales following these steps:

1. Navigate to the **Sales by Postal Code** sheet.
2. Double-click on **Postal Code** under **Dimensions**. Tableau automatically adds Postal Code to the **Detail** of the **Marks** card and **Longitude (generated)** and **Latitude (generated)** to Columns and Rows. The **Mark** type is set to a circle by default and a single circle is drawn for each postal code at the correct latitude and longitude. You may also notice an indicator for the**1 unknown** postal code.
3. Drag **Sales** from **Measures** to the **Size** shelf on the **Marks** card. This causes each circle to be sized according to the sum of sales for that postal code.
4. Drag **Profit** from **Measures** to the **Color** shelf on the **Marks** card. This encodes the mark color to correspond to the sum of profit. You can now see the geographic location of profit and sales at the same time. This is useful because you will see some locations with high sales and low profit that may require some action.

The final view should look like this after making some fine tuned adjustments to size and color detailed:

Sometimes, you'll want to adjust the marks on symbol map to make them more visible. Some of the options are as follows:

- If marks are overlapping, click on the **Color** shelf and set transparency to somewhere between 50% and 75%. Additionally, add a dark border. This makes the marks stand out and you can often discern any overlapping marks much better.
- If marks are too small, click on the **Size** shelf and adjust the slider. You can also double-click on the Size value legend and edit the details of how Tableau assigns size.
- If marks are too faint, double-click on the **Color** legend and edit the details of how Tableau assigns color. This is especially useful when you are using a continuous field that defines a color gradient.

A combination of tweaking the size and using **Stepped Color** and **Use Full Color Range**, as shown here, produced the final result for this example:

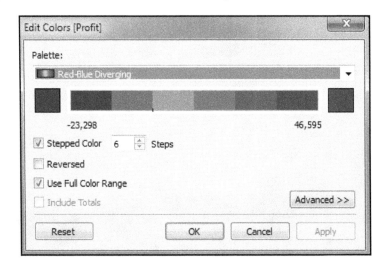

Unlike filled maps, symbol maps allow you to use size to visually encode aspects of the data. Symbol maps also allow for greater precision. In fact, if you have latitude and longitude in your data, you can very precisely plot marks at a street address level of detail. This type of visualization allows you to map locations that do not have clearly defined boundaries. Notice that if you were to change the mark type from **Automatic to Filled Map** in the preceding view, you would get an error message indicating that filled maps are not supported at the level of detail in the view.

Using Show Me

Show Me is a powerful component of Tableau, which is used to arrange selected and active fields into the arrangement required for the selected visualization type. The **Show Me** toolbar displays small thumbnail images of different types of visualizations, thus allowing you to create visualizations with a single click. Based on the fields you select in the data pane and the fields which are already in the view, **Show Me** will enable possible visualizations and highlight a recommended visualization. Let's explore the features of **Show Me** using these steps:

1. Navigate to the **Show Me** sheet.
2. If the **Show Me** pane is not expanded, click on the **Show Me** button in the upper-right corner of the toolbar to expand the pane.

3. Press and hold the *Ctrl* key while clicking on the **Postal Code**, **State**, and **Profit** fields in the data pane to select each of those fields. With those fields highlighted, **Show Me** should look similar to this screenshot:

Notice that the **Show Me** window has enabled certain visualization types such as text tables, heat maps, symbol maps, filled maps, and bar charts. These are the visualizations that are possible, given the fields are already in the view in addition to any selected in the data pane. **Show Me** highlights the recommended visualization for the selected fields and also gives a description of what fields are required as you hover over each visualization type. Symbol maps, for example, require one geographic dimension and up to two measures.

Other visualizations are grayed out, such as line charts and histograms. **Show Me** will not create these visualization types with the fields that are currently in the view and selected in the data pane. Hover over the grayed out line charts in **Show Me**. **Show Me** indicates that line charts require one or more measures, which you have selected, but also require a date field, which you have not selected.

Tableau will actually draw line charts with fields other than dates. **Show Me** gives you options for what is typically considered a good practice for visualizations. However, there may be times when you know a line chart would accurately show your data. Understanding how Tableau renders visualizations based on fields and shelves instead of always relying on **Show Me** will give you a much greater flexibility in your visualizations and will allow you to rearrange things when **Show Me** doesn't give the exact results you want. At the same time, you will need to cultivate an awareness of good visualization practices.

Show Me can be a powerful way to quickly iterate through different visualization types as you search for insights into the data. But as a data explorer, analyst, and storyteller, you should consider **Show Me** as a helpful guide giving suggestions. You may know that a certain visualization type will answer your questions more effectively than the suggestions of **Show Me**. You may also have a plan for a visualization type that will work well as part of a dashboard, but isn't even included in **Show Me**.

You will be well on your way to learning and mastering Tableau when you can use **Show Me** effectively, but feel just as comfortable building visualizations without it. **Show Me** is powerful for quickly iterating through visualizations as you look for insights and raise new questions. It is a wonderful teaching and learning tool useful for starting with a standard visualization that you can further customize.

Be careful not to use it as a crutch without understanding how visualizations are actually built from the data. Take time to evaluate why certain visualizations are or are not possible. Pause to see what fields and shelves were used when you selected a certain visualization type.

Conclude the **Show Me** example by experimenting with **Show Me** by clicking on various visualization types, looking for insights into the data that may be more or less obvious based on the visualization type. Circle views and box and whisker plots show the distribution of postal codes for each state. Bar charts easily expose several postal codes with negative profit.

Bringing everything together in a dashboard

Dashboards are often interactive and allow end users to explore different facets of the data. Tableau makes it very easy to use multiple visualizations together on a dashboard. In Tableau, a dashboard is a collection of views, filters, parameters, images, and other objects that work together to communicate a data story.

Dashboards serve as a wide variety of purposes and can be tailored for a wide variety of audiences. Consider the following possible dashboards:

- A summary level view of profit and sales to allow executives to have a quick glimpse into the current status of the company
- An interactive dashboard allowing sales managers to drill into sales territories to identify threats or opportunities
- A dashboard allowing doctors to track patient re-admissions, diagnosis, and procedures in order to make better decisions about patient care
- A dashboard allowing executives of a real-estate company to identify trends and make decisions for various apartment complexes
- An interactive dashboard for loan officers to make lending decisions based on portfolios broken down by credit ratings and geographic location

Let's take a look at an example that introduces the foundational concepts:

1. Navigate to the **Superstore Sales** sheet, which is a blank dashboard. The sidebar on the left now shows options for building a dashboard instead of the data pane that was visible in the worksheet:

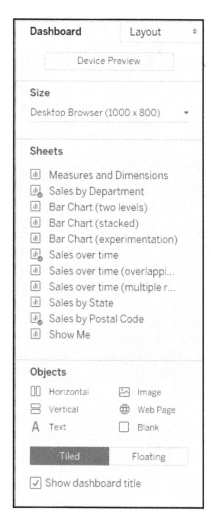

The dashboard window consists of several key components. The left sidebar contains two tabs:

- A **Dashboard** tab for sizing options, and adding sheets and objects to the dashboard
- A **Layout** tab for adjusting the layout of various objects on the dashboard

The **Dashboard** pane contains options for previewing based on target device, sizing options, and a list of all visible sheets (views) in the dashboard. You can add these sheets to a dashboard by dragging and dropping. As you drag the view, a light gray shading will indicate the location of the sheet in the dashboard once it is dropped. You can also double-click on any sheet and it will be added automatically.

The next section lists multiple additional objects that can be added to the dashboard. **Horizontal** and **Vertical** layout containers will give you finer control over the layout, and text allows you to add text labels and titles. **Images** and even embedded web content can be added. Finally, a **Blank** object allows you to preserve blank space in a dashboard or can serve as a place holder.

You cantoggle toselect whether new objects will be added as **Tiled** or **Floating**. **Tiled** objects will snap into a tiled layout next to other tiled objects or within layout containers. Floating objects will float on top of the dashboard in successive layers.

Building your dashboard

Now, let's build a dashboard:

1. Successively, double-click on each sheet listed in the **Dashboard** section on the left: **Sales by Department**, **Sales over time**, and **Sales by Postal Code**. Notice that double-clicking on the object adds it to the layout of the dashboard.

When a worksheet is first added to a dashboard, any legends, filters, or parameters that were visible in the worksheet view will be added to the dashboard. If you wish to add them in at a later point, select the sheet in the dashboard and click on the little drop-down caret in the upper-right corner. Nearly every object has a drop-down caret providing many options for fine tuning the appearance and controlling the behavior. Take note of the various UI elements that become visible for selected objects on the dashboard, as shown here:

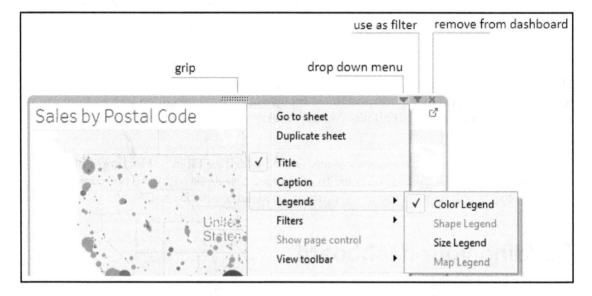

2. Add a title to the dashboard by checking **Show Title** in the lower-left corner of the sidebar. Make sure that nothing is selected in the dashboard (such as a view or legend), otherwise the **Show Title** checkbox will likely apply to the selection. If necessary, click in a gray area off the dashboard or a blank area in the left sidebar to clear any objects selections. You may edit the title by double-clicking on it.

3. Select the **Sales by Department** sheet in the dashboard and click on the drop-down caret in the upper-right corner. Go to**Fit | Entire View**. The fit options describe how the visualization should fill any available space.

Be careful when using various fit options. If you are using a dashboard with a size that has not been fixed or if your view dynamically changes the number of items displayed based on interactivity, then what might have once looked good might not fit the view nearly as well.

4. Select the **Sales** size legend by clicking on it. Use the remove UI element to remove the legend from the dashboard.

5. Select the **Profit** color legend by clicking on it. Use the grip to drag the legend and place it under the map.

6. For each view, **Sales by Department**, **Sales by Postal Code**, and **Sales over time**, select the view by clicking in an empty area in the view. Then click on the **Use as Filter** UI element to make that view an interactive filter for the dashboard. Your dashboard should look similar to this:

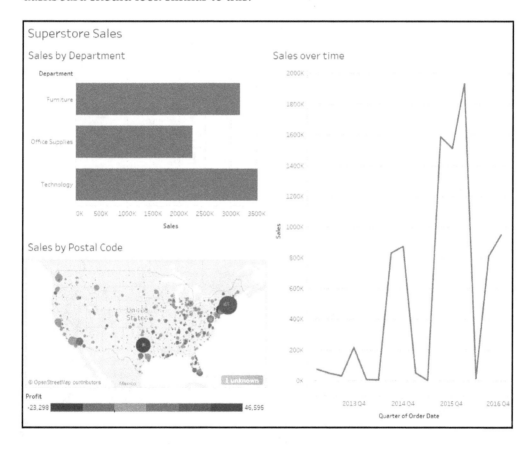

7. Take a moment to interact with your dashboard. Click on the various marks, such as the bars, states, and points of the line. Notice that each selection filters the rest of the dashboard. Clicking on a selected mark will deselect it and clear the filter. Notice that selecting marks in multiple views cause filters to work together. For example, selecting the bar for **Furniture** in **Sales by Department** and **2016 Q4** in **Sales over time,** allows you to see all the postal codes that had furniture sales in the first quarter of 2016:

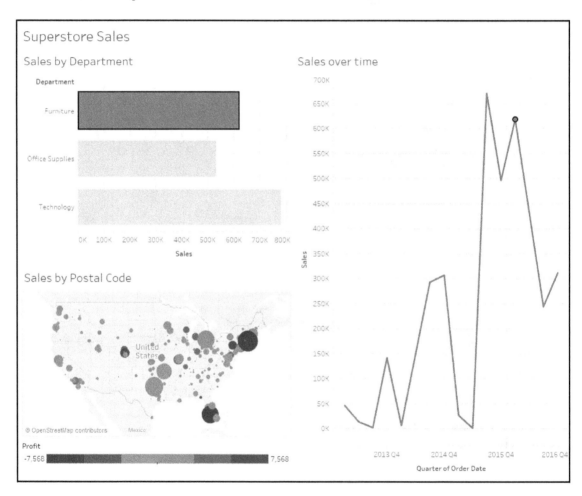

You have now created a dashboard that allows for interactive analysis. As an analyst for the Superstore chain, your visualizations allowed you to explore and analyze the data. The dashboard you created can be shared with the management as a tool to help them see and understand the data in order to make better decisions. When a manager selects the Furniture department, it immediately becomes obvious that there are locations where sales are quite high, but profit is actually a loss. This may lead to decisions such as a change in marketing or a new sales focus for that location. Most likely it will require additional analyses to determine the best course of action. In that case, Tableau will empower you to continue the cycle of discovery, analysis, and storytelling.

Summary

Tableau's visual environment allows for a rapid and iterative process of exploring and analyzing data visually. You've taken your first steps in understanding how to use the platform. You connected to data and then, explored and analyzed it using some foundational visualization types such as bar charts, line charts, and geographic visualizations. Along the way, you focused on learning the techniques and understanding key concepts such as the difference between measures and dimensions, and discrete and continuous fields. Finally, you put all the pieces together to create a fully functional dashboard that allows an end user to understand your analysis and make discoveries of their own.

In the next chapter, we will add a few more interactive components to our views. Interactivity in Tableau can be achieved in many different ways using filters, parameters, and calculated fields to give the users of our dashboards more control over what is being shown in the charts.

2
Interactivity

Tableau shows you various ways to experiment with visualization through interactivity. Interactivity in Tableau encourages the users to ask more questions, find solutions to these questions, and even pique their curiosity into what more the viz can offer.

Tableau provides us various ways to achieve interactivity. In this chapter, we will explore interactivity in more detail by adding a few interactive components to our views. We will use filters, parameters, and calculated fields that will allow the users of our dashboards to control what is shown in the charts.

This chapter will cover the following topics:

- Creating a motion chart
- Creating a dynamic column/row trellis chart
- Creating a top/bottom N filter
- Comparing one to everything else
- Dynamically displaying dimensions
- Dynamically displaying and sorting measures

Creating a motion chart

A motion chart, as its name suggests, is a chart that displays the entire trail of changes in data over time by showing movement using the X and Y-axes.

It is very much similar to the doodles in our notebooks which seem to come to life after flipping through the pages. It is amazing to see the same kind of movement in action in Tableau using the **Pages**shelf. It is work that feels like play. On the **Pages** shelf, when you drop a field, Tableau creates a sequence of pages that filters the view for each value in that field.

Tableau's page control allows us to flip pages, enabling us to see our view come to life. With three predefined speed settings, we can control the speed of the flip. The three settings include one that relates to the slowest speed, the others to the fastest speed. We can also format the marks and show the marks or trails, or both, using page control.

In our viz, we have used a circle for marking each year. The circle that moves to a new position each year represents the specific country's new population value. These circles are all connected by trail lines that enable us to simulate a moving time series graph by setting the mark and trail histories both to show in page control:

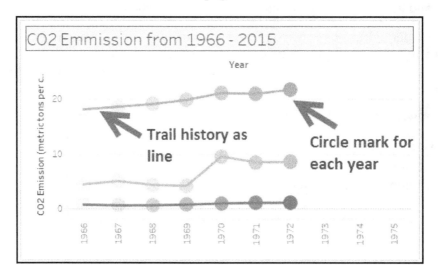

Let's create an animated motion chart showing the population change over the years for a selected few countries:

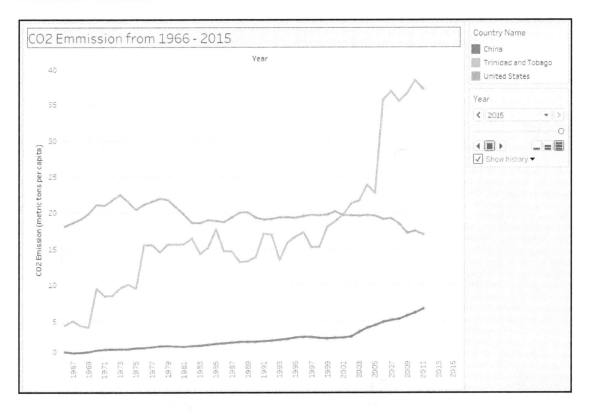

1. Open the `Motion Chart` worksheet and connect to the `CO2 (Worldbank)` data source:

2. Open **Dimensions** and drag **Year** to the **Columns** shelf.
3. Open **Measures** and drag **CO2 Emission** to the **Rows** shelf.

4. Right-click on the **CO2 Emission** axis, and change the title to **CO2 Emission (metric tons per capita)**:

5. In the **Marks** card, click on the dropdown to change the mark from **Automatic** to **Circle**.
6. Open **Dimensions** and drag **Country Name** to **Color** in the **Marks** card.
7. Also, drag **Country Name** to the **Filter** shelf from Dimensions
8. Under the **General** tab of the **Filter** window, while the **Select from list** radio button is selected, select **None**.

9. Select the **Custom value list** radio button, still under the **General** tab, and add **China**, **Trinidad and Tobago**, and **United States**:

10. Click **OK** when done. This should close the **Filter** window.
11. Open **Dimensions** and drag **Year** to **Pages** for adding a page control to the view.
12. Click on the **Show history** checkbox to select it.

13. Click on the drop-down beside **Show history** and perform the following steps:

Select **All** for **Marks to show history for**
Select **Both** for **Show**

14. Using the **Year** page control, click on the forward arrow to play. This shows the change in the population of the three selected countries over the years.

In case you ever want to loopback the animation, you can click on the dropdown on the top-right of your page control card, and select **Loop Playback**:

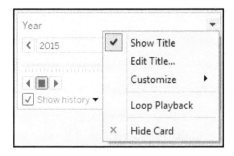

Note that Tableau Server does not support the animation effect that you see when working with motion charts using Tableau Desktop. Tableau strives for zero footprint when serving the charts and dashboards on the server so that there is no additional download to enable the functionalities. So, the play control does not work the same. No need to fret though. You can click manually on the slider and have a similar effect.

Creating a dynamic column/row trellis chart

A **trellis chart, also known as a** panel chart or grid chart, is a small multiple chart composed of multiple similar, small charts that allow for easier adjacent comparison of the items being visualized.

We will add a parameter to a typical small multiple that will allow the consumer of the view to decide or experiment with the number of adjacent columns that would be most effective for the data analysis.

Note that by default, a chart becomes a small multiple when sliced into discrete dimensions. By adding at least one discrete dimension to the **Columns** shelf, and another to the **Rows** shelf, we can create a small multiple with columns and rows.

To display small charts with the use of a specific number of columns and rows, we can introduce a discrete dimension in **Columns** and then, calculate how many rows will result based on the number of columns. The discrete dimension in **Columns** is based on what the user enters in the # of Columns parameter.

The following formula is used for the calculated field called Columns:

```
Columns                          Population (WDI 1966-2016)

IIF([Index]%[# of Columns]==0,
    [# of Columns],
    [Index]%[# of Columns]
  )
```

To create a trellis chart with a # of Columns parameter value, we need to technically assign each small graph a number. This is achieved by using the INDEX() function used in the Index calculated field. This assigns a sequential number to each value specified in the Compute Using. This formula then takes the index assigned to each country and checks for the modulo based on the parameter value. The modulo operator is the %, and this operator finds the remainder after dividing the number by another number.

To visualize this, let's assume that the # of Columns parameter value is 4. The corresponding values are as follows:

Country	INDEX()	INDEX() % 4	Column	Row
Afghanistan	1	1	1	
Albania	2	2	2	
Algeria	3	3	3	
American Samoa	4	0	4	
Andorra	5	1	1	
Angola	6	2	2	

The number of rows are indirectly defined by the number of columns. The country's Index value is divided by the # of Columns parameter value based on which row number a country would be placed. This row number is placed by the Rows calculated field:

```
Rows                        ☐ Population (WDI 1966-2016)

(INT((([Index]-1)/[# of Columns])) + 1
```

The resulting row values are as follows:

Country	INDEX()	(INDEX()-1) / 4	((INDEX()-1) / 4) + 1	Column	Row
Afghanistan	1	0	1	1	1
Albania	2	0	1	2	1
Algeria	3	0	1	3	1
American Samoa	4	0	1	4	1
Andorra	5	1	2	1	2
Angola	6	1	2	2	2

The dynamic column/row trellis chart is really just a play on modulo and integer division. To confirm, when we plug in 4 as our parameter, our chart looks like this, with the headers for **Rows** and **Columns** turned on:

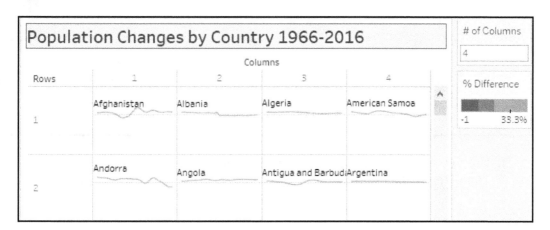

Let's create a parameter for our trellis chart that will help us adjust the number of columns and, indirectly, rows:

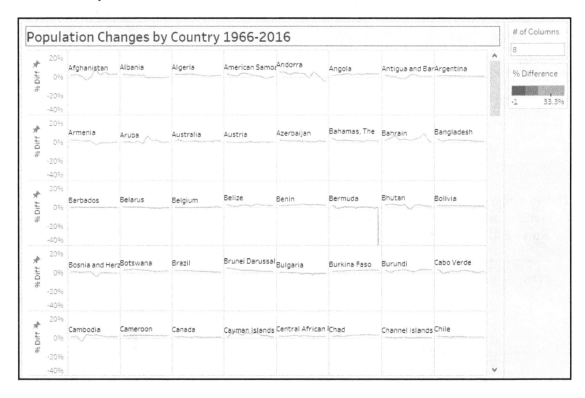

1. Use the worksheet called **Trellis**, and connect to the `Population (WDI 1966-2016)` data source:

2. Open **Dimensions** and drag **Year** to the **Columns** shelf.
3. Right-click on the **Year** pill in the **Columns** shelf, and select **Continuous**.
4. Open **Measures** and drag **Population** to the **Rows** shelf.

5. Right-click on the **SUM(Population)** pill in the **Rows** shelf, and under **Quick Table Calculation**, select **Percent Difference**:

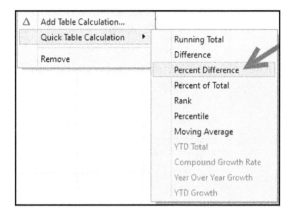

6. Control drag the **SUM(Population)** pill in your **Rows** shelf to the **Color** shelf.
7. Right-click on the color legend and choose **Edit Colors**. Check **Stepped Color**, and enter 4 as the value for **Steps**:

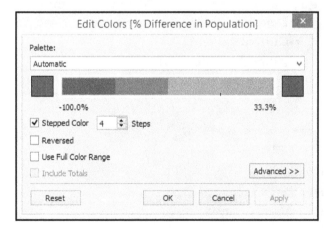

8. Right-click on the color legend and choose **Edit Title**. Change the color legend title to % Difference.
9. Open **Dimensions** and drag **Country Name** to **Label** in the **Marks** shelf.

10. Right-click on the arrow beside the**Dimensions** section in the sidebar, and select **Create Parameter**:

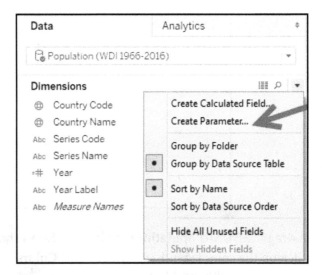

11. Create a parameter called `# of Columns` with the following settings:
    - **Data type: Integer**
    - **Current value**: 8
    - **Allowable values: All**

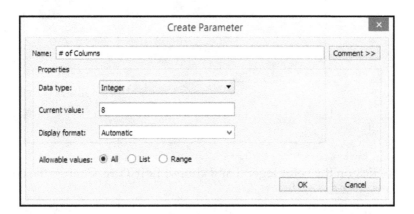

12. Show the parameter control for **# of Columns**. You can do this by right-clicking on the parameter, and selecting **Show Parameter Control**:

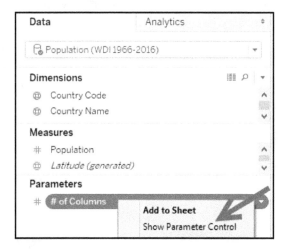

13. Create a calculated field called `Index`, with the following formula:

```
INDEX()
```

14. Create a calculated field called `Columns`, with the following formula:

```
IIF([Index]%[# of Columns]==0,
    [# of Columns],
    [Index]%[# of Columns]
    )
```

15. Create a calculated field called `Rows`, with the following formula:

```
(INT((([Index]-1)/[# of Columns])) + 1
```

16. Open **Measures** and drag the calculated field **Columns** to the **Columns** shelf, to the left of **Year**.

17. Right-click on the **Columns** pill in the **Columns** shelf, and select **Compute Using** and then **Country Name**:

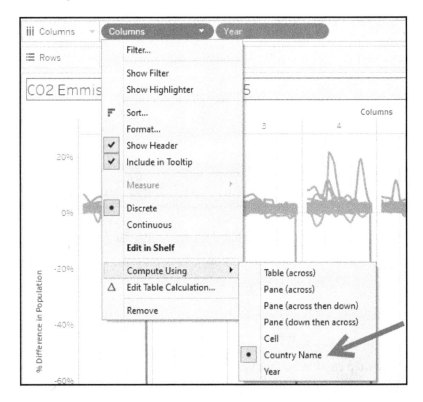

18. Change the **Columns** pill to discrete by right-clicking on this pill, and selecting **Discrete**.

19. Open **Measures** and drag the calculated field **Rows** to the **Rows** shelf, to the left of **SUM(Population)**.

20. Right-click on the **Rows** pill in the **Rows** shelf, and select **Compute Using |** **Country Name**.

21. Change the **Rows** pill to discrete by right-clicking on this pill, and selecting **Discrete**.

22. Click on **Label** in the **Marks** card, and use the following settings:
    - **Marks to Label: Line Ends**
    - **Options: Allow labels to overlap other marks**
    - **Options: Label start of line**
    - **Alignment: Custom**

23. Right-click on the **Columns** heading and choose **Hide Field Labels for Columns**:

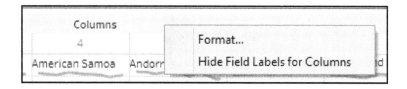

24. Right-click on the **Rows** pill in the **Rows** shelf and uncheck **Show Header**.
25. Right-click on the **Year** pill in the **Columns** shelf and uncheck **Show Header**.
26. Right-click on the % **Difference in Population** axis and:
    - Change the **Title** to `$ Diff`

- Change **Range** to **Fixed**, starting at -0.4

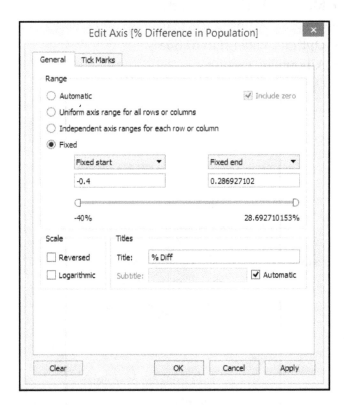

27. Go to the **Format** menu, and choose **Lines**. This will show a formatting sidebar.
28. Under the tabs **Sheet**, **Rows**, and **Columns**, set the **Grid Lines** to **None**. Close the formatting sidebar when done.
29. Test the parameter. Change the column size and confirm that the chart adjusts the number of columns shown.

Creating a top/bottom N filter

By creating a top/bottom N filter, we allow the end users to select whether they want to display the top *N* countries (that is, countries with the most CO2 emissions) or bottom *N* countries (that is, countries with the least CO2 emissions). To do this, we need to use a parameter that determines if they went to the top or bottom.

To ascertain which countries belong to the top or bottom, we use the **Rank** table calculation function. We determine whether the rank sorting is in ascending or descending order using the **Country CO2 Rank** calculated field. If we select Top,SUM([CO2 Emission]) is sorted in descending order (that is, the most first) and if we select Bottom,SUM([CO2 Emission]) itis sorted in ascending order (that is, the least first):

```
Country CO2 Rank            ⬒ CO2 (Worldbank)

IF [Top or Bottom?] = "Top"
THEN RANK(SUM([CO2 Emission]), 'desc')
ELSEIF [Top or Bottom?] = "Bottom"
THEN RANK(SUM([CO2 Emission]),'asc')
END
```

Placing the Country CO2 Rank calculated field with the rank calculation as a discrete field between Year and Country Name is an important step to make sure that the ranking works. This can thus limit the scope per year, letting us reset the ranking for each year.

 Note that we cannot place a green (or continuous) pill between two blue (discrete) pills, so this field also needs to be discrete.

We have also reused the Country CO2 Rank pill in the Rows shelf. We can easily change which years are to be shown on the chart by copying it to our Filter shelf.

Since the pill is discrete, by default when we copy it, the pill shows all the values as check boxes:

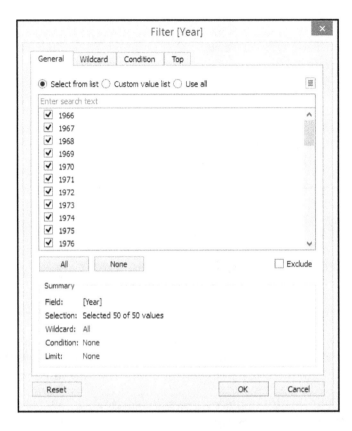

Leaving the **Year** filter as **Discrete** is quite tedious and annoying, having to check or uncheck each box every time the year range needs to change. Hence, we change this copied field to **Continuous** as the **Discrete** field is not very user friendly.

Copying pills with table calculations around, and changing some of them to discrete and perhaps changing some of them back to continuous is a pretty common trick. We change the fields as we need them. If you need to make changes, you need to remember you may need to change them in the other copies because when you copy, that pill becomes another pill that is no longer connected to the original.

Let's create a bar chart that can display the top *N* or bottom *N* countries based on CO2 emissions, a **world development indicator** (**WDI**) tracked by the World Bank:

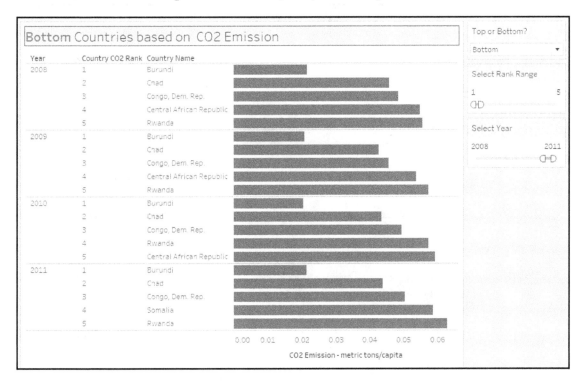

Use the worksheet called `Top N Bottom N`, and connect to the `CO2 (Worldbank)` data source:

1. Open **Dimensions** and drag the **Year** to the **Rows** shelf.
2. Also, drag **Country Name** to the **Rows** shelf, to the right of the **Year** pill.
3. Open **Measures** and drag **CO2 Emission** to the **Columns** shelf.
4. Right-click the arrow beside the **Dimensions** section in the side bar, and select **Create Parameter**.

5. Create a string parameter called `Top or Bottom?` with the following settings:

6. Show the parameter control for `Top or Bottom?`. You can do this by right-clicking on the parameter, and selecting **Show Parameter Control**.

7. Create a calculated field called `Country CO2 Rank`, with the following formula:

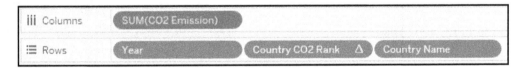

```
Country CO2 Rank                    □ CO2 (Worldbank)

IF [Top or Bottom?] = "Top"
THEN RANK(SUM([CO2 Emission]), 'desc')
ELSEIF [Top or Bottom?] = "Bottom"
THEN RANK(SUM([CO2 Emission]),'asc')
END
```

8. Drag the new calculated field **Country CO2 Rank** to the **Rows** shelf. By default, since this is a continuous field, it can only be placed to the right of **Country Name** and will produce an axis.
9. Right-click on the **Country CO2 Rank** in the **Rows** shelf and select **Discrete**. This will change the pill color from green to blue.
10. Move the discrete **Country CO2 Rank** pill and place it between **Year** and **Country Name**. Your Rows and Columns shelves should now look as follows:

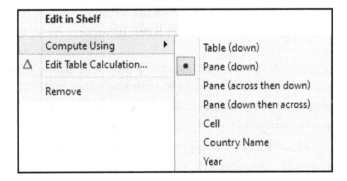

11. Right-click on the **Country CO2 Rank** pill, and change the **Compute Using |Pane (down)**:

12. Control drag the blue **Country CO2 Rank** in the **Rows** shelf to the **Filters** shelf to copy this pill.

13. Click on **OK** to accept the defaults in the **Filters** window that appears. This leaves all the countries selected by default.
14. Right-click on the **Country CO2 Rank** pill in the **Filters** shelf and select **Continuous**.
15. Change the range in the window that appears to show 1 to 5:

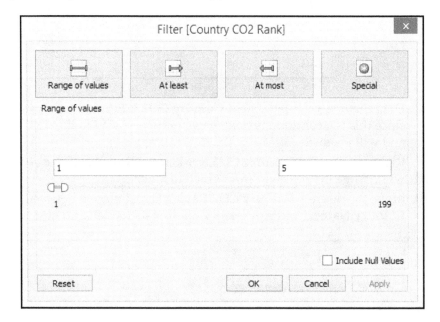

16. After you click **OK**, notice that the color of the **Country CO2 Rank** pill in the **Filters** card changes from blue to green.
17. Right-click on the **Country CO2 Rank** filter and select **Show Filter**.
18. Right-click on the **Country CO2 Rank** filter, and select **Edit Title**. Change the title to Rank.
19. Control and drag the **Year** from the **Rows** shelf to the **Filters** shelf to create a copy of it. Accept all the defaults in the filter window that comes up.
20. Right-click on the **Year** pill in the **Filters** shelf and select **Continuous**.
21. Change the range in the window that appears to show 2008 to 2011.
22. Right-click on the **Year** filter and select **Show Filter**.
23. Edit the **CO2 Emission** axis. Change the title to CO2 Emission - metric tons/capita.

24. Test the `Top or Bottom?` parameter. Check that when you select **Top**, the graph shows the highest emitting countries. When you select **Bottom**, the graph should show the least emitting countries.

Comparing one to everything else

We can compare one item against all other items in a chart or vizin Tableau, thanks to the addition of LOD expressions starting in V9.

LOD expressions

LOD expressions were introduced in Tableau V9. They simplify what used to be complicated calculations before their introduction. If we did not have access to LODs, the problem we solved might have required a blend, or a sub-query to the data source.

The syntax for LOD expressions is as follows:

```
{[FIXED | INCLUDE | EXCLUDE] <dimension declaration > : <aggregate
expression>}
```

While powerful, one of the limitations of LOD expressions is that the dimension declaration must be a persistent field. We can overcome it, but this requires creating additional fields that may be used only within the LOD expression.

Tableau V10 now allows expressions to be used instead of dimension field names. So, for example, if you wanted to fix sales per year, you can simply use the YEAR function in your LOD expression:

```
{ FIXED YEAR([Order Date]):SUM([Sales])}
```

LOD expressions are useful and efficient in many scenarios. If you're new to LOD expressions, or looking to understand them better, I encourage you to check out the following resources:

- Top 15 LOD expressions (http://bit.ly/top15LOD)
- Understanding level of detail expressions (http://bit.ly/UnderstandingLOD)

Let's create a bar chart that shows how much more or less athletes earned compared to a selected athlete:

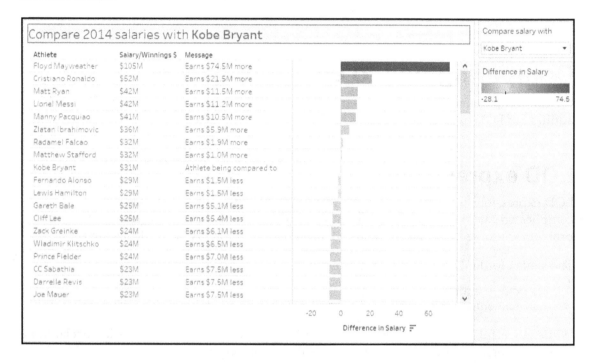

Use the worksheet called `Compare one against everything else` and connect to the `Top Athlete Salaries (Global Sport Finances)` data source:

1. Right-click the arrow beside the **Dimensions** section in the sidebar, and select **Create Parameter**.

2. Create a string parameter called `Compare salary with` the following settings:

3. Click on the **Add from Field** button, and choose the data source **Top Athlete Salaries (Global Sport Finances)**, and then select **Athlete**:

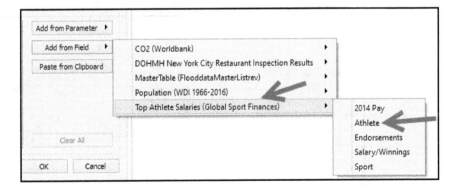

4. Click on **OK** when done.
5. Show the parameter control for **Compare salary with**. You can do this by right-clicking on the parameter, and selecting **Show Parameter Control**.

6. Create a calculated field called **Selected Athlete Salary**, which uses the following **LOD** (**Level of Detail**) expression:

```
Selected Athlete Salary                    Top Athlete Salaries (Global Sport Finances)

//this is a fixed LOD expression
{
    SUM(
        IF [Athlete] = [Compare salary with]
        THEN [Salary/Winnings $]
        ELSE 0
        END
    )
}
```

7. Create another calculated field called `Difference in Salary`, which uses the following formula:

```
Difference in Salary                    Top Athlete Salaries (Global Sport Finances)

SUM([Salary/Winnings $]) - SUM([Selected Athlete Salary])
```

8. Create one more calculated field called `Message`, which determines what string message to display depending on the calculated salary difference. The formula is as follows:

```
Message                    Top Athlete Salaries (Global Sport Finances)

IF [Difference in Salary] < 0
THEN "Earns $" +
    STR(ROUND(ABS([Difference in Salary]),1))  + "M less"
ELSEIF [Difference in Salary] > 0
THEN "Earns $" +
    STR(ROUND(ABS([Difference in Salary]),1)) + "M more"
ELSEIF [Difference in Salary] = 0
        AND ATTR([Athlete]) = [Compare salary with]
THEN "Athlete being compared to"
ELSEIF [Difference in Salary] = 0
        AND ATTR([Athlete]) = [Compare salary with]
THEN "Earns the same"
ELSEIF ISNULL([Difference in Salary])
THEN "N/A"
END
```

9. From **Dimensions**, drag **Athlete** to the **Rows** shelf.
10. From **Measures**, drag **Salary/Winnings $** to the **Rows** shelf, to the right of **Athlete**.
11. Right-click on the **SUM(Salary/Winnings $)** pill in the **Rows** shelf, and select **Discrete** to show this as a text column beside **Athlete**.
12. From **Measures**, drag **Message** to the **Rows** shelf, to the right of **SUM(Salary/Winnings $)**.
13. From **Measures**, drag **Difference in Salary** to the **Columns** shelf. This should produce a bar chart.
14. This is what you should now have in your **Rows** and **Columns** shelves:

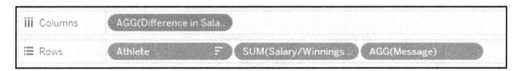

15. From **Measures**, drag **Difference in Salary** to **Color** in the **Marks** card.
16. Right-click on the **Athlete** pill in the **Rows** shelf, and select **Sort**.
17. Sort the **Athlete** field in **Descending** order, using the **Difference in Salary** field:

18. Click **OK** when done.
19. Test the parameter. Select different athletes and confirm that the bars and message are adjusted based on the difference between the selected athlete's salary compared to everyone else in the list.

Now, let's compare how much more or less athletes make compared to one athlete we select. This calculation may seem simple but is quite tricky taking into account how Tableau works. In Tableau, by default, the grain (or granularity) of measures depends on the dimensions that are present in the view. So, for example, the granularity of the following measure **SUM(Salary/Winnings $)** in the **Columns** shelf is per **Sport**:

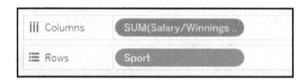

We can further slice **SUM(Salary/Winnings $)** by adding another dimension. In the following example, it means that the measure is now by **Sport** and by **Athlete**:

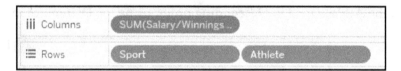

By default, the data fields used in any of the cards and shelves affects the level of detail presented in a Tableau chart. We can make the level of detail different from what is in the canvas using LOD expressions.

Let us start by attempting to display the salary differences between the selected athlete in the Compare salary with parameter and the rest of the athletes using a simple SUM formula:

```
Selected Athlete Salary Non LOD        Top Athlete Salaries (Global Sport Finances)

SUM
(
  IF [Athlete] = [Compare salary with]
  THEN [Salary/Winnings $]
  ELSE 0
  END
)
```

When we select **Kobe Bryant**, we can only view his salary. The salary for the rest of them appears to be zero. This is because when we use the non-LOD calculated field, we are not able to compare his salary with other athletes. This will result in incorrect salary differences:

Athlete	Salary/Winnings $	Selected Athlete Salary Non LOD
Floyd Mayweather	$105M	0
Cristiano Ronaldo	$52M	0
Matt Ryan	$42M	0
Lionel Messi	$42M	0
Manny Pacquiao	$41M	0
Zlatan Ibrahimovic	$36M	0
Radamel Falcao	$32M	0
Matthew Stafford	$32M	0
Kobe Bryant	$31M	30.5
Fernando Alonso	$29M	0
Lewis Hamilton	$29M	0

The solution to this is to use a FIXED LOD expression to keep this number static. Just use the previous formula and enclose it in curly braces:

The syntax for LOD expressions is as follows:

```
{[FIXED | INCLUDE | EXCLUDE] <dimension declaration > : <aggregate
expression>}
```

We can omit the `FIXED` by not keeping the LOD expression fixed to any specific dimensions. On applying this to our view, we can see that Kobe Bryant's salary is persisted for each row:

Compare 2014 salaries with **Kobe Bryant**			
Athlete	Salary/Winnings $	Selected Athlete Salary Non LOD	Selected Athlete Salary LOD
Floyd Mayweather	$105M	0	30.5
Cristiano Ronaldo	$52M	0	30.5
Matt Ryan	$42M	0	30.5
Lionel Messi	$42M	0	30.5
Manny Pacquiao	$41M	0	30.5
Zlatan Ibrahimovic	$36M	0	30.5
Radamel Falcao	$32M	0	30.5
Matthew Stafford	$32M	0	30.5
Kobe Bryant	$31M	30.5	30.5
Fernando Alonso	$29M	0	30.5
Lewis Hamilton	$29M	0	30.5

This makes calculating the difference easier because the calculated field with LOD expression maintains the chosen athlete's salary:

The reason behind enclosing the `Selected Athlete Salary` calculated field in `SUM` when it is already a `SUM` is because as far as Tableau is concerned, an LOD expression is still a non-aggregated field. If we tried using this without an aggregation and subtracting this from an aggregated expression, we would get the classic error of mixing aggregate and non-aggregate fields:

Simply enclose the field with the LOD expression in an aggregated function, such as SUM, MIN, or MAX. The SUM, MIN, or MAX of one value is still that value, so it will not affect the calculation and it allows us to get around the mixed aggregation error.

We also created another calculated field for a text message displaying as a column. This calculated field, called Message, uses several IF...ELSEIF statements to see if the salary difference is more, less, or equal, and composes the appropriate string message to be displayed:

```
Message                          Top Athlete Salaries (Global Sport Finances)

IF [Difference in Salary] < 0
THEN "Earns $" +
     STR(ROUND(ABS([Difference in Salary]),1))  + "M less"
ELSEIF [Difference in Salary] > 0
THEN "Earns $" +
     STR(ROUND(ABS([Difference in Salary]),1)) + "M more"
ELSEIF [Difference in Salary] = 0
        AND ATTR([Athlete]) = [Compare salary with]
THEN "Athlete being compared to"
ELSEIF [Difference in Salary] = 0
        AND ATTR([Athlete]) = [Compare salary with]
THEN "Earns the same"
ELSEIF ISNULL([Difference in Salary])
THEN "N/A"
END
```

Dynamically displaying dimensions

Normally, when we create our charts, we choose the dimensions and measures to display and place them on the appropriate shelves or cards.

For example, if we wanted to show flood damage by **Country**, our **Rows** and **Columns** shelves would look like this:

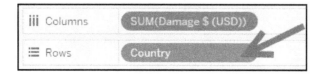

If we wanted to show it by **Main Flood Cause**, we would replace the **Country** pill in the **Rows** shelf with **Main Flood Cause**:

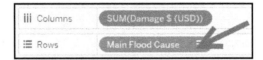

We will introduce a parameter so that our end users can decide which dimension they want used in the **Rows** shelf. The parameter called `Dimension to Display` elicits the choice from our end users. Once the choice is made, a calculated field identifies which dimension should be used:

```
Selected Dimension                          MasterTable (FicoddataMasterListrev)

CASE [Dimension to Display]
     WHEN "Country"
     THEN [Country]
     WHEN "Main Flood Cause"
     THEN [Main Flood Cause]
     WHEN "Register #"
     THEN STR([Register #])
END
```

This calculated field needs to replace the dimension pill we have in the **Rows** shelf:

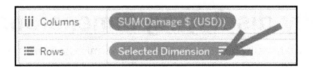

With dimension changes due to the parameter choice changes, what is being displayed can now be dynamic, with the calculated field **Selected Dimension** in place.

Let's explore how to display different dimensions in the same graph using a parameter and calculated field:

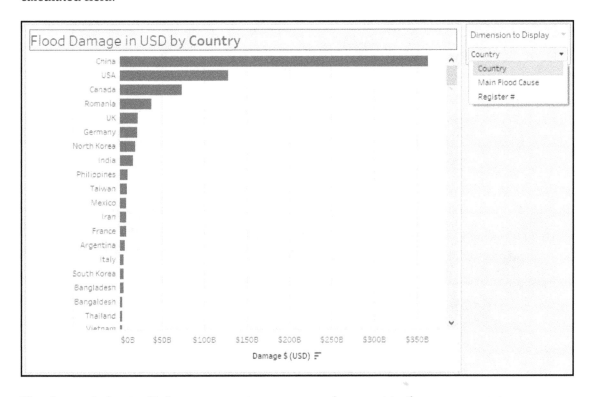

Use the worksheet called `Dynamic Dimension,` and connect to the `MasterTable` `(FlooddataMasterListrev)` data source:

1. Right-click the arrow beside the **Dimensions** section in the sidebar, and select **Create Parameter**.

2. Create a string parameter called `Dimension to Display` with the following settings:

3. Show the parameter control for `Dimension to Display`. You can do this by right-clicking on the parameter, and selecting **Show Parameter Control**.

4. Create a calculated field called `Selected Dimension`, with the following formula:

```
CASE [Dimension to Display]
    WHEN "Country"
    THEN [Country]
    WHEN "Main Flood Cause"
    THEN [Main Flood Cause]
    WHEN "Register #"
    THEN STR([Register #])
END
```

5. From **Dimensions**, drag the calculated field **Selected Dimension** to the **Rows** shelf:

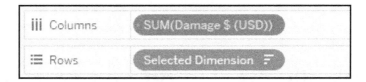

6. From **Measures**, drag **Damage $ (USD)** to the **Columns** shelf.
7. Right-click on the **SUM(Damage $ (USD))** pill in the **Columns** shelf, and select **Format**.
8. In the side bar, change the **Numbers** in the **Scale** section, and select **Currency (Custom)** with the following additional settings:
   - Zero (0) decimal places
   - **Units** in **Billions (B)**

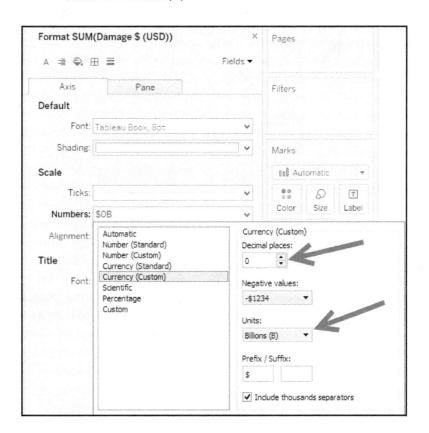

9. Hover your mouse pointer over the **Damage $ (USD)** axis and click the sort icon once to sort the bars in descending order.

10. Test the parameter. Ensure that as you change the parameter selection, the labels for the bars also change.

Dynamically displaying and sorting measures

Dynamically displaying and sorting measures puts the end users in the driver's seat and allows them to change the measures being displayed as required, as well as how the measures are sorted.

Normally, we place the measures we want to display in the shelves or cards. However, they need to be enabled to specify their choice through a parameter to allow end users the flexibility to change this on demand. The parameter Sort by is used in a calculated field that determines the actual measure to be used in the visualization, as well as the appropriate aggregation function:

```
Chosen Sort by                     MasterTable (FlooddataMasterListrev)

CASE [Sort by]
    WHEN "Total Damage $ (USD)"
    THEN SUM([Damage $ (USD)])
    WHEN "Total Dead"
    THEN SUM([Dead])
    WHEN "Avg Magnitude"
    THEN AVG([Magnitude (M)**])
    WHEN "Total Duration in Days"
    THEN SUM([Duration in Days])
END
```

Let's create another parameter called Sort direction to be used in a calculated field called Chosen Sort by with direction that either keeps the value of the calculated field Chosen Sort by is if ascending, or reverses it by multiplying it by -1 if descending:

Chosen Sort by with direction		MasterTable (FlooddataMasterListrev)

```
CASE [Sort direction]
    WHEN "Ascending"
    THEN [Chosen Sort by]
    ELSE [Chosen Sort by] * -1
END
```

This calculated field is to be used with the sort direction for the **Country** dimension.

The respective calculated fields trigger the change in the chart due to the parameter choices change, and show the appropriate measure and sort direction.

One trick when working with dynamic measures is adding the parameter in the same shelf as the dynamic measure:

This allows for the actual measure name to be displayed as a header in the view:

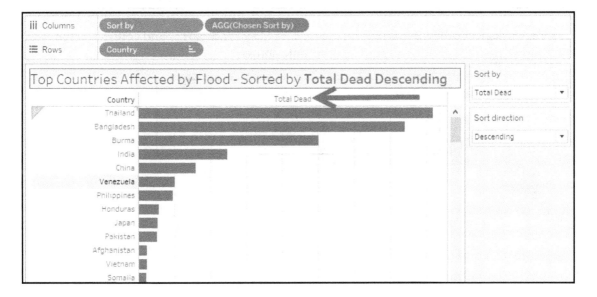

Let's walk through the strategy of displaying and sorting measures based on user selection:

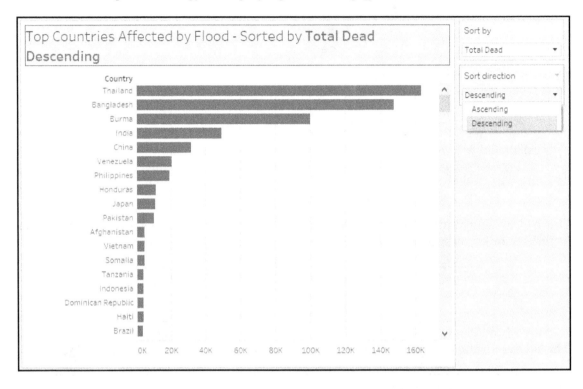

Use the worksheet called `Dynamic Measure Display and Sort`, and connect to the `MasterTable (FlooddataMastListrev)` data source:

1. Right-click the arrow beside the **Dimensions** section in the side bar, and select **Create Parameter**.

2. Create a string parameter called Sort by with the following settings:

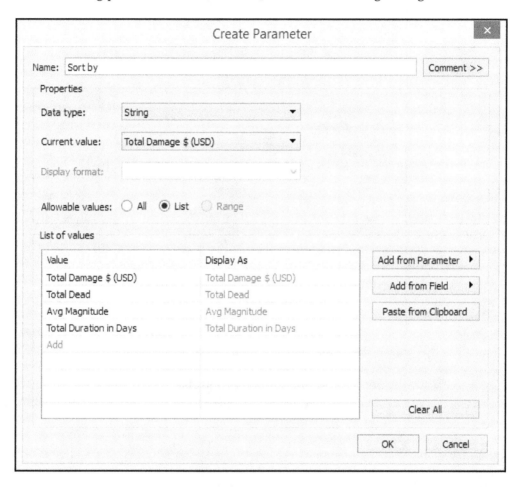

3. Show the parameter control for **Sort by**. You can do this by right-clicking on the parameter, and selecting **Show Parameter Control**.

4. Create another parameter called `Sort direction` with the following settings:

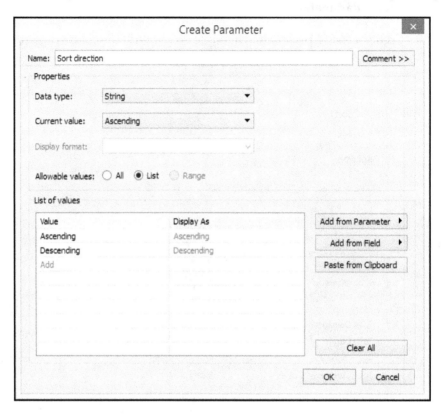

5. Show the **Sort direction** parameter control.
6. Create a calculated field called `Chosen Sort by` with the following formula:

```
Chosen Sort by                    MasterTable (FlooddataMasterListrev)

CASE [Sort by]
    WHEN "Total Damage $ (USD)"
    THEN SUM([Damage $ (USD)])
    WHEN "Total Dead"
    THEN SUM([Dead])
    WHEN "Avg Magnitude"
    THEN AVG([Magnitude (M)**])
    WHEN "Total Duration in Days"
    THEN SUM([Duration in Days])
END
```

7. Create another calculated field called Chosen Sort by with direction, which takes into account the selected direction:

8. From **Measures**, drag the calculated field **Chosen sort by** to the **Columns** shelf.
9. From **Dimensions**, drag **Country** to the **Rows** shelf.
10. Right-click on the **Country** pill in the **Rows** shelf, and select **Sort**.
11. Sort the **Country** based on the calculated field **Chosen sort by with direction** in **Ascending** order:

12. Click **OK** when done.
13. From **Measures**, drag **Chosen sort by** to the **Filters** shelf.
14. Choose **Special**, and select **Non-null values**:

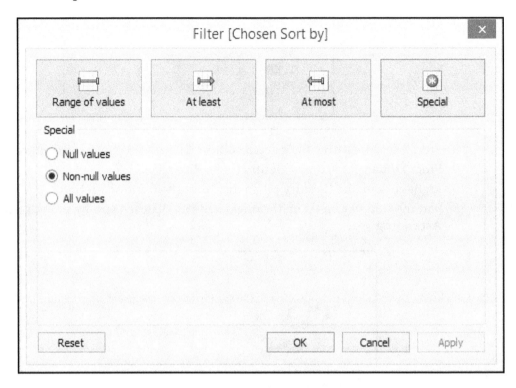

15. From **Dimensions**, drag **Country** to the **Filters** card.
16. Under the **General** tab, check the **Exclude** option, and select **Null**. Notice that selecting something when the **Exclude** option is checked adds a strike through to the selected item, meaning that item will be excluded:

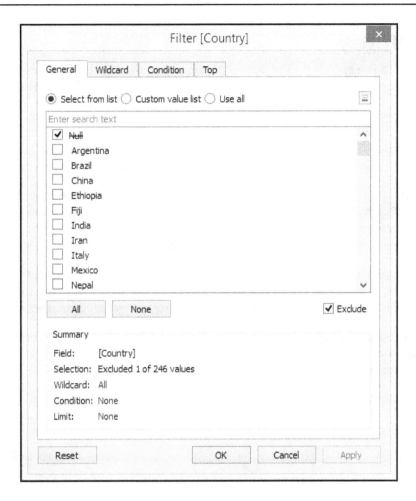

17. Click **OK** when done.
18. Test the parameters. Ensure that as you change the parameter selection, the measures and the sorting change accordingly.

Summary

Interactivity is a crucial part of data analysis that allows the user to stay engaged at all times, generate queries, and solve them without breaking the flow of the analysis.

We explored various ways to integrate interactivity in Tableau. One of the ways included how to create a motion chart using the **Pages** shelf. We also created a parameter that helped us adjust the number of columns for our trellis chart. This allowed us to experiment as to how many adjacent columns would be most effective for data analysis.

We also created a top/bottom N filter to allow the end user to select whether they want to display the top N countries with the most CO_2 emissions or the bottom N countries with the least CO_2 emissions. In comparing one to everything else, Tableau made it easier to compare one item against all other items in a chart or viz.

We also explored how to dynamically display different dimensions in the same graph using a parameter and calculated field. Dynamically displaying and sorting measures walked through the strategy of displaying and sorting measures based on user selection.

In the next chapter, you will learn about moving from foundational to advanced visualizations. The chapter will demonstrate the kind of problems that can be solved with different types of visualizations.

3
Moving from Foundational to More Advanced Visualizations

Now that you are ready to set out on a journey building advanced visualizations, know that advanced does not necessarily mean difficult and complex. Tableau makes it easy to create them. The goal is to communicate data, not obscure it in needless complexity.

These visualizations are advanced in the sense that you will need to understand when they should be used, why they are useful, and how to leverage the capabilities of Tableau to create them. Additionally, many of the examples introduce some advanced techniques to extend the usefulness of foundational visualizations.

Most of the examples in this chapter are designed so that you can follow along. Take time to understand how the combinations of different field types that you place on different shelves change the way headers, axes, and marks are rendered. Experiment with, and even deviate from, the instructions from time to time just to see what else is possible. You can always use Tableau's Back button to return to following the example.

We will cover the following major categories of visualizations in this chapter:

- Comparing values across different dimensions
- Visualizing dates and times
- Relating parts of the data to the whole
- Visualizing distributions
- Visualizing multiple axes to compare different measures

You will notice the lack of a spatial location or geographic category in the preceding list. Mapping was introduced in `Chapter 1`, *Creating Your First Virtualization and Dashboard* and we'll cover some advanced geographic capabilities in `Chapter 9`, *Advanced Visualizations, Techniques, Tips, and Tricks.*

The complete examples are included in the `Chapter 3 workbook`. You can also use the data sources in that workbook to work through the examples on your own.

Comparing values across different dimensions

When you compare the differences in measured values across different categories, you might find yourself asking the following questions:

- How much profit did we generate in each department?
- How many views did each web page get?
- How many patients did each doctor see?

In each case, you are looking to make a comparison (among departments, websites, or doctors) in terms of some quantitative measurement (profit, number of views, and count of patients).

Bar charts

The following figure is a simple bar chart:

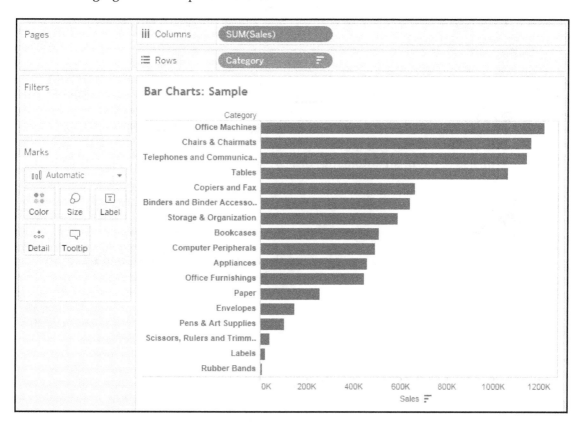

In the preceding figure, we have compared the sum of sales for each category of item sold in a chain of stores. **Category** is used as a discrete dimension in the view, which defines row headers (because it is discrete) and slices the sum of sales for each category (because it is a dimension). **Sales** defines an axis (because it is continuous) and is summed (because it is a measure) for each category.

Note that the bar chart is sorted with the category that has the highest sales at the top and the lowest at the bottom. Sorting a bar chart often adds a lot of value to the analysis because it makes it easier to make comparisons and see the ranking order; for example, it is easy to see that **Bookcases** have more total sales than **Computer Peripherals** even though the bar lengths are close. If this chart had not been sorted it might have not been as obvious.

We can sort a view in multiple ways:

- We can click on one of the sort icons on the toolbar, which will result in an automatic sorting of the dimensions based on the measure that defined the axis. Changes in data or filtering that result in a new order will be reflected in the view, as follows:

- We can also click on the sort icon on the axis, which will become visible when you hover over the axis and then remains in place when you enable the sort. This will also result in an automatic sort, as follows:

- We can use the drop-down menu on the active dimension field and select **Sort** to view and edit sorting options. We can also select **Clear sort** to remove any sorting:

- We can drag and drop row headers to manually rearrange them. This will result in a manual sort that does not get updated with data refreshes.

Any of these sorting methods are specific to the view and will override any default sort method that you defined in the metadata.

Bar chart variations

A basic bar chart can be extended in many ways to accomplish various objectives. We can consider the following variations:

- Bullet chart to show progress towards a goal or target
- Bars in a bar chart to show the progress towards a target
- Highlighting categories of interest

Bullet chart - Showing progress towards a goal

Let's say that you are an enterprise manager and you've set the following profit targets for your regional managers:

Region	Profit target
Central	600,000
East	350,000
South	100,000
West	300,000

You maintain these goals in a spreadsheet and would like to see a visualization that tells you how the actual profit compares with your goals.

A **bullet graph** (sometimes also called a **bullet chart**) is a great way to visually compare a primary measure (in this case, profit) with a secondary measure (in this case, target profit). We'll use two data sources which contain the **Superstore Sales** and the **Profit Targets** spreadsheet data source to visualize the relationship between actual and target profit, in the following steps:

1. Navigate to the **Bullet Chart: Progress toward a goal** sheet.

2. Using the **Superstore Sales** connection, create a basic bar chart of the sum of **Profit** per **Region**:

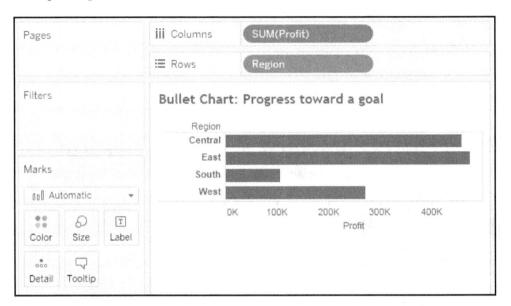

3. In the left data pane, select the **Profit Targets** connection and click to highlight the **Profit Target** field in the data pane.

4. Open **Show Me** and select the bullet graph. At this point, Tableau has already created a bullet graph using the fields in the view and the **Profit Target** field you selected. You'll observe that the **Region** field has been used in the data blend to link the two data sources and it is already enabled because the **Region** field was used in the view, as shown in the following screenshot:

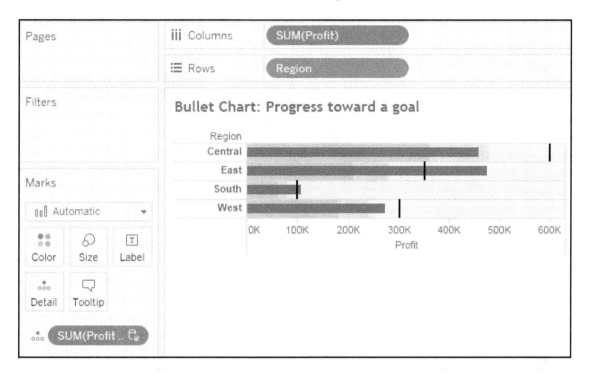

When you use **Show Me** to create a bullet chart you may sometimes find that Tableau uses the fields in reverse order from what you intend (with the wrong measure defining the axis and bars and the other defining the reference line). If this happens, simply right-click on the axis and select **Swap reference line fields**.

You can now clearly see that the **Central** and **West** regional managers are falling short of the goal you set. Bullet graphs make use of reference lines. (If you are interested, right-click the axis and select **Edit Reference Line** to explore the reference lines Tableau created.)

Bar in Bar charts

You can also use the Bar in Bar chart to show progress towards a goal, as follows:

Let's create this view; continue in the same workbook and follow these steps:

1. Navigate to the **Bar in Bar** sheet.
2. Drag and drop **Profit** from the **Superstore Sales** data source on to the horizontal axis in the view (which is the same as dropping it onto the **Columns** shelf).
3. Drag and drop **Region** onto **Rows**.

4. Drag the **Profit Target** field from the **Profit Targets** data source and drop it directly onto the horizontal axis. Since you are dropping one measure (**Profit Target**) onto the same space (in this case, an axis) that was being used by another measure (**Profit**), Tableau substituted the special fields **Measure Names** and **Measure Values**.

> Any time you want two or more measures to share the same space within a view, you can use **Measure Names** and **Measure Values**.
>
> **Measure Names** is a special dimension field that Tableau adds to every data source; is a place holder for the names of measures. You can place it in the view anywhere you would place another dimension.
>
> **Measure Values** is a special measure field that Tableau adds to every data source that is a place holder for the values of other measures. You can use it in almost any way you would use any other measure.

> When these special fields are in use, you will see a new **Measure Values** shelf in the workspace. This shelf contains all the measures that are referenced by **Measure Names** and **Measure Values**. You can add and remove measures from this shelf as well as rearrange the order of any on the shelf.
>
> You can also drag and drop the **Measure Names** and **Measure Values** fields directly from the data pane into the view. Many times, it is easier to remember that if you want two or more measures to share the same space, all you have to do is simply drag and drop the second onto the same space that is occupied by the first. For example, if you want multiple measures to define a single axis, drag and drop the second measure to the axis. If you want two or more measures to occupy the pane, drop the second onto the pane.

5. Move the **Measure Names** field from the **Rows** shelf to the **Color** shelf and edit the colors in the legend (double-click on the legend or use the drop-down arrow on the legend) and set **Profit** to orange and **Profit Target** to light gray).You now have a stacked bar chart with a different color for each measure name being used:

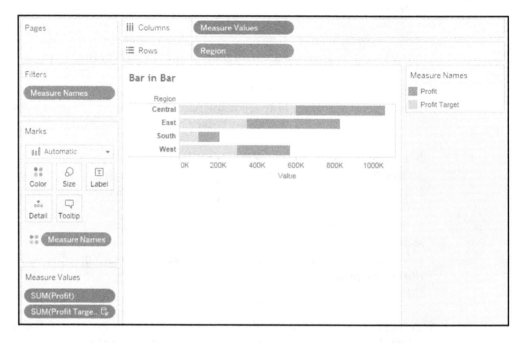

6. Copy the **Measure Names** field from **Color** to the **Size** shelf (hold *Ctrl* while you drag a field in the view and drop it on another shelf in the view). This creates different sizes for each bar segment.
7. Tableau's default is to stack marks. In this case, you do not want the bars to be stacked. Instead, you want them to overlap. To change the default behavior, from the menu, navigate to **Analysis | Stack Marks | Off**.

The order of the measures in the **Measure Values** shelf will determine which marks appear on top. If the gray bars are on top of the orange bars, you can switch the order of the fields. Your view should now look like the bar chart in the first screenshot in this section. You can further enhance the visualization using the following options:

- **Adding a border to the bars**: You can add a border to the bars by clicking on the **Color** shelf and using the **Border** option

- **Adjusting the size range to reduce the difference between the large and small extremes**: You can adjust the size range to reduce the difference between the large and small extremes by double-clicking on the **Size** legend (or using the caret drop-down and selecting **Edit** from the menu)
- **Adjusting the sizing of the view**: You can adjust the sizing of the view by hovering over the canvas, just over the bottom border until, the mouse cursor changes to a sizing cursor, then click and drag to resize the view

Highlighting categories of interest

Let's say one of your primary responsibilities at the Superstore is to monitor the sales of **Tables** and **Bookcases**. You don't necessarily care about the details of other categories, but you do want to keep a track of how tables and bookcases compare with other categories. You might design something similar to the following screenshot:

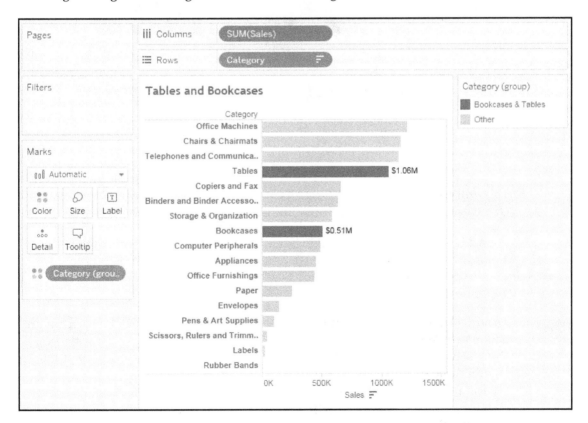

Now you will be able to immediately see where **Tables and Bookcases** are compared to other categories as sales figures change day by day. Let's create this view by following these steps:

1. Navigate to the **Tables and Bookcases** sheet.
2. Place **Category** on **Rows** and **Sales** on **Columns**. Sort the bar chart in descending order.
3. Click on the bar mark in the view for **Tables** and, while holding the *Ctrl* key, click on the bar for **Bookcases**.
4. Hover over one of the selected bars and from the **Tool tip** menu click on the **Create Group** button (which looks like a paperclip), as follows:

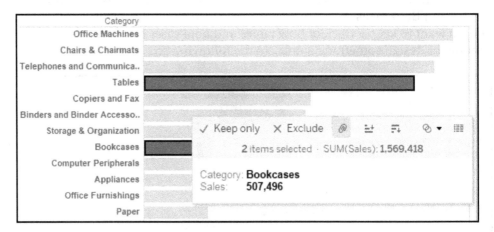

5. This will create a group, which results in a new dimension, named **Category** (group), in the data pane. Tableau automatically assigns this field to **Color**.

   Ad hoc groups are powerful in Tableau. You can create groups in the view or using the menu for a dimension in the data pane and navigating to **Create | Group**. Unlike previous versions, Tableau 10 allows you to use groups in calculations.

6. To add a label, only to the **Tables** and **Bookcases** bars, right-click on each bar and navigate to **Mark label | Always show**. The label for the mark will always be shown, even if other labels are turned off for the view or the label overlaps marks on other labels.
7. We can format the label using the drop-down menu on the **Sales** field on **Columns**, selecting **Format**. Switch to the left formatting pane and, under **Default | Numbers**, select **Currency (Custom)** and set the **Units** to **Millions (M)**.

As an alternative to labels, you can add annotations to **Views** in Tableau:

- **Annotations:**

  Annotations can be used to display values of data and free-form text to draw attention or give explanation. There are three kinds of annotations in Tableau: Mark, Point, and Area.

- **Mark:**

  Mark annotations are associated with a specific mark (such as a bar or shape) in the view. The annotation can display any data associated with the mark. It will be shown in the view as long as that mark is visible.

- **Point:**

  Point annotations are associated with a specific point as defined by one or more axes in the view. The annotation can display values, which define the X and/or Y location of the point. It will be shown in the view as long as the point is visible.

- **Area:**

  Area annotations are associated with an area in the view. They are typically shown when at least part of the area defined is visible.

Visualizing dates and times

Often in your analysis you will want to understand when something happened. You'll ask questions such as:

- When did we gain the newest customers?
- What times of day have the highest call volumes?
- What kinds of seasonal trends do we see in sales and profit?
- Fortunately, Tableau makes this kind of visual discovery and analysis easy

The built-in date hierarchy

When you are connected to a flat-file, relational, or extracted data source, Tableau provides a robust built-in date hierarchy for any date field.

Cubes/OLAP connections do not allow for Tableau hierarchies. You will want to ensure that all the date hierarchies and date values that you need are defined in the cube.

To see this in action, continue with the `Chapter 3`, *Moving from Foundational to More Advanced Visualizations* workbook, navigate to the **Built-in Date Hierarchy** sheet, and create a view similar to the one shown here by dragging and dropping **SUM(Sales)** to **Rows** and **YEAR(Order Date)** to **Columns**:

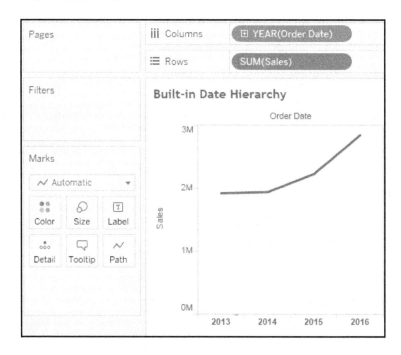

Note that even though the **Order Date** field is a date, Tableau, by default shows sales by **YEAR**. Additionally, the field in Columns has a + icon indicating that the field is a part of a hierarchy which can be expanded. When you click the + icon, additional levels of the hierarchy are added to the view. Starting with **Year**, this includes Year **Quarter** | **Month** | **Day**. When date and time is selected in the field, you can further drill down into **Hour**, **Minute**, **Second**. Any part of the hierarchy can be moved within the view or removed from the view completely.

You can specify how a date field should be used in the view, by right-clicking the date field or using the drop-down menu and selecting various date options.

 As a short-cut, you can right-click drag and drop a date field into the view to get a menu of options for how the date field should be used prior to the view being drawn.

The options for a date field look as follows:

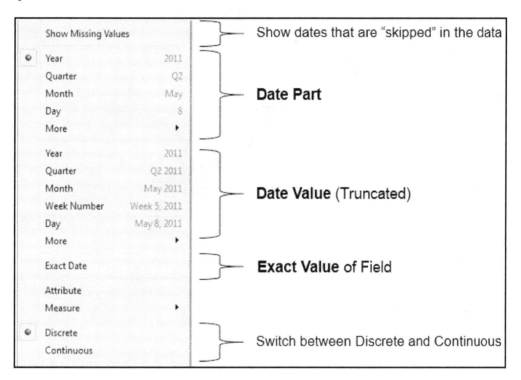

The three major ways in which we can use a date field are as follows:

- **Date Part**: The field will represent a specific part of the date, such as the **Quarter** or **Month**. The part of the date is used by itself and without reference to any other part of the date. That means that November 8, 1980, when used as a month date part, is simply November:

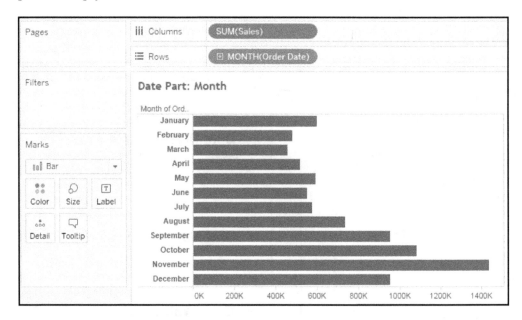

- **Date Part** view: The bar for November represents the sum of sales for all Novembers, regardless of the year or day.

- **Date Value**: The field will represent a date value, but rolled up or truncated to the level you select. For example, if you select a **date value** of Month, then November 8, 1980 gets truncated to the month and year and is November 1980:

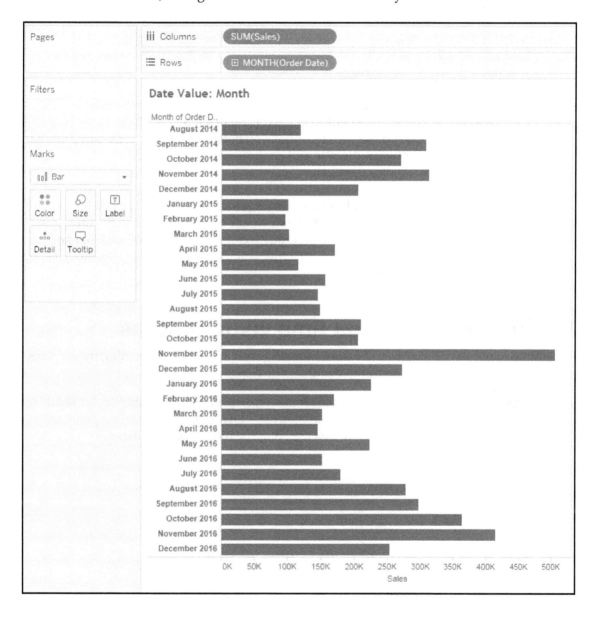

The preceding screenshot, for example, includes a bar for the sum of sales for November 2012 and another bar for November 2013. All individual dates within the month have been rolled up, so sales for November 1, 2013 and November 11, 2013 are all summed under November 2013:

- ExactDate: This field represents the exact date value (including the time if applicable) in the data. This means that November 8, 1980 2:01 AM is treated differently from November 8, 1980 3:08 PM

It is important to note that any of the preceding options can be used as discrete or continuous fields. Date parts are discrete by default. Date values and exact dates are continuous by default. However, you can switch them between discrete and continuous as needed to allow for flexibility in the visualization.

For example, you must have an axis (requiring a continuous field) to create a reference line. Also, Tableau will only connect lines at the lowest level of row or column headers. Using a continuous date value instead of multiple discrete date parts will allow you to connect lines across multiple years, quarters, and months.

Variations of date and time visualizations

The ability to use various parts and values of dates (even mixing and matching them) gives you a lot of flexibility in creating unique and useful visualizations.

For example, using the month and date part for columns and the year date part for color gives a time series that makes year over year analysis quite easy. The year date part has been copied to a label so the lines could be labeled in the following screenshot:

Clicking on any of the shelves on the **Marks** card will give you a menu of options. Here **Label** has been clicked and the label was adjusted to show only at the start of each line.

The following screenshot is another example of using date parts on different shelves to achieve a useful analysis. This kind of visualization can be useful when looking at patterns across different parts of time, such as hours in a day or weeks in a month:

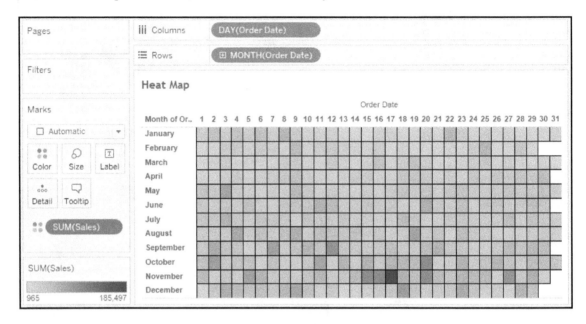

The **Heat Map** view shows the sum of sales for the intersection of each day and each month. Year has not been included in the view, so this is an analysis of all years in the data and allows us to see if there are any seasonal patterns or hotspots. Observe that placing a continuous field on the **Color** shelf resulted in Tableau completely filling each intersection of **Row** and **Columns** with the shade of color that encoded the sum of sales. Clicking on the **Color** shelf gives some fine-tuning options, including the option to add borders to marks. Here, a black border has been added to help distinguish each cell.

Gantt charts

Gantt charts can be incredibly useful for understanding any series of events with duration, especially if those events have some kind of relationship. Visually, they are very useful for determining if certain events overlap, have a dependency, or take a longer or shorter time than other events. For example, next is a Gantt chart that shows a series of processes, some of which are clearly dependent on others:

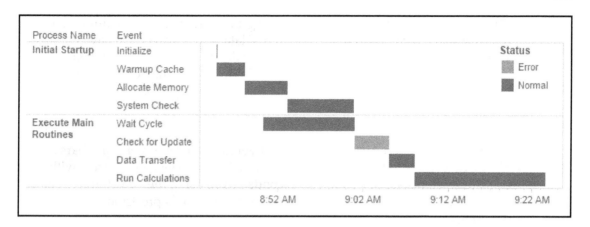

Gantt charts can be created fairly easily in Tableau. Tableau uses the Gantt mark type, which places a Gantt bar starting at the value defined by the field defining the axis. The length of the Gantt bar is set by the field on the **Size** card.

Let's create an example where you want to visualize the time it takes from an order being placed to the time the order is shipped by following these steps:

1. Place **Order Date** on **Columns** as a continuous **Exact Date** or as a **Day** value (not day part). Note that Tableau's automatic default for the mark type is Gantt bars:

2. Place **Order ID** on **Rows**. The result is a row for each order and the Gantt bar shows the date of the order.
3. Filter the view for October 2016. Accomplish this by dragging and dropping the **Order Date** field on the **Filters** shelf. Select the **Month/Year** option and then choose the single month and year from the list.

4. The length of the Gantt bar is set by placing a field with a value of duration on the **Size** shelf. There is no such field in this data set. However, we have the **Ship Date** and we can create a calculated field for the duration. Select **Analysis** from the menu and click on **Create Calculated Field...**. Name the field Days to Ship and enter the following code:

```
DATEDIFF('day', [Order Date], [Ship Date])
```

When plotted on a date axis, the field defining the length of Gantt bars always needs to be in terms of days. If you want to visualize events with duration measured in hours or seconds, avoid using the 'day' argument for DATEDIFF because it computes whole days and loses precision in terms of hours and seconds.

Instead, calculate the difference in hours or seconds and then convert back to days. The following code converts the number of seconds between a start and end date and then divides it by 86,400 to convert the result into days (including fractional parts of the day):

```
DATEDIFF('second', [Start Date], [End Date]) / 86400
```

5. The new calculated field will appear under **Measures** in the data pane. Drag and drop the field onto the **Size** shelf. You now have a Gantt chart showing when orders were placed. There is, however, one problem. Some orders include more than one item and you are showing the sum of days to ship. This means that if one item took 5 days to ship and another item in the same order took 7 days, the length of the bar shows 12 days for the order. If both items took 5 days and were shipped at the exact same time, the length of the bar indicates 10 even though the order really only took 5 days.

6. To correct this, decide if you want to show the minimum number of days or the maximum number of days for each order, then right-click on the **Days to Ship** field on the **Marks** card or use the drop-down menu and select **Measure |** **Minimum** or **Measure | Maximum**. Alternately, you might decide to add RowID, ItemID, or Item to the **Detail** of the **Marks** card.

Your final view should look similar to the following screenshot:

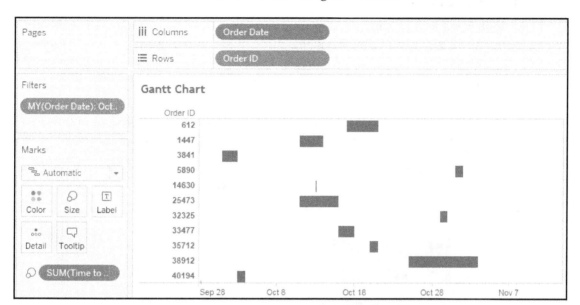

 Often, you'll want to sort a Gantt chart so the earliest start dates appear first. Do this via the drop-down menu of the dimension on rows and select **Sort**. Sort it in ascending order by the minimum of the date field.

Relating parts of the data to the whole

As you explore and analyze data, you'll often want to understand how various parts add up to a whole. For example, you'll ask questions such as:

- How many patients with different admission statuses (inpatient, outpatient, observation, ER) make up the entire population of patients in the hospital?
- What percentage of total national sales is made in each state?
- How much space does each file, sub-directory, and directory take up on my hard disk?

These types of question are asked about the relationship between the part (patient type, state, and file/directory) and the whole (entire patient population, national sales, and hard disk). There are several types of visualizations and variations that can aid you in your analysis.

Stacked bars

We took a look at stacked bars in Chapter 1, *Creating Your First Visualization and Dashboard* where we noted one significant drawback: it is difficult to compare values across categories for any bar other than the bottom-most bar (for vertical bars) or left-most bar (for horizontal bars). The other bar segments have different starting points, so lengths are difficult to compare.

In this case, however, we used stacked bars to visually understand the makeup of the whole. We are less concerned with visually comparing across categories.

Let's say a bank manager wants to understand the makeup of their lending portfolios. They might start with a visualization similar to the following screenshot:

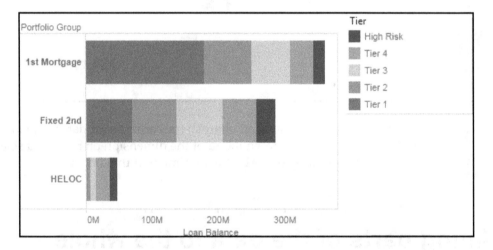

This gives a decent view of the makeup of each portfolio. However, in this case the bank manager already knows that the bank has more balance in first mortgage loans than fixed second loans. But they want to understand if the relative makeup of the portfolios is similar. And specifically, do the **High Risk** balances constitute a higher percentage of balances in any portfolio?

Let's consider this alternative:

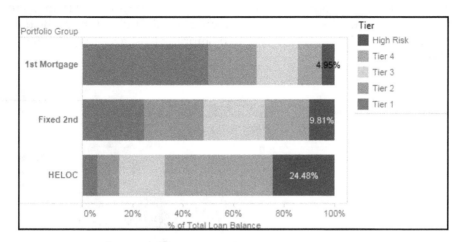

None of the data has changed, but the bars now represent the percentage of the total of each portfolio. You can no longer compare the absolute values, but comparing the relative breakdown of each portfolio has been made much easier. The bank manager may find it alarming that nearly 25% of the balance of **HELOC** loans is in the high-risk category when the bar segment looked fairly small in the first visualization.

Creating this kind of visualization is relatively easy in Tableau. It involves using quick table calculations that only take a few clicks to implement.

Continuing with the Chapter 03 workbook, follow these steps:

1. Create a stacked bar chart by placing **Department** on **Rows**, **SUM(Shipping Cost)** on **Columns**, and **Ship Mode** on **Color**.

2. Duplicate the **SUM(Shipping Cost)** field on **Columns** by either holding *Ctrl* while dragging the **Shipping Cost** field to a spot on **Columns** immediately to the right of its current location, or by dragging and dropping it from the data pane to **Columns**. At this point, you have two Shipping Cost axes that, in effect, duplicate the view:

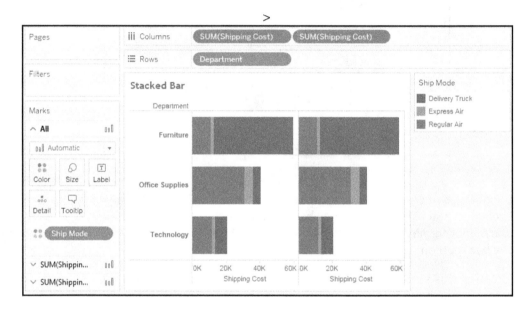

3. Using the drop-down menu of the second **Shipping Cost** field, navigate to **Quick Table Calculation** | **Percent of Total**. This table calculation runs a secondary calculation on the values returned from the data source to compute a percentage of the total. You will need to further specify how that total should be computed.

4. Using the same drop-down menu, navigate to **Compute Using** | **Ship Mode**. This tells Tableau to compute the percent of total for **Ship Mode** within a given department. This means that the values will add up to 100% for each department.

5. Turn on labels by clicking the **Abc** button on the top toolbar. This turns on the default labels for each mark:

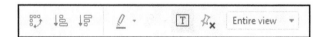

6. Right-click on the second axis, which is now labeled **% of Total Shipping Cost**, and select **Edit Axis....** Then set the range as fixed with a fixed start at 0 and a fixed end at 1. Since you know the totals will add up to 100%, this fixes the axis in a way that allows Tableau to draw the bar all the way across:

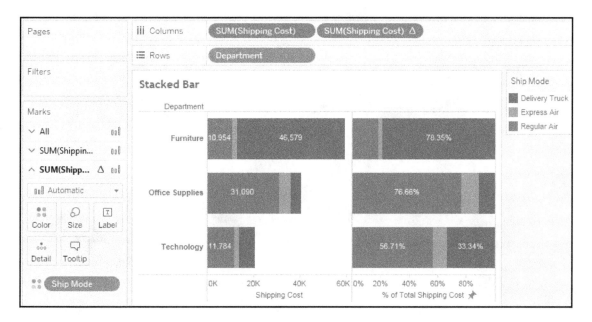

Treemaps

Treemaps are particularly useful when you have hierarchies and dimensions with high cardinality (a high number of distinct values). They use a series of nested rectangles to represent hierarchical relationships of parts to the whole.

Here is an example of a treemap that shows how sales of each **Item** add up to give total sales by **Category**, then **Department**, and finally total sales overall. Profit has been encoded by **Color** to add additional analytical value to the visualization. It is now easy to pick out items with negative profit and relatively high sales when placed in the context of the whole:

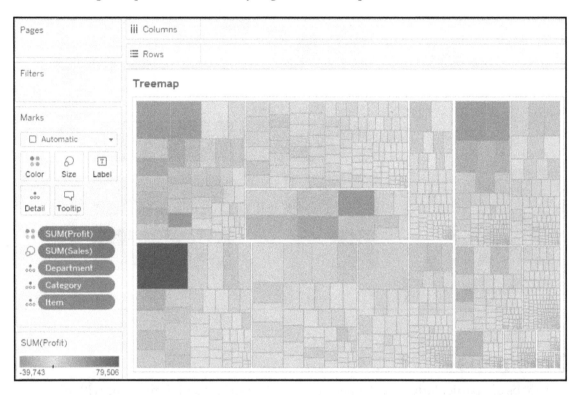

To create a treemap, you simply need to place a measure on the **Size** shelf and a dimension on the **Detail** shelf. You can add additional dimensions to the level of detail to increase the detail of the view. Tableau will add borders of varying thickness to separate the levels of detail created by multiple dimensions. Note that in the previous view you can easily see the division of departments, categories, and items. You can adjust the border of the lowest level by clicking on the **Color** shelf.

The order of the dimensions on the **Marks** card defines the way the treemap groups the rectangles. Additionally, you can add dimensions to rows or columns to slice the treemap into multiple treemaps. The end result is effectively a bar chart of treemaps:

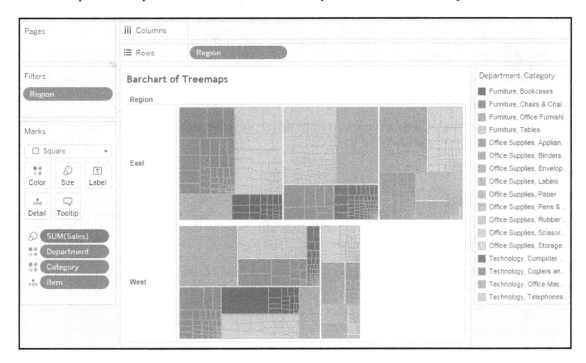

The preceding treemap not only demonstrates the ability to have multiple rows (or columns) of treemaps, it also demonstrates the technique of placing multiple fields on the **Color** shelf. This can only be done with discrete fields. You can assign two or more colors by holding the Shift key while dropping the second field on **Color**. Alternately, the icon or space to the left of each field on the **Marks** card can be clicked to change which shelf is used for the field:

Treemaps, along with packed bubbles, word clouds, and a few other chart types, are called non-Cartesian chart types. This means they are drawn without an *X* or *Y* axis and do not even require row or column headers. To create any of these chart types:

Make sure no continuous fields are used on **Rows** or **Columns**.

Use any field as a measure on **Size**.

Change the mark type based on the desired chart type: Square for treemap, Circle for packed bubbles, or Text for word cloud (with the desired field on Label).

Area charts

Think of a line chart and then fill in the area beneath the line. If you have multiple lines, then stack the filled areas on top of each other. That's how you might think of an area chart.

As an example, consider a visualization of delinquent loan balances being analyzed by the bank manager:

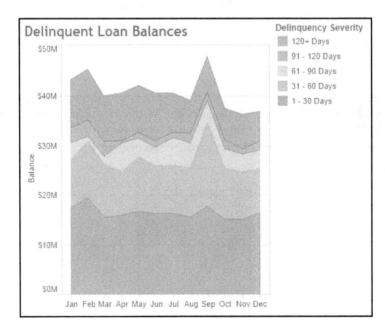

This area chart shows delinquency balances over time. Each band represents a different severity of delinquency. In many ways, the view is aesthetically pleasing, but it suffers from some of the same weaknesses as the stacked bar chart. Since all but the bottom band have different starting locations month to month, it is difficult to compare the bands between months. For example, it is obvious that there is a spike in delinquent balances in September. But is it in all bands? Or is one of the lower bands pushing the higher bands up? Which band has the most significant spike?

Now consider this similar view:

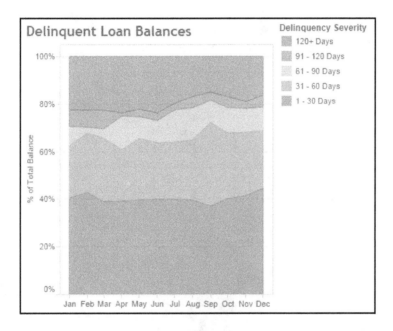

This view uses a quick table calculation similar to the stacked bars. It makes it clear that the percent of balances within the **31 - 60 Days** delinquent range increased in September. However, it is no longer clear that September represents a spike in balances. If you were telling a story with this data, you would want to carefully consider what either visualization might represent or misrepresent.

Creating an area chart is fairly simple. Simply create a line chart or time series as you have done previously and then change the mark type on the **Marks** card to Area. Any dimensions on **Color**, **Label**, or **Detail** shelves will create slices of an area that will be stacked on top of each other. The **Size** shelf is not applicable to an area chart.

You can define the order in which the areas are stacked by changing the sort order of the dimensions on the shelves of the **Marks** card. If you have multiple dimensions defining slices of area, you can additionally re-arrange them on the **Marks** card or in the **Color** shelf to further adjust the order.

Pie charts

To create a pie chart, change the mark type to **Pie**. This will give you an **Angle** shelf which you can use to encode a measure. Whatever dimension(s) you place on the **Marks** card (typically on the **Color** shelf) will define the slices of the pie:

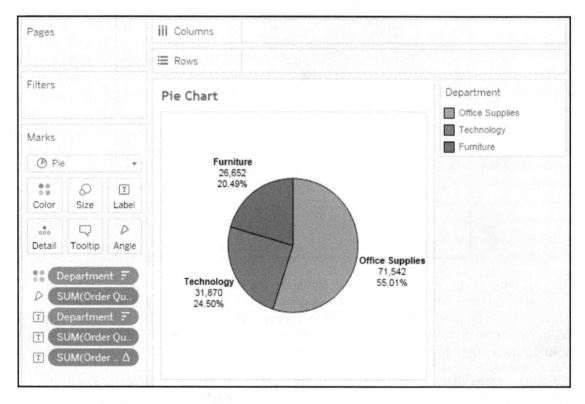

Notice that the preceding pie chart uses the sum of order quantity to define the angle of each slice; the higher the sum of order quantity, the wider the slice. The **Department** dimension slices the measure and defines slices of the pie. This view also demonstrates the ability to place multiple fields on the **Label** shelf. The second **SUM(Order Quantity)** field is the percentage of total table calculations you have seen earlier.

Note that pie charts are limiting. If you choose to use pie charts, try to limit the number of slices to two or three. Any more than that, and pie charts become difficult to understand. Instead, a better alternative would be to consider a bar chart or something similar.

Also, as a best practice, sort slices by sorting the dimension that defines the slices. In the previous example, the **Department** dimension has been sorted by descending sum of order quantity, using the drop-down menu option. This causes slices to be ordered from largest to smallest and allows anyone reading the chart to easily see which slices are larger, even when the size and angles are nearly identical.

Visualizing distributions

Often, simply understanding totals, sums, and even the breakdown of part to the whole only gives a piece of the overall picture. Many times, you'll want to understand where individual items fall within a distribution of all similar items.

You might find yourself asking questions such as:

- How long do most of our patients stay in the hospital? Which patients fall outside the normal range?
- What's the average life expectancy for components in a machine and which components fall above or below that average? Are there any components with extremely long or extremely short lives?
- What are the most students test score for passing preceding or following test?

All these questions have similarities as you are asking for an understanding of where individuals (patients, components, students) were in relation to the group. In each case, you most likely have a relatively high number of individuals. In data terms, you have a dimension (patients, components, and students) with high cardinality (a high number of distinct individual values) and some measure (length of stay, life expectancy, and test score) you'd like to compare. Using one or more of the following visualizations might be one of the best ways to visualize this kind of data.

Circle charts

Circle charts are one way to visualize a distribution. Consider the following view, which shows how each state compares to other states within the same region in terms of total profit:

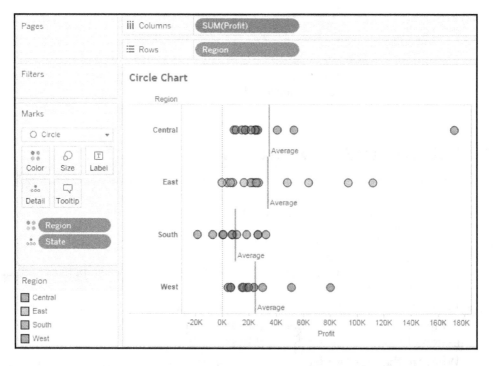

Here you can easily see that certain states do far better or far worse than others in terms of profit. More than that, you can see whether a state has made or lost money and how much above or below the regional average it was.

After placing the fields on shelves shown previously, simply change the mark type from **Automatic** (which was a Bar mark) to **Circle**. **Region** defines the rows and each circle is drawn at the level of state, which is in the level of **Detail** on the **Marks** card. Finally, to add the average lines, simply switch to the **Analytics** tab of the left sidebar and drag the **Average Line** to the view, specifically dropping it on the **Cell** option, as shown:

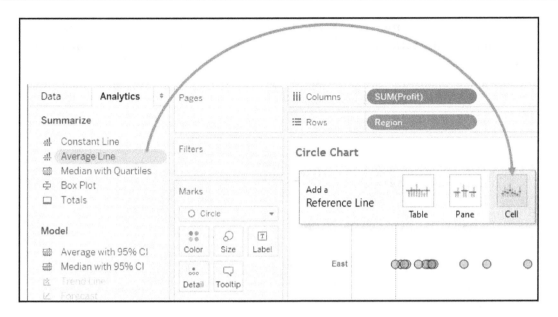

You can additionally click on one of the resulting average lines and select **Edit** to find fine-tuning options such as labeling.

Jittering

When using views such as circle plots (or other similar visualization types), you'll often see that marks overlap, which can lead to obscuring the true story. Do you know for certain, just by looking, that there are only two states in the **South** region that are unprofitable? Or could there be two or more circles exactly overlapping? One way of minimizing this is to click on the **Color** shelf and add some transparency and a border to each circle. Another approach is a technique called jittering.

Jittering is a common technique in data visualization involves adding a bit of intentional noise to a visualization to avoid overlap without harming the integrity of what is communicated. Alan Eldridge and Steve Wexler are among those who pioneered techniques for jittering in Tableau.

Various jittering techniques, such as using `Index()` or `Random()` functions, can be found by searching for jittering on the Tableau forums or Tableau jittering using a search engine.

Here, for example, is one approach that uses the `Index()` function, computed along **State**, as a continuous field on **Rows**. Since `Index()` is continuous (green) it defines an axis and causes the circles to spread out vertically. Now you can see each individual mark more clearly and have a higher level of confidence that overlap is not obscuring the true picture of the data. You can use jittering techniques on many different kinds of visualizations:

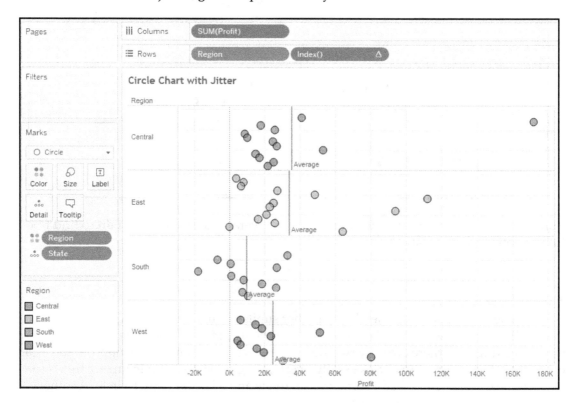

In the previous view, the vertical axis created by the `Index()` field is hidden. You can hide an axis or header by using the drop-down menu of the field defining the axis or header and unchecking **Show Header**. Alternately, you can right-click on any axis or header in the view and select the same option.

Box and whisker plots

Box and whisker plots add additional information and context to distributions. They show the upper and lower quartile and whiskers that extend to either 1.5 times the upper/lower quartile or to the maximum/minimum values in the data. This allows you to see which data points are close to normal and which are outliers.

The following is the original circle chart from the preceding section, with the addition of boxes and whiskers:

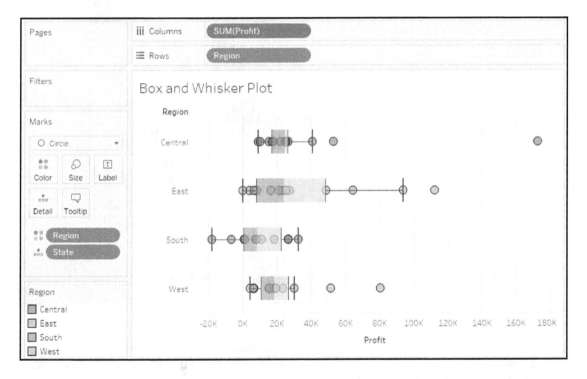

To add **Box and Whisker Plot**, use the **Analytics** tab on the left sidebar and drag **Box Plot** to the view.

Histograms

Another way of showing a distribution is to use a histogram. A histogram looks similar to a bar chart, but the bars show the count of occurrences of a value. For example, standardized test auditors looking for evidence of grade tampering might construct a histogram of student test scores. Typically, a distribution might look similar to this:

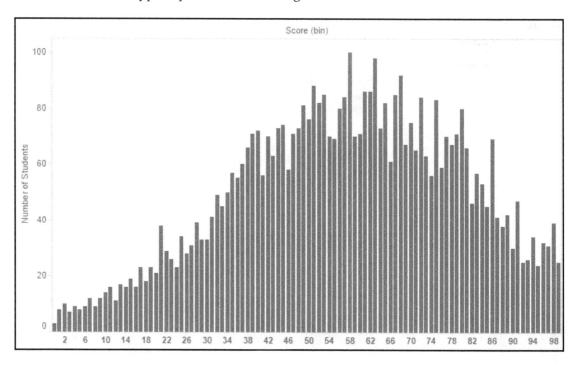

The test scores are shown on the X-axis and the height of each bar shows the **Number of Students** that made that particular score. A typical distribution should have a fairly recognizable bell curve with some students doing poorly, some doing extremely well, and most falling towards somewhere in the middle.

What if auditors saw something similar to the following?

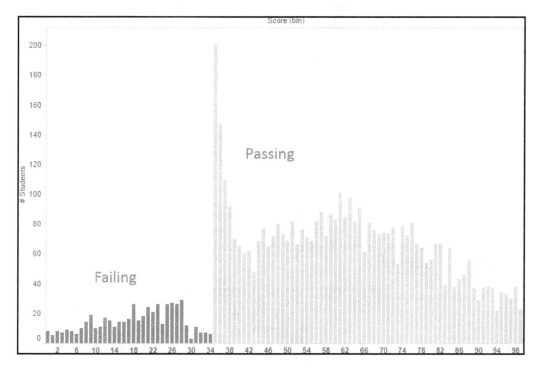

Something is clearly wrong. It appears that graders may have bumped up students who were just shy of passing to barely passing. Histograms are very useful in catching anomalies similar to this.

Let's say you'd like to create a histogram to show you a distribution of items according to the number of days it took to ship the item. Tableau includes the ability to easily create bins, which makes creating histograms easy.

Bins are ranges of measure values that can be used as dimensions to slice the data. You can think of bins as buckets. For example, you might look at test scores by 0-5%, 5-10%, and so on or people's ages by 0-10, 10-20, and so on. You can also set the size or range of the bin when it is created and edit it at any point. Tableau will also suggest a size of the bin based on an algorithm that looks at the values present in the data. Tableau will use uniform bin sizes for all bins.

Create bins using steps similar to these:

1. Decide the numeric field for which you'd like to see a distribution. In this case, use the drop-down menu for the **Days to Ship** calculated measure we created earlier and select **Create Bins**. Set the size of the bin to **1** in the resulting dialog box and click on **OK**:

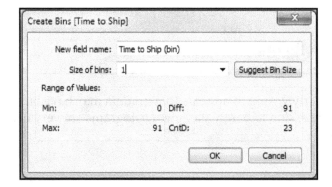

2. This creates a bin field, named **Days to Ship (bin)** under **Dimensions** in the data pane. Drag and drop this field on **Columns**. This gives you a column for each possible value of the number of days to ship.
3. You'll need to decide what you want to count for each bucket and place that on **Rows**. Do you want to know how many distinct customers fell into each bucket? Then you'd use customer ID or customer name aggregated as **COUNTD**. If you want to know how many total items fell into each bucket (and not just the unique ones) you could use a **Count of Item ID** or the **Number of Records** field.

Here is an example of a histogram showing the number of days to ship and how many items took that long:

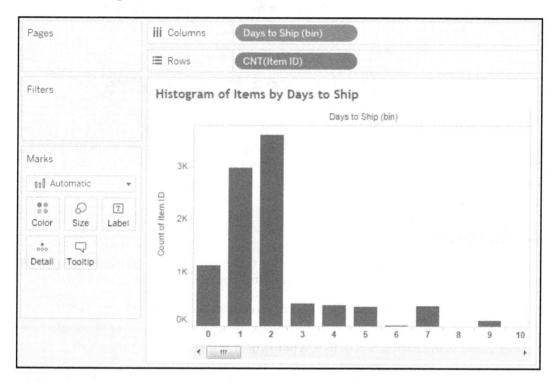

Most items took anywhere from 0 to 2 days to ship, with a sharp decline in the number of items that took 3 or more days to ship.

Just like dates, the bin field in the view has a drop-down menu that includes an option for **Show Missing Values**. This option is on by default. In the previous view, you'll note that there are no items that took **8** days to ship, but **8** is still shown. This can be very useful to avoid distorting the visualization and for identifying what values don't occur in the data.

Histograms can be created very easily using **Show Me**. Simply navigate to **single measure** | **Histogram** | **Show Me**. It will create the bin and place the required fields on the view. You can adjust the size of a bin using the Edit option from the drop-down menu in the data pane.

Visualizing multiple axes to compare different measures

Often, you'll need to use more than one axis to compare different measures, understand correlation, or analyze the same measure at different levels of detail. In these cases, you'll use the visualizations with more than one axis.

Scatterplot

A scatterplot is an essential visualization type for understanding the relationship between two measures. Consider a scatterplot when you find yourself asking questions such as:

- Does how much I spend on marketing really make a difference in sales?
- How much does power consumption go up with each degree of heating/cooling?
- Is there any correlation between hours of study and test performance?

Each of these questions seeks to understand the correlation (if any) between two measures. Scatterplots are great for seeing these relationships and also in locating outliers.

Consider the following scatter plot that looks at the relationship between the measures: the sum of **Sales** (on the X axis) and the sum of **Profit** (on the Y axis):

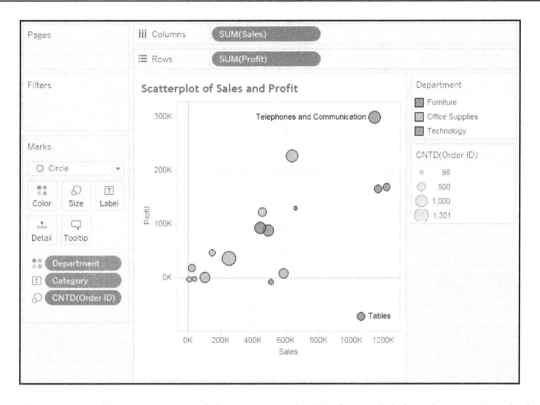

The dimensions of **Department** and **Category** on the **Marks** card define the view Level of Detail. **Color** has been used to make it easy to see the department where the category belongs. Each mark in the view represents the total sales and total profit for a particular **Category** in a particular **Department**. The **Size** of each circle indicates the number of distinct orders for that category/department. The scatterplot points out an issue with Tables. They have high sales, but are unprofitable. Telephones on the other hand have high sales and high profits.

Dual axis

One very important feature in Tableau is referred to as a dual-axis chart. Scatter plots use two axes, they are X and Y. You've already seen using **Measure Names** and **Measure Values** to show more than one measure on a single axis. You saw in the stacked bar example that placing multiple continuous (green) fields next to each other on **Rows** or **Columns** results in multiple side by side axes. Dual axis, on the other hand, means that a view is using two axes that are opposite each other with a common pane.

For example, this view is using a **Dual Axis of Sales and Profit**:

Notice several key features of the view:

- The **Sales** and **Profit** fields on **Rows** indicate that they have a dual axis by sharing a flattened side.
- The **Marks** card is now an accordion-like control with an **All** section and a section for **Sales** and **Profit**. You can use this to customize marks for all measures or specifically customize marks for either **Sales** or **Profit**.
- **Sales** and **Profit** both define Y axes that are on opposite sides of the view.

Note that the peaks of the lines might lead you to believe that **Sales** and **Profit** were roughly equal in value at certain points. That is hardly likely to be the case. Indeed, it is not. Instead the axes are not in sync. Sales of $1,000,000 roughly align with profit of just over $200,000. To fix this, right-click on the **Profit** axis and select **Synchronize Axis**.

You must set the synchronize option using the secondary axis (**Profit** in the preceding example). If the **Synchronize Axis** option is ever disabled on the secondary axis, it is likely that the two fields defining the axes are different numeric types.

For example one may be an integer, while the other may be a decimal. To enable the synchronize option, you'll need to force a match of the types by either changing the data type of one of the fields (using the drop-down menu of the field) or by creating a calculated field that specifically casts one of the fields to the matching type, using a conversion function, such as INT() or FLOAT().

To create a dual axis, drag and drop two continuous (green) fields next to each other on **Rows** or **Columns**, then use the drop-down menu on the second and select **Dual Axis**. Alternately, you can drop the second field onto the canvas, opposite the existing axis.

Dual axis can be used with any continuous field that defines an axis. This includes numeric fields, date fields, and latitude or longitude fields that define a geographic visualization. In the case of latitude or longitude, simply copy one of the fields and place it immediately next to itself on the **Rows** or **Columns shelf**. Then select the **Dual Axis** using the drop-down menu.

Combination charts

Combination charts extend the use of dual axes to overlay different mark types. This is possible because the **Marks** card will give options for editing all marks or customizing marks for each individual axis.

Multiple mark types are available any time two or more continuous fields are located beside each other on **Rows** or **Columns**. This means that you can create views with multiple mark types, even when you are not using a dual axis.

As an example of a combination dual-axis chart, consider the following visualization:

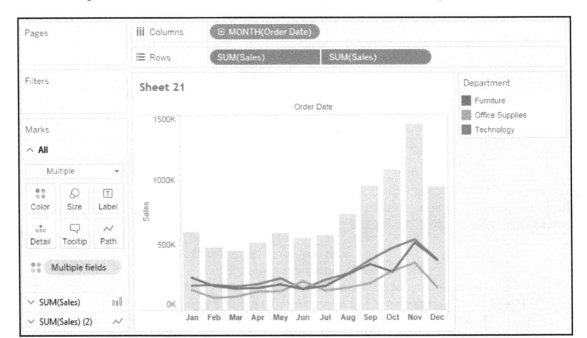

This chart uses a combination of bars and lines to show the total sales over time (using bars) and the breakdown of sales by department over time (using lines). This kind of visualization can be quite effective for giving additional context in detail.

There are several things to note about this view:

- The field on the **Color** shelf is listed as **Multiple Fields** and is gray on the **Marks** card. This indicates that different fields have been used for **Color** for each axis on **Marks**.
- The view demonstrates the ability to mix levels of detail in the same view. The bars are drawn at the highest level (total sales for each month) while the lines have been drawn at a lower level (department sales for each month).
- The view demonstrates the ability to use the same field (**Sales**, in this case) multiple times on the same shelf (**Rows**, in this case).
- The second axis (the Sales field on the right) has the header hidden to remove redundancy from the view. You can do this by unchecking **Show Header** from the drop-down menu on the field in the view or right clicking the axis or header you wish to hide.

- The months have been formatted to show abbreviations. This was done via the drop-down menu of the **Month(Order Date)** field on **Columns**, selecting **Format** and selecting the desired format of the field for headers.

Dual axis and combination charts open up a wide range of possibilities for mixing mark types and levels of detail and are very useful for generating unique insights.

Summary

We've covered quite a bit of ground in this chapter! You should now have a good grasp of when to use certain types of visualizations. The types of questions you ask of the data will often lead you to a certain type of view. You've explored how to create these various types and how to extend basic visualizations using a variety of advanced techniques such as calculated fields, jittering, multiple mark types, and dual axis. Along the way we've also covered some details on how dates work in Tableau and using the special **Measure Names** and **Measure Values** fields.

The ability to create calculations in Tableau opens up endless possibilities for extending analysis of the data, calculating results, customizing visualizations, and creating rich user interactivity. We'll dive deep into how we can put worksheets together to create dashboards and story points.

4
Dashboards and Story Points

In this chapter, we will tackle how we can put worksheets together to create dashboards and story points. Dashboards are containers for worksheets to relay information and insights in a more holistic manner. Story points, on the other hand, allow you to organize your topics and ideas for a presentation. This chapter has a section on dashboards and story points, and goes through the concepts and terminologies used in this area.

In this chapter, we will cover the following topics:

- Creating a filter action
- Creating a URL action
- Creating an infographic-like dashboard

Creating a filter action

Dashboards in Tableau allow multiple worksheets to be put together to provide a more comprehensive view of the insights you are trying to provide. Dashboards also allow additional interactivity between the worksheets, and even other dashboards, using what are called **actions**. Tableau supports three actions: filter, highlight, and URL.

A filter action enables one view to narrow down the information shown in other views, either in the same dashboard or different dashboards. Adding filter actions is a great way to make Tableau dashboards more interactive. It allows the user of the dashboard to focus on specific items by narrowing down other views and only retaining values based on what they selected. It also encourages end users to explore datasets more, and see how each of the graphs varies based on how they filter them.

We will use the filter action with the quick icon that is made available within the worksheet's options. This icon was introduced in Tableau V9.2:

We can also enable this option by using the drop-down arrow and selecting **Use as Filter**:

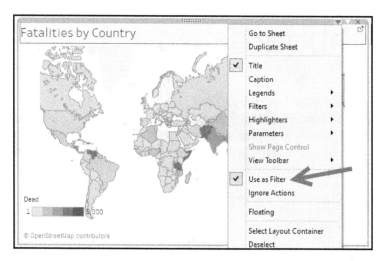

When a sheet is enabled as a filter, Tableau autogenerates a filter action which filters all other worksheets in the dashboard using the values that were selected in the sheet:

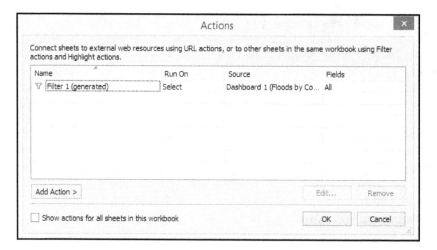

The following are the settings for the autogenerated filter action:

Note that the source and target are the current dashboard. The filter happens on **Select**, which triggers the action when the consumer of the dashboard clicks on a label or mark from the source sheet. The fields that are used for filtering are all fields that are common among the worksheets.

There are two other options under **Run action on:Hover** and **Menu**. **Hover** triggers the action when the mouse pointer is moved over a label or mark, while **Menu** shows a hyperlink after a label or mark is clicked.

We can also create the filter actions manually by going to the **Dashboard** menu, and selecting **Actions...**:

When setting up the action, the target can be a different dashboard altogether.

When setting up actions that allow your end users to jump from one dashboard to another, ensure you provide a way to go back to the previous dashboard. This can be done by creating another filter action, and reversing the source and destination dashboards.

Pay attention to the source and target item icons:

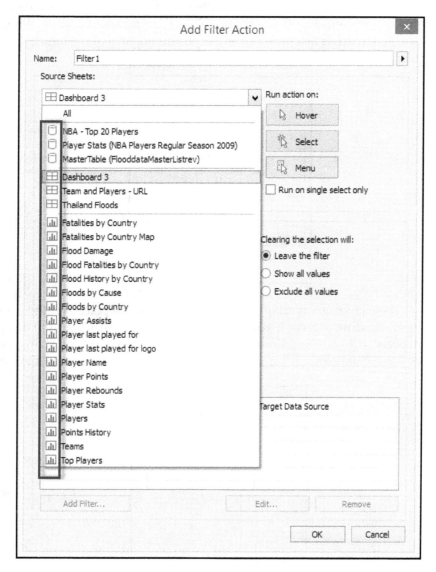

Typically, we target dashboards instead of individual sheets. In addition, when we target an individual sheet that is not in the dashboard, the action would take them to that specific worksheet. This may create a confusing effect, especially if the look and feel of the dashboard is different from that of the individual sheet.

We have used a mix of **Tiled** and **Floating** components in this exercise. **Tiled** makes all the components (worksheets, containers, legends, filters, and so on) occupy a single layer in a grid. All of these components together occupy 100% of the dashboard space. When components are tiled, there is no control over the position or size of the items:

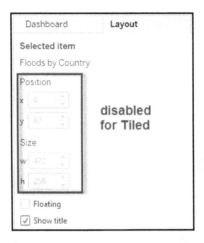

Floating allows these layers to overlap each other, and either be placed on the front or at the back of any sheet. **Floating** is great if you want to have more control over the design of your dashboards, especially if you are following more stringent constraints on sizing, such as needing to print the dashboard on letter or legal paper, or targeting specific devices:

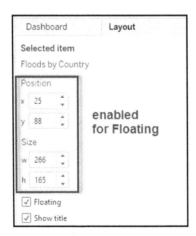

Floating is also great for placing legends, parameters, and filters nearer the views they refer to. By default, these components are placed on the right-hand section of the dashboard. However, this placement may be disruptive if the view they relate to is not within the proximity of the control.

We also made use of filters (not filter action, but filter control). When you add a filter to the dashboard, it is possible to change the scope of that filter to affect not only the worksheet it belongs to, but other worksheets as well:

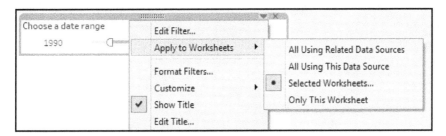

As can be seen in the screenshot, the **Apply to Worksheets** menu shows four options:

- **Only This Worksheet**
- **Selected Worksheets...**
- **All Using This Data Source**
- **All Using Related Data Sources**

These options illustrate how flexible filters can be. It is possible for one filter to affect multiple selected sheets, or even all sheets that share the same data source. In Tableau V10, the option **All Using Related Data Sources** was introduced, which allows the filter to work across different data sources. This is a very welcome addition, as this simplifies filtering in dashboards. In previous versions, the only ways to filter across different data sources were either using filter actions or creating parameters and calculated fields in all related sheets.

Now, let's use one of the sheets in our dashboard to filter all other sheets in the dashboard:

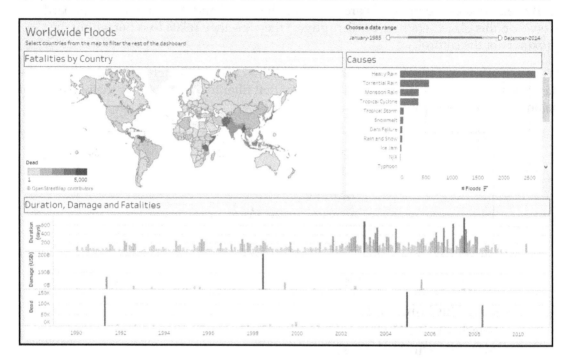

We will use the following worksheets:

- Floods by Country
- Floods by Cause
- Flood Damage

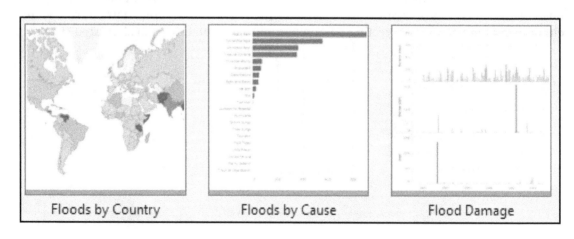

1. At the bottom of your Tableau design area are **Sheet** tabs. There are three tabs with plus signs, which allow you to create a new sheet, dashboard, and story point respectively. Click on the middle icon with the grid to create a new dashboard:

2. When in the dashboard design area, the sidebar becomes a dashboard bar, showing the available worksheets and other dashboard components.

3. Check the **Show dashboard title** checkbox, located at the bottom of the **Objects** section. This will show the dashboard title text box in the dashboard:

4. Change the dashboard title to show the following:

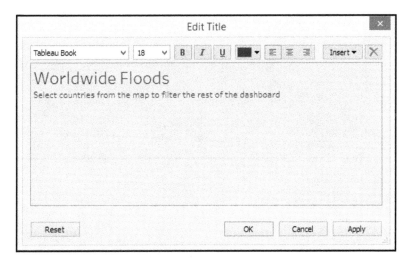

5. Right-click on the dashboard title, and select **Format Title**. Choose a light gray background to the title.

6. If needed, adjust the height of the dashboard title so the whole text is visible.

7. Under the **Objects** section, ensure that **Tiled** is selected and not **Floating**.

8. Under the **Sheets** section in the **Dashboard** tab, drag the related worksheets onto the dashboard:

   - Drag `Floods by Country`. By default, when **Tiled** is selected, this will occupy the whole dashboard space

   - Drag the `Flood Damage` worksheet and place it below `Floods by Country`. When you drag it, you will notice certain areas will get shaded. Release your mouse only when the shaded area is underneath the `Floods by Country` worksheet

   - Drag `Floods by Cause` to the right of `Floods by Country` and above `Flood Damage`:

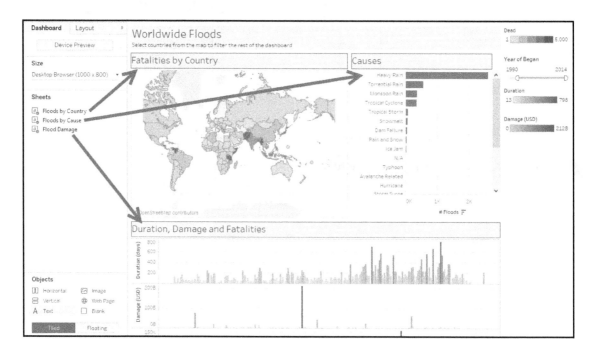

9. Increase the width of the `Fatalities by Country` so it is wider than the `Floods by Cause` worksheet.

10. Remove the **Duration** and **Damage (USD)** color legends by clicking on the **X** mark:

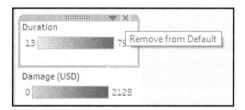

11. Set the **Dead** color legend to **Floating**. You can do this by selecting the color legend, which will show the legend's gray border. Click on the drop-down arrow in the top-right corner, and select **Floating**. Selecting the **Floating** option will take the legend out of the grid and allow it to be layered on top of other items in the dashboard:

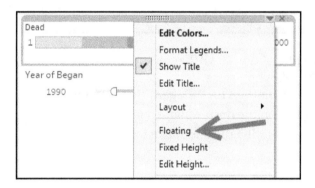

12. Place the **Dead** color legend closer to the `Fatalities by Country` map worksheet, closer to the bottom-left area so it does not cover any countries in the map:

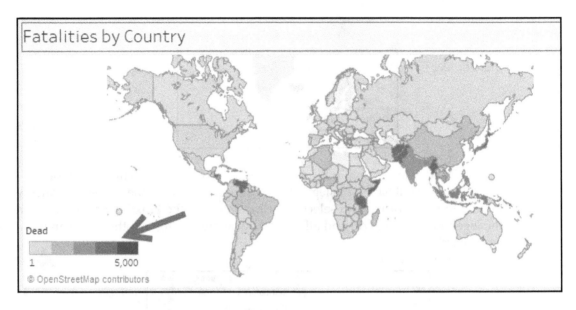

13. Change the title of the **YEAR(Began)** filter to `Choose a date range`. To do this, perform the following steps:
    - Click on the **YEAR(Began)** filter to show the gray border
    - Click on the drop-down menu on the top-right corner
    - Select **Edit Title** and make the changes

14. Change the scope of the date filter to all worksheets in the dashboard:
    - Click on the drop-down of the filter, and choose **Apply to Worksheets**, and then **Selected Worksheets...**
    - Click the **All on dashboard** button in the **Apply Filter to Worksheets** window that appears. Click on **OK** when done:

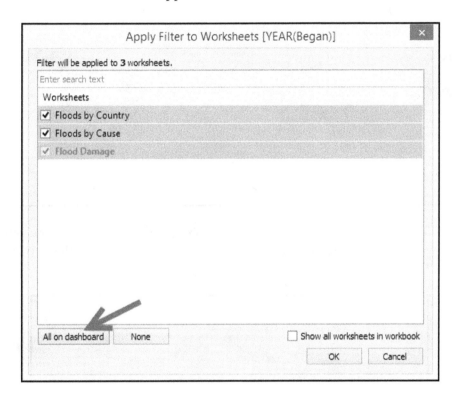

15. Format the filter to have light gray shading using the same color as the dashboard title. You can do this by selecting the filter and clicking on the drop-down arrow on the top-right corner. From here, you can choose **Format Filters**. You can change the shading from the formatting sidebar that appears.

16. Click on the drop-down of the date filter, and choose **Float**. Place the filter in the top-right corner of the dashboard, beside the dashboard title:

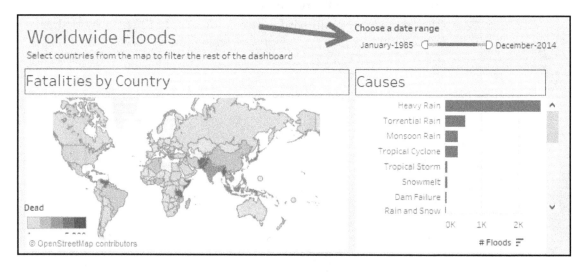

17. Click on the `Floods by Country` worksheet, and click on the funnel icon that appears in the top-right corner. This enables the map to filter all the worksheets in the dashboard:

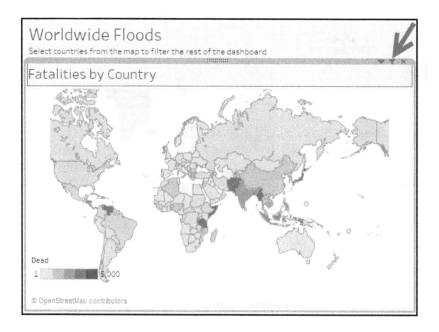

18. Change the dashboard name to `Flood Dashboard`. You can double-click on the **Dashboard** tab, and rename from there.

19. Test the dashboard. Use the presentation mode (or press *F7* key) to see what the end users will see. Click on countries in the map and/or change the date range in the filter. Confirm that the rest of the worksheets are filtered by that country.

Creating a URL action

The URL action opens up a world of possibilities. It allows us to specify a URL that our dashboard can navigate to, either using the user's default web browser or using a web page placeholder that exists in the dashboard. If there is a web page object in the dashboard, the URL action displays the web page in that object. If there is no web page object, the URL is opened in the default web browser.

Adding a URL action can add a lot of value to a dashboard because it can allow additional information to be searched or fetched, in addition to the information the dashboard already offers.

Increase the width of `Fatalities by Country` so it is wider than the `Floods by Cause` worksheet.

As with the other actions, the URL action can be used with **Select**, **Hover**, or **Menu**. **Menu** is quite popular as this creates a hyperlink for each URL action, almost simulating a drop-down menu from a web page. The hyperlink can be customized, and can include values we have in the dashboard:

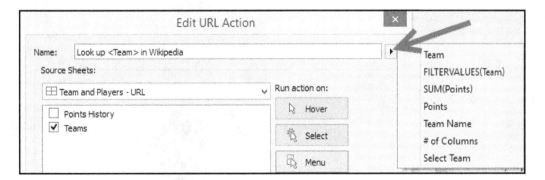

To feed values from our dashboard to the target URL, the target URL must be able to accept parameters at the URL string called the GET parameters.

Be aware that when websites are embedded, the behavior may change as the providers change their agreement, code, and so on. For example, a while back, it was pretty easy to embed YouTube videos onto Tableau dashboards and play them on Tableau Desktop. However, this behavior has changed and the dashboard is now required to be published to Tableau Server/Online/Public before the video plays.

Another aspect to consider when embedding web pages in Tableau dashboards is using the mobile version of the page, when available. Otherwise, many web pages tend to show all the extraneous headers and footers, which may make the page look odd or out of place.

One limitation is if you have multiple URLs and want to direct them to different web page objects in your dashboard: you cannot. You also cannot choose to open the web page in a new window if you have a web page object in your dashboard.

Let's create a dashboard that uses a URL action to look up information about an NBA team from Wikipedia:

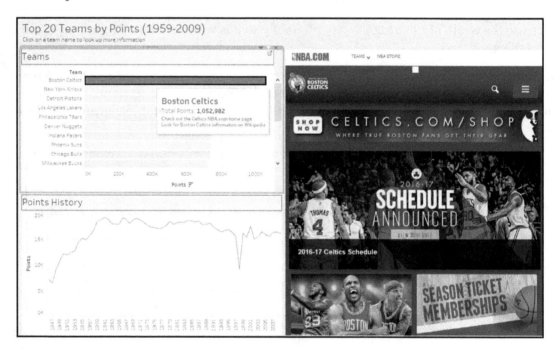

We will use the following worksheets:

- Teams
- Points History

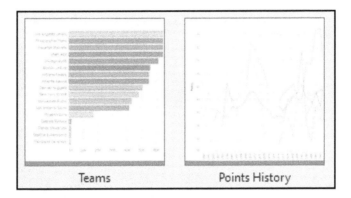

Teams   Points History

1. At the bottom of your Tableau design area are three tabs with plus signs, which allow you to create a new sheet, dashboard, and story point respectively. Click on the middle icon with the grid to create a new dashboard:

2. When in the dashboard design area, the sidebar becomes a **Dashboard** bar, showing the available worksheets and other dashboard components.
3. Change the dashboard name to Team and Players – Embed URL.
4. Check the **Show dashboard title** checkbox. This will show the dashboard title text box in the dashboard:

5. Change the dashboard title to show the following:

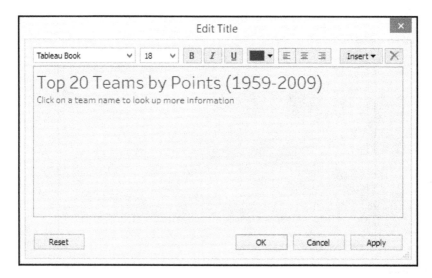

6. Right-click on the dashboard title, and select **Format Title**. Choose a light gray background to the title.
7. If needed, adjust the height of the dashboard title so the whole text is visible.
8. Under the **Objects** section, ensure that **Tiled** is selected and not **Floating**.
9. Click on the **Dashboard** menu, and choose **Format**.
10. Under **Dashboard Shading**, change the color beside **Default** to a light color. This will set the dashboard background color:

11. Drag the worksheets from the **Dashboard** tab, under the **Sheets** section, onto the dashboard:
    - Drag the `Teams` worksheet. By default, when **Tiled** is selected, this worksheet will occupy the whole dashboard space
    - Drag **Web Page** from the **Objects** section to the right of `Teams`
    - Drag `Points History` below Teams, but to the left of the web page component:

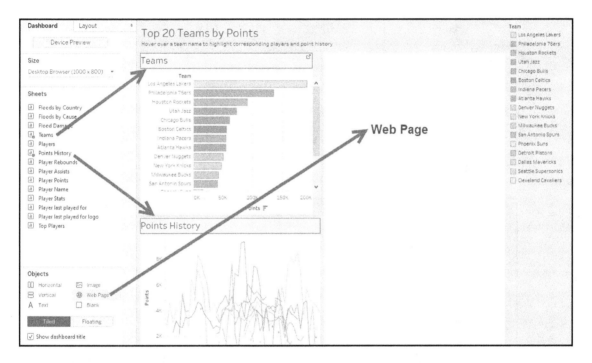

12. Click the color legend to activate it, and select the X in the top-right corner to remove it from the dashboard.

13. Click on the **Dashboard** menu and select **Actions...**:

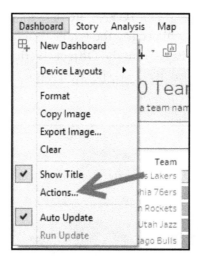

14. In the **Actions** window, click on **Add Action >**, and choose **URL...**:

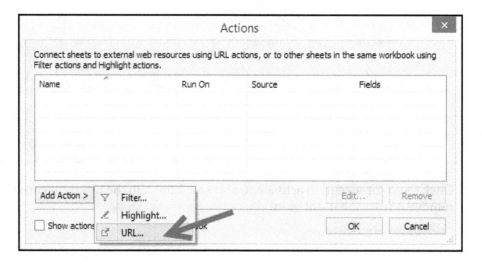

15. In the Add URL Action window, do the following:
    - Change the **Name** to `Check out the <Team> NBA.com home page`
    - Change the **Run action on:** to **Menu**
    - Add the URL `http://www.nba.com/<Team>/`

- Click **OK** to close the window:

16. Add another URL action with the following settings:
    - Change the **Name** to `Look for <Team> information on Wikipedia`
    - Change the **Run action on:** to **Menu**
    - Add the URL `http://www.nba.com/<Team>/`:

17. Add a filter action with the following settings:
    - Change the **Name** to `Filter dashboard for <Team>`
    - Change the **Run action on:** to **Select**
    - Under **Source Sheets**, ensure **the Team and Players - URL** dashboard is selected (icon should be the grid), and the `Teams` worksheet is checked.
    - Under **Target Sheets**, ensure the **Team and Players - URL** dashboard is selected (icon should be the grid), and the `Points History` worksheet is checked:

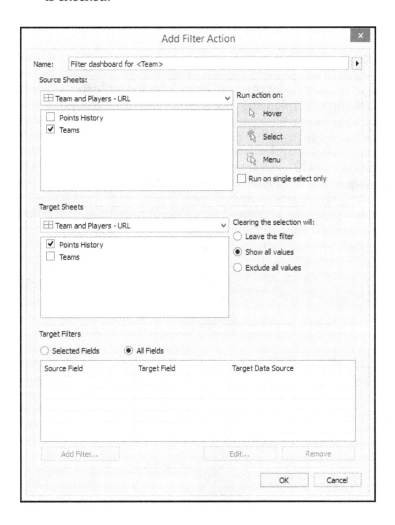

18. Test the dashboard. Use the presentation mode (or press *F7* key) to see what the end users will see. Confirm that when you hover over any of the teams in the bar chart, you see the corresponding points history for that team highlighted in the time series graph, as well as the players on that team highlighted in the scatter plot.

Creating an infographic-like dashboard

Infographics is a shortened term for information graphics, which is a way to visualize data using a lot of graphics and is designed to make the visuals more graphic and eye-catching. Tableau has the components to add more visual elements into a dashboard and make it look more like a typical infographic.

Creating an infographic-like dashboard in Tableau can be quite involved. Often, this task will encompass creating multiple worksheets with individual components or pieces of information, and putting these all together creatively so that the design elements flow according to the infographic design.

Just a word of caution: the URL cannot come from a secondary data source, in the case of blended data sources; it has to be from the primary data source.

Let's create an infographic-like dashboard that incorporates free-form images and text. We will have a fairly simplistic take on the infographic possibility with Tableau, but it should give you a clearer idea on how to do it. If you check the individual worksheets that we will use, many of them will have a single piece of information; for example, one worksheet will contain only the name of the player and another worksheet will contain only the logo of the team that player last played with:

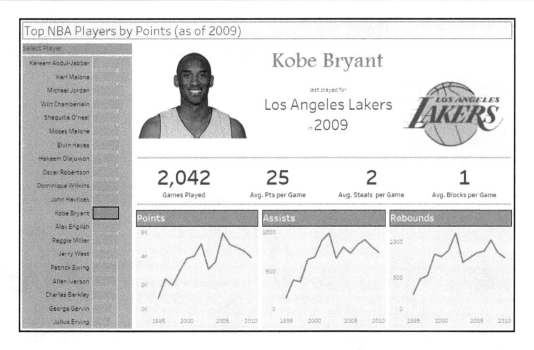

We will use the following worksheets:

- Top Players
- Player Points
- Player Assists
- Player Rebounds
- Player Name
- Player Stats
- Player last played for

- Player last played for logo

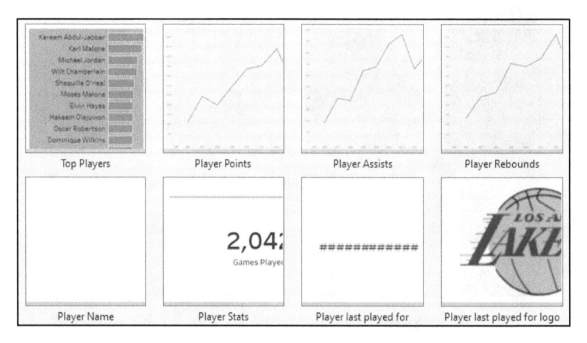

1. Create a new dashboard.
2. Check the **Show dashboard title** checkbox. This will show the dashboard title text box in the dashboard.
3. Change the dashboard title to Top NBA Players by Points (as of 2009).
4. Ensure that **Tiled** is selected under the **Objects** section.
5. Drag the Top Players worksheet to your dashboard. By default, this will occupy the whole space of the dashboard.

6. From the **Objects** section, drag a **Blank** object to the right of the `Top Players` worksheet. Adjust the width of the **Blank** object so that it occupies about 75% of the space:

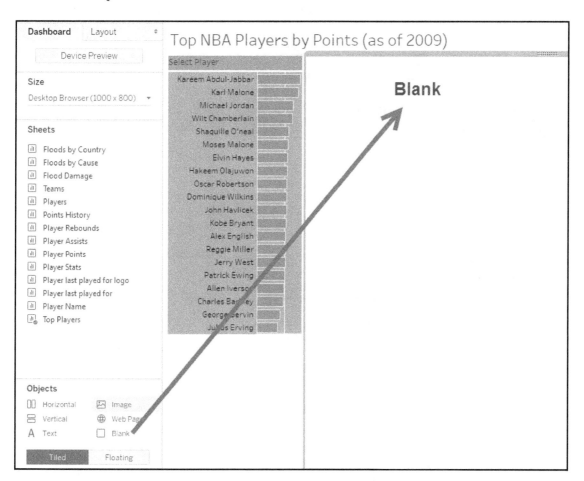

7. Drag the **Player Stats** worksheet and place it below the **Blank** space, to the right of the Top Players worksheet.

8. Click on the drop-down of the Player Stats worksheet. Under **Fit**, choose **Entire View**:

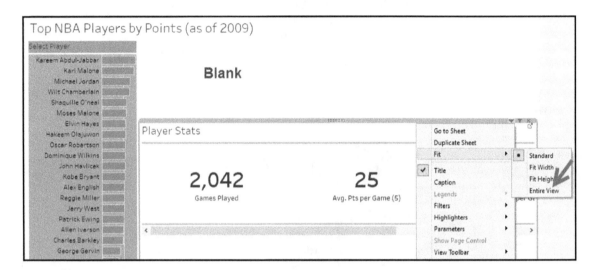

9. Under **Objects**, drag **Horizontal** (which is a layout container) and place it underneath the Player Stats worksheet, to the right of the Top Players worksheet.

10. Under **Objects**, drag another **Blank**. Place it underneath **Horizontal Layout Container**:

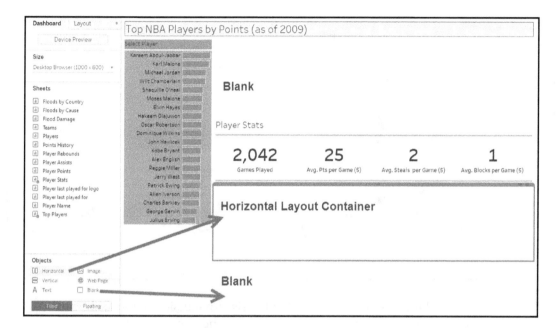

11. Hide the title for Player Stats. To do this, you can right-click on the Player Stats title, and choose **Hide Title**.

12. Drag the following player worksheets:
    - Drag the Player Points worksheet and place it on the horizontal layout container. By default, it will occupy all the space in that layout container
    - Drag the Player Rebounds worksheet and place it to the right of the Player Points worksheet

- Drag the `Player Assists` worksheet and place it in the middle of the `Player Points` and `Player Rebounds` worksheets:

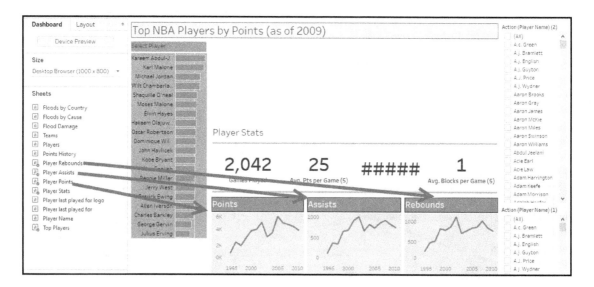

13. Remove all filters that were added to the right-hand side of the dashboard. You can do this by selecting the respective filters, and clicking on the X mark.

14. Under **Objects**, select **Floating**.

15. Add the following as floating objects; a screenshot of the expected layout is provided as well:

    - Add a web page to the top. Leave the URL as blank for now. We will add the URL action later
    - Drag `Player Name` to the right of the **Blank** web page
    - Drag `Player last played for,` and place it below the `Player Name` worksheet

- Drag `Player last played for` to the right of `Player Name` and `Player last played for`:

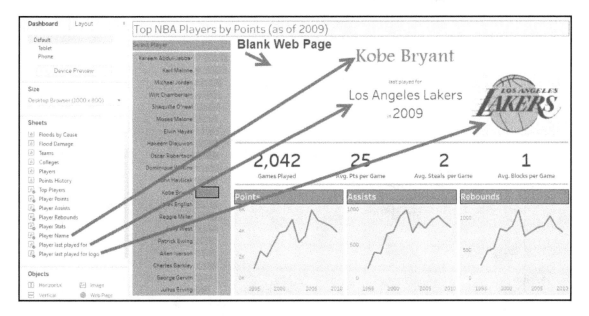

16. Click on the **Dashboard** menu, and select **Actions...**.

17. Add a URL action with the following settings:
    - Change the **Name:** to `Player Image`.
    - Change the **Run action on:** to **Select**.
    - Set the **URL** to **<Image URL>**:

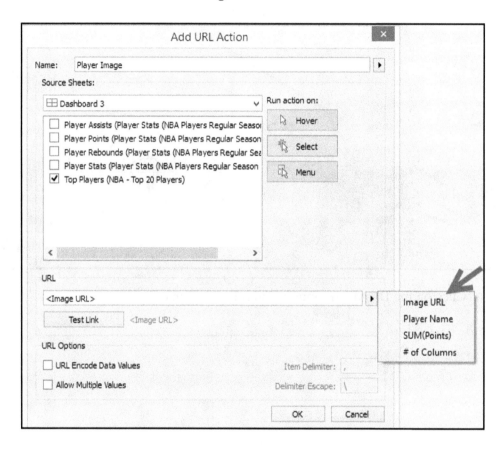

18. Test to ensure that the image is showing properly. Click on any player name, and the image of that player should show up:

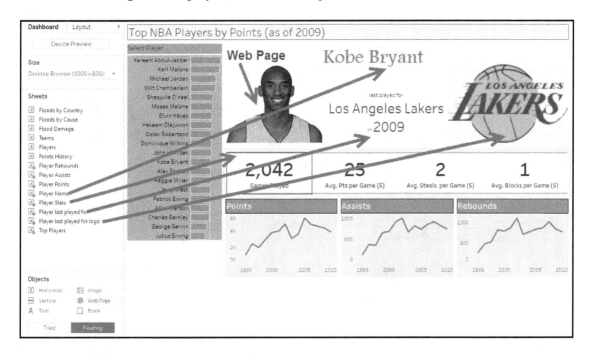

19. Click on the `Top Players` worksheet to select it. Click on the drop-down on the top-right corner, and under **Fit**, choose **Entire View**.

20. Drag another **Blank** object and place it underneath the `Top Players` worksheet. Line up this **Blank** object to the other **Blank** object under the **Player Points** row:

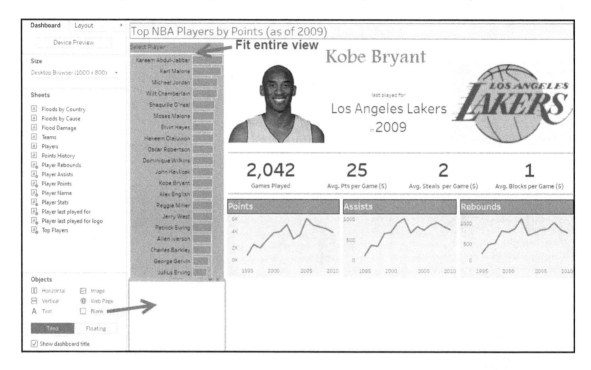

21. Change the dashboard name to `Top NBA Players by Points`.

Creating story points

Story points help you organize your points and thoughts for a presentation. They allow us to organize our topics and views into a sequence of points that aid in presenting data. Story points can leverage any views or dashboards in the workbook and use any of those in each point.

You may have done this in the past using different software applications. This, however, would have required you to export the worksheets and dashboards as images so they can be embedded into the presentation application. This does limit the interactivity, and you really lose the advantages that Tableau brings to the table.

Tableau is largely an interactive tool, and allows for the exploration of information. As you select, you may see other views get filtered. As you hover, you may get highlights. Story points allow you to present, as well as retain, the interactive components of Tableau. It provides a seamless flow of discussion and analysis.

If you need to incorporate images and custom text, you will need to create a dashboard first with those objects and then use them in the story points.

What we explore here is just a starting point. Story points are completely dependent on your data story, your goal, and your audience. Although the formatting options for story points are fairly limited, you can still create very organized, interactive, and compelling presentations using Tableau's story points.

Let's explore where fatal floods have happened over time using Tableau's story points:

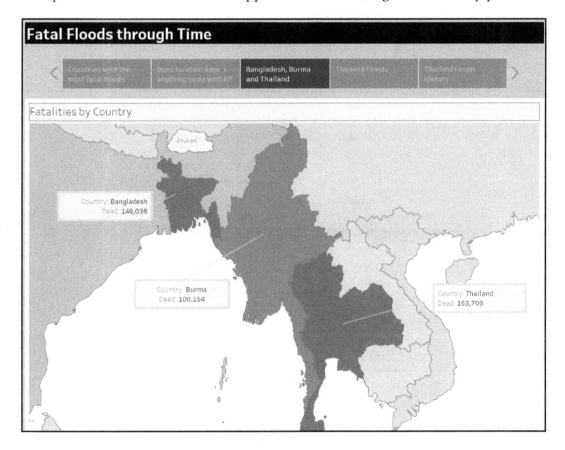

We will use the following worksheets:

- Fatalities by Country
- Fatalities by Country Map
- Flood History by Country

We are also going to use the following dashboard, which shows **Thailand Floods** data:

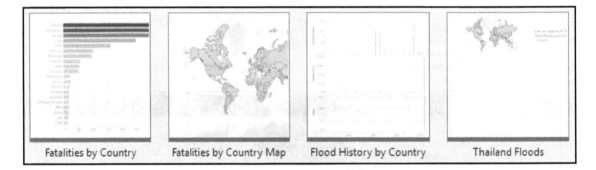

| Fatalities by Country | Fatalities by Country Map | Flood History by Country | Thailand Floods |

1. Create a new story point. You can click on the **New Story Point** tab, which looks like a book with a plus sign, at the bottom of the canvas:

2. Double-click on the title, and change the story title to Fatal Floods over Time.

3. Click on the **Story** menu at the top, and select **Format**:

4. Format the story using the following settings:
   - **Story Shading** to gray
   - **Story Title | Font:** to **22**pt bold, **Tableau Bold** font family, white color
   - **Story Title | Shading:** to black
   - **Navigator | Font:** to **10**pt, **Tableau Book** font family
   - **Navigator | Shading:** to dark red:

5. Change the **Story size** to **Automatic**:

6. Click on **New Blank Point** to create a new story point:

- Change the text of the navigator to `Countries with the most fatal floods`
- Drag the `Fatalities by Country` worksheet to the story point canvas:

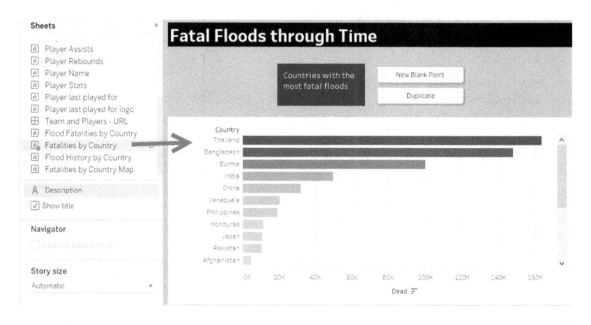

7. Click on **New Blank Point** to create another point:
   - Set the new title to `Does location have anything to do with it?`
   - Drag the `Fatalities by Country` worksheet, which is a filled map, to the current story point canvas:

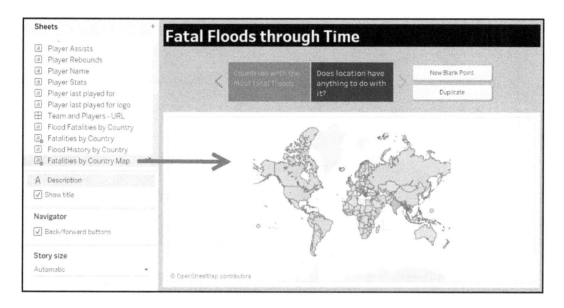

8. Zoom to where the reddest areas are. You can do this by clicking on the map's view toolbar, and using the magnifying lens to zoom to the area:

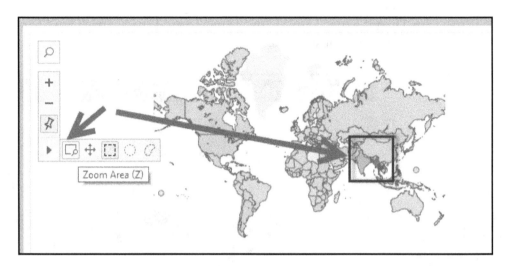

9. Add mark annotations to the three countries with the reddest colors - Bangladesh, Burma, and Thailand. Leave the default text on the mark annotations, which should include the country name and the total fatalities for those countries:

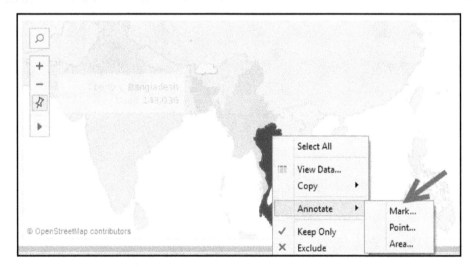

10. Right-click on each of the annotation boxes and select **Format**. Add a thick gray border to each of the annotations.

11. Click on **Save as a New Point** to save this view as a new point.

12. Change the text on this new point to Bangladesh, Burma, and Thailand:

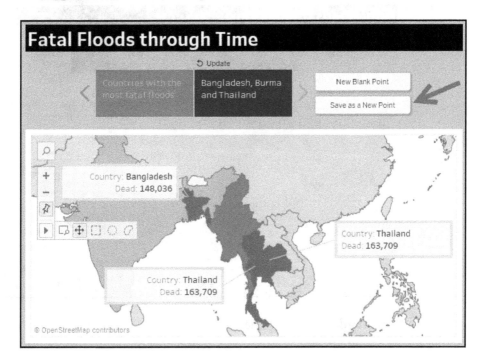

13. Click on **New Blank Point**, and change the text to Thailand Floods.

14. Drag the **Thailand Floods** dashboard from the **Sheets** onto this new story point:

15. Click on **New Blank Point**, and change the text to `Thailand Floods History`.

16. Drag the `Flood History by Country` worksheet onto the story point:

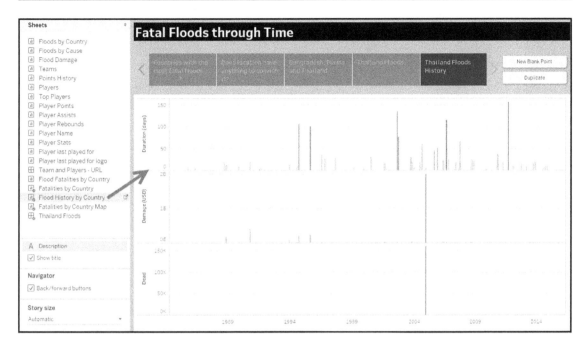

17. Click on the presentation mode, or press *F7* key, and test the story points. You can click on the navigator or simply use the left and right arrows in your keyboard to move through the points.

Summary

In this chapter, we have seen how we can use actions in dashboards to allow added interactivity between the worksheets. We created a filter action that filtered the information shown in other views using the same or different dashboards. We then created a URL action that allowed us to specify a URL that our dashboard can navigate to for looking up information about an NBA team from Wikipedia.

We also created an infographic-like dashboard for the top NBA players by points using free-form images and text with Tableau. Lastly, we covered Tableau's story points that allowed us tolook at fatal floods and where they have taken place over time.

In the next chapter, we will look at data preparation that can help clean and reshape data.

5
Data Preparation

Before we can utilize the analytic power of Tableau, the very first step is connecting with the data. In a perfect world, we would have perfect, clean data that we could easily analyze in Tableau. But alas, in reality, the data that we need to use will most likely need to be cleaned, transformed, and managed before we can effectively use it in Tableau.

Tableau's philosophy with data preparation is to enable anyone at anytime to make fundamental changes to their data connection. This means the capabilities need four key attributes to empower you:

- **Smart**: They should apply automatically and have a deep sense of the data
- **Fast**: They need to operate at near real time even on big data
- **Repeatable**: They need to allow for changes to the underlying data, such as new values, rows, and columns
- **Flexible**: They need to allow you to make significant changes at any time while preserving your work

There are tools that exclusively help clean and reshape data. Many refer to these as **ETL** (**Extract**, **Transform**, and **Load**) tools. While Tableau is not an ETL tool, it has the ability to help clean or prepare data if it is not possible to clean or prepare it at the data source.

In this chapter, we will cover the following topics:

- Using the Data Interpreter and pivots
- Using the legacy Jet driver
- Using schema.ini to resolve data type issues
- Pivoting columns

- Using unions
- Using joins
- Using blends

Using the Data Interpreter and pivots

Tableau works best with clean, tall, and narrow data instead of short and wide data. The same measures should ideally be provided in a single column instead of spread out.

Let's clean up the following spreadsheet on Canada International Student Permits and ready it for Tableau:

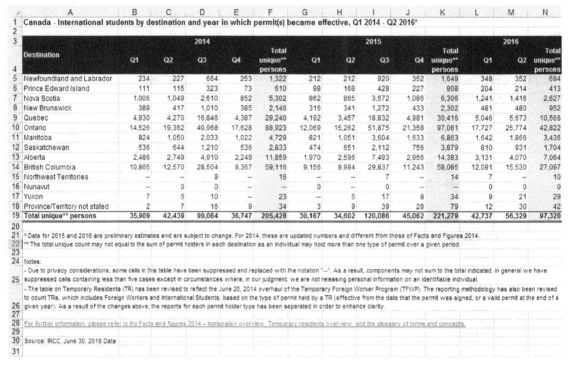

	A	B	C	D	E	F	G	H	I	J	K	L	M	N
1	Canada - International students by destination and year in which permit(s) became effective, Q1 2014 - Q2 2016*													
2														
3				2014					2015				2016	
4	Destination	Q1	Q2	Q3	Q4	Total unique** persons	Q1	Q2	Q3	Q4	Total unique** persons	Q1	Q2	Total unique** persons
5	Newfoundland and Labrador	234	227	664	253	1,322	212	212	920	352	1,649	348	352	694
6	Prince Edward Island	111	115	323	73	610	98	168	428	227	908	204	214	413
7	Nova Scotia	1,006	1,049	2,610	852	5,302	862	865	3,672	1,086	6,306	1,241	1,416	2,627
8	New Brunswick	389	417	1,010	385	2,146	316	341	1,272	433	2,302	481	480	952
9	Quebec	4,930	4,270	16,846	4,387	29,240	4,192	3,457	18,832	4,981	30,416	5,046	5,673	10,566
10	Ontario	14,526	19,362	40,968	17,628	88,923	12,069	15,262	51,875	21,358	97,061	17,727	25,774	42,822
11	Manitoba	824	1,050	2,033	1,022	4,729	821	1,051	3,604	1,633	6,863	1,642	1,866	3,436
12	Saskatchewan	536	644	1,210	536	2,833	474	651	2,112	756	3,879	810	931	1,704
13	Alberta	2,486	2,749	4,910	2,249	11,859	1,970	2,596	7,493	2,956	14,383	3,131	4,070	7,064
14	British Columbia	10,865	12,570	28,504	9,367	59,116	9,156	9,994	29,837	11,243	58,085	12,091	15,530	27,097
15	Northwest Territories	--	--	9	--	16	--	--	7	--	14	7	--	10
16	Nunavut	--	0	0	--	--	0	--	0	--	--	0	0	0
17	Yukon	7	6	10	--	23	--	5	17	8	34	9	21	29
18	Province/Territory not stated	2	7	16	9	34	3	9	39	28	79	12	30	42
19	Total unique** persons	35,909	42,439	99,064	36,747	205,428	30,167	34,602	120,086	45,062	221,279	42,737	56,329	97,320
20														
21	* Data for 2015 and 2016 are preliminary estimates and are subject to change. For 2014, these are updated numbers and different from those of Facts and Figures 2014.													
22	** The total unique count may not equal to the sum of permit holders in each destination as an individual may hold more than one type of permit over a given period.													
23														
24	Notes:													
25	- Due to privacy considerations, some cells in this table have been suppressed and replaced with the notation "--". As a result, components may not sum to the total indicated. In general we have suppressed cells containing less than five cases except in circumstances where, in our judgment, we are not releasing personal information on an identifiable individual.													
26	- The table on Temporary Residents (TR) has been revised to reflect the June 20, 2014 overhaul of the Temporary Foreign Worker Program (TFWP). The reporting methodology has also been revised to count TRs, which includes Foreign Workers and International Students, based on the type of permit held by a TR (effective from the date that the permit was signed, or a valid permit at the end of a given year). As a result of the changes above, the reports for each permit holder type has been separated in order to enhance clarity.													
27														
28	For further information, please refer to the Facts and figures 2014 – Immigration overview: Temporary residents overview, and the glossary of terms and concepts.													
29														
30	Source: IRCC, June 30, 2016 Data													
31														

1. Download the file from the Citizenship and Immigration Canada website using the following URL:

   ```
   http://www.cic.gc.ca/opendata-donneesouvertes/data/IRCC_IS_0004_E.
   xls
   ```

2. Connect to the Excel file in this example. Make sure you choose **Excel** from the **To a File** section:

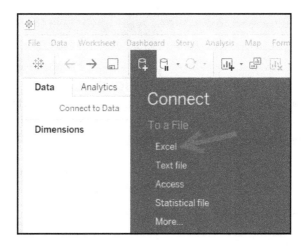

3. When you first connect to this Excel file, this is what you will see:

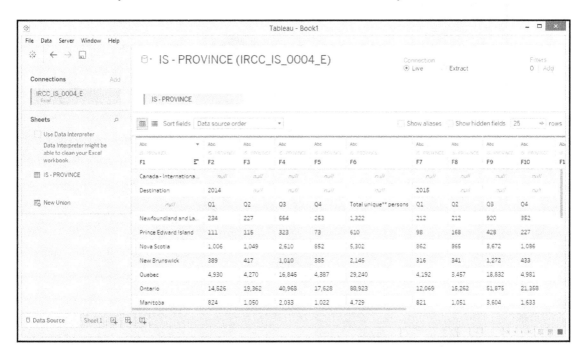

4. The original Excel file is a common type of file that many data professionals have to work with. The Excel file has a header and a footer, and the measures are spread across the columns. The number of international students--a measure--is spread out across 13 columns.

This file needs to be cleaned up:

- The header and footer needs to be removed
- Year values need to be a dimension, since these are descriptors for the measure
- The measure, which is the number of international students, needs to be placed in a single column

1. Check the checkbox beside **Use Data Interpreter**. Note that when this checkbox is checked, the label changes to **Cleaned with Data Interpreter**:

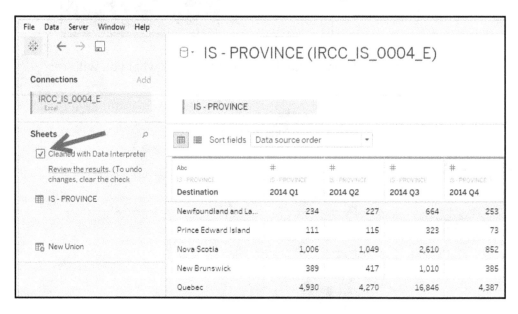

2. Select all fields except for **Destination**.

When we use the Tableau Data Interpreter, it will clean up the headers and footers, but will not clean up the year dimension and the measure for the number of international students. When we run the Data Interpreter, we can also choose to review the results by clicking on the provided link. The first tab, presented here, provides the key to what the Data Interpreter does:

	A	B	C	D	E	F	G	H	I	J	K	L
2		**Key for Understanding the Data Interpreter Results**										
3												
4												
5		Use the key to understand how your data source has been interpreted.										
6		To view the results, click a worksheet tab.										
7		Note: Tableau never makes changes to your underlying data source.										
8												
9												
10												
11		Key:										
12		Data is interpreted as column headers (field names).										
13		Data is interpreted as values in your data source.										
14		Data derived from a merged cell is interpreted as value in your data source.										
15		Data is ignored and not included as part of your data source.										
16		Data has been excluded from your data source.										
17		Note: To search for all excluded data, use CRTL +F on Windows										
18		or Command F on the Mac, and then type '***DATA REMOVED***'.										
19												
20												
21		If the Data Interpreter has interpreted the Tableau data source incorrectly, close the spreadsheet,										
22		and then clear the Cleaned with Data Interpreter check box from the Data Source page.										
23		If the Tableau data source continues to be interpreted incorrectly or for general information										
24		about why some data was removed by the Data Interpreter, refer to										
25		Resolving Common Issues with Data Interpreter Results										
26		Help Tableau improve the Data Interpreter by emailing your file to support@tableau.com										
27		or filing a support request with an attached file at:										
28												
29		http://tableau.com/support/request										

3. To further clean our data source, we need to pivot the remaining so year the values and number of international students are stored in single columns. While the fields are selected, right-click and choose **Pivot**:

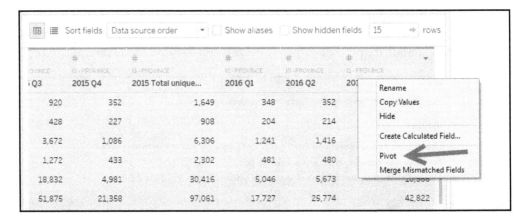

4. Right-click the new fields to rename them:
    a. Change **Pivot Field Names** to **Period**
    b. Change **Pivot Field Values** to **International Students**:

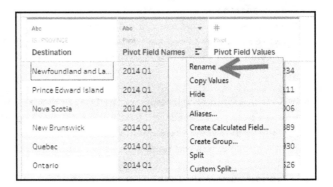

    c. Click on **Add** underneath **Filters**:

5. In the **Select a field:** option, choose **Period**:

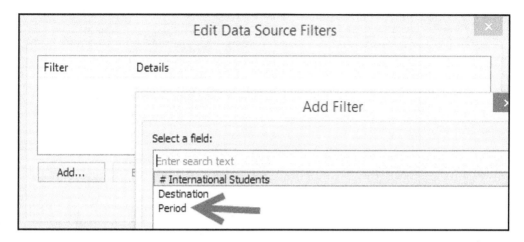

6. In the filter window for **Period**, under the **Wildcard** tab, type `Total` and check the **Exclude** checkbox:

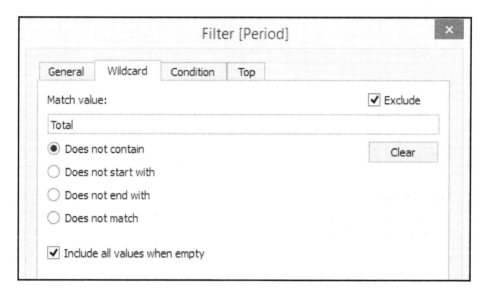

7. Once you click **OK**, you should see the following in the **Edit Data Source Filters** box:

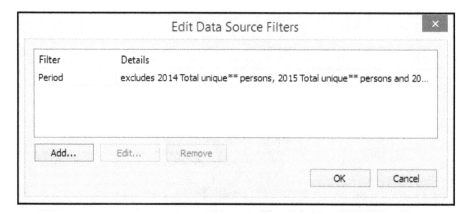

8. Click on **OK** when done.The original Excel file has some total fields, which we excluded, so that we can keep the granularity of the measure consistent; for example, we would not want to sum all the measures and the field for total unique persons.

9. Under **Filters**, click on **Edit** to add one more filter:

10. This time, choose the **Destination** field.

11. In the filter window for **Destination**, under the **Wildcard** tab, type Total and check the **Exclude** checkbox.

12. Once you click **OK**, you should see the following in the **Edit Data Source Filters** box:

13. In the preview pane, click on the **Abc** symbol above **Destination** and change **Geographic Role** to **State/Province**:

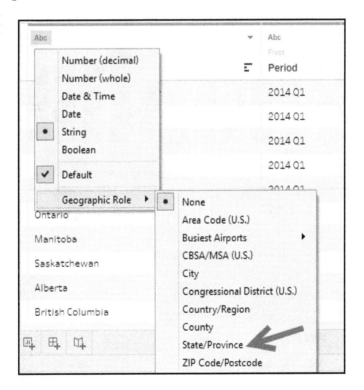

14. From here, we can create a new sheet and create visualizations that are easier to work with in Tableau. The following screenshot depicts the number of students per period:

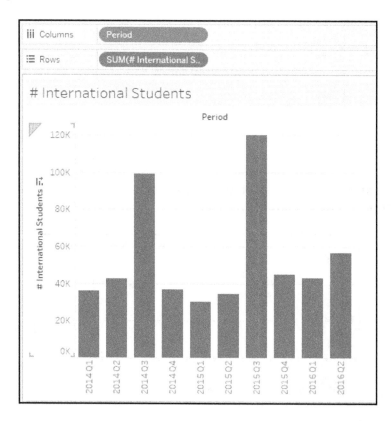

15. Since we have geocoded the **Destination** and assigned it the **State/Province** geographic role, we can also create a filled map to see where students are going:

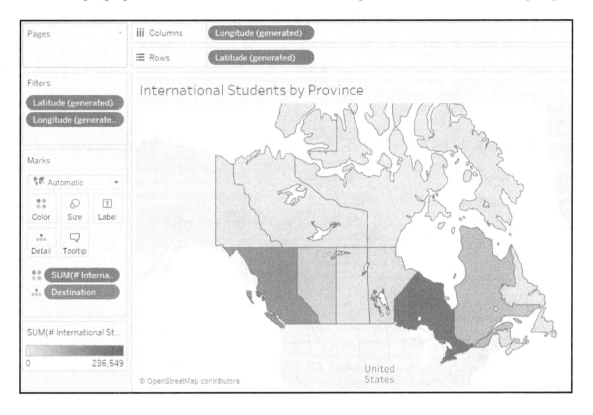

16. Although the **Destination** field is geocoded to **State/Province**, we will still need the **Country** information before we can successfully create a map. For this data set, we can simply set the country manually by going to the Mapmenu item, and selecting **Edit Locations**. We can set this to **Canada**:

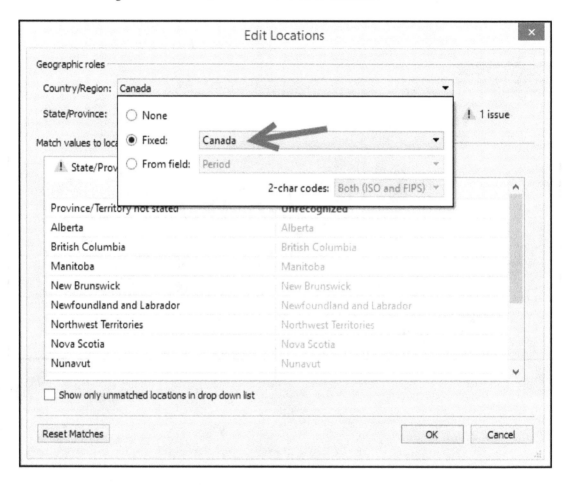

17. Alternatively, we can create a field for **Country** and use that in the geocoding.

18. You can probably see that there is additional cleanup and transformation that can be done. **Period**, for example, can be split further into year and quarter. We can even go as far as creating a date for the start of the period. This can be done using a calculated field:

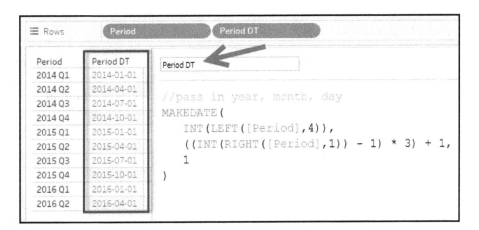

Using the legacy Jet driver

Let's use the New York Restaurant Inspections Excel file and use the legacy Jet driver to shape the file so that we can have both the inspection date and grade date in the same column.

The challenge here is that we often have a universal notion of date, that is, a date is a day that isn't specific to any events. We may want to summarize or aggregate measures based on this universal notion of dates. However, in reality, dates may exist in different fields with different contexts, and this can limit our ability to work on them as a single unit.

In the Excel file for this recipe, we want to count how many restaurants were inspected and how many were graded for a specific date. The Excel file does not have a generic date field that allows us to count how many were inspected or graded. Thus, we need to re-shape our data so that **Inspection Date** and **Grade Date** exist in one column instead of two.

If we are using an Excel file as our data source, we can potentially use the legacy Jet connection, which allows custom SQL statements against the Excel file.

The legacy connection option was introduced in Tableau 8.2. You can learn more about this in the Tableau KB article *Differences between Legacy and Default Excel and Text File Connections*, which can be found at `http://onlinehelp.tableau.com/current/pro/desktop/en-us/help.htm` `#upgrading_connection.html`.

Download the file from the New York City Open Data website using the following URL:

```
https://nycopendata.socrata.com/Health/DOHMH-New-York-City-Restaurant-
Inspection-Results/xx67-kt59/data
```

Once you have downloaded the data, save the file as `DOHMH_New_York_City_Restaurant_Inspection_Results.xls` (Microsoft Excel 97-2003 worksheet). Note that the records may have been updated between the time of writing and the time of your download:

1. Click on **New Data Source** icon, and choose **Excel**:

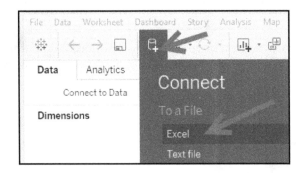

2. Choose `DOHMH_New_York_City_Restaurant_Inspection_Results.xls`, and select **Open with Legacy Connection**:

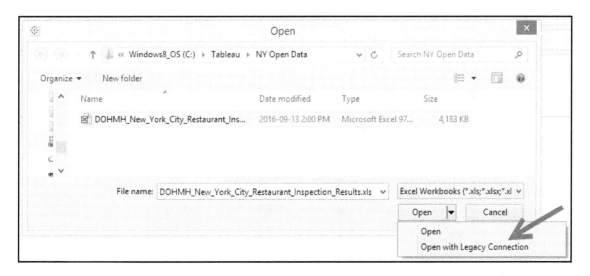

3. In the **Connections** window, remove the existing connection to the one sheet in the Excel file:

4. Drag **New Custom SQL** to the main connection pane:

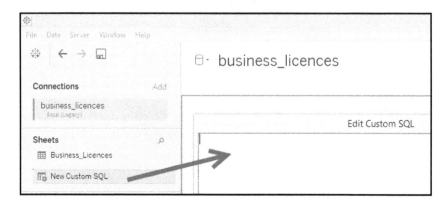

5. Add the following code to the **Edit Custom SQL** window:

```
SELECT
[DBA],
[CAMIS],
[CUISINE DESCRIPTION],
[INSPECTION DATE],
[GRADE DATE],
[INSPCTION DATE] AS [Date],
'Inspected' AS [Type]
FROM [DOHMH New York City Restaurant$]
UNION ALL
SELECT
[DBA],
[CAMIS],
[CUISINE DESCRIPTION],
[INSPECTION DATE],
[GRADE DATE],
[GRADE DATE] AS [Date],
'Graded' AS [Type]
FROM [DOHMH New York City Restaurant$]
```

6. In the preview window, click on the **Abc** symbol above the **Date** field and select **Date** to change the data type to Date:

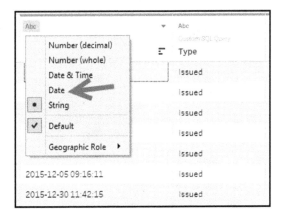

When we query our Excel spreadsheet, each tab will be treated as a table and referenced as the worksheet name with a $ symbol at the end and enclosed in square brackets, like so: [DOHMH New York City Restaurant$].

QuerySurge has a good short tutorial on using SQL against Excel spreadsheets here: http://bit.ly/QuerySurge-SQL-against-Excel.

What we will do in this query is stack two copies of the original data set on top of each other using the UNION ALL set operator, and introduce two new fields - **Date** and **Type**. This forces one field to contain the two dates we are interested in.

The first set uses **INSPECTION DATE** as the value for:**Date**, and **Inspected** as the value for **Type**. The second set uses **GRADE DATE** as the value for **Date**, and **Graded** as the value for **Type**. If you need to add additional fields for your analysis, you can simply add the field names to both SELECT statements.

Once we have the fields in place, we can analyze and visualize our data. For example, we can create a time series graph with trend lines. Since we have a single date field to consider, we can simply drag that **Date** field and create a continuous axis. Since we also have a single field to differentiate what event that date was related to, we can use that in **Color** in the **Marks** card to create two separate lines for the **Graded** and **Inspected** events:

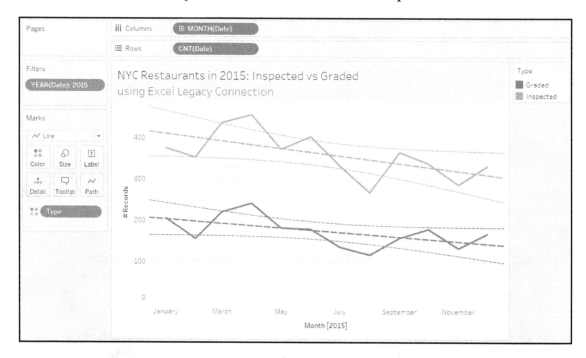

The measure in this example is **CNT(Date)** because **Date** will have a value if it is related to the event, and null (and will not be counted) if it is not.

Be careful when doing other kinds of analysis. Since we stacked two copies of our data set, we essentially doubled our record count.

We are only using the legacy connection because our data source is an Excel file. If your data source is different, for example, if you are using a relational data source, you can re-shape the data using those data source's query mechanisms. In a relational data source, you may be able to do a union or a self-join at the data source level before the data is consumed by Tableau.

Tableau 10 introduces a new feature called cross database join, which we can also consider. Cross database join allows you to connect to multiple data sources and join them from within the Tableau connection interface. In the following example, we have essentially connected to the same Excel worksheet three times:

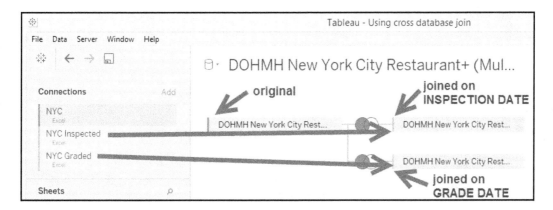

Each connection is a left join. The first one connects mainly based on the **INSPECTION DATE**. There are other fields being considered in the join to ensure we are only matching the correct records. Otherwise, we will end up with something called a cross join and may match one record to all other records of restaurants that were inspected on the same date:

The second one connects mainly based on the **GRADE DATE**. As with the previous join, we also still need to consider other fields in the join to avoid mismatching records:

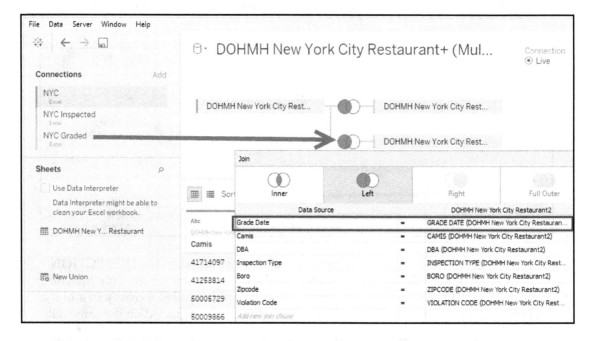

Once the connections are set up, we can create a similar visualization to the one we created using the legacy connection. The following visualization uses a slightly different approach. Since our measures come from different data sources, we are using a dual axis graph for the **COUNT of INSPECTION DATE**s from one data source, and **COUNT of GRADE DATE**s from another data source:

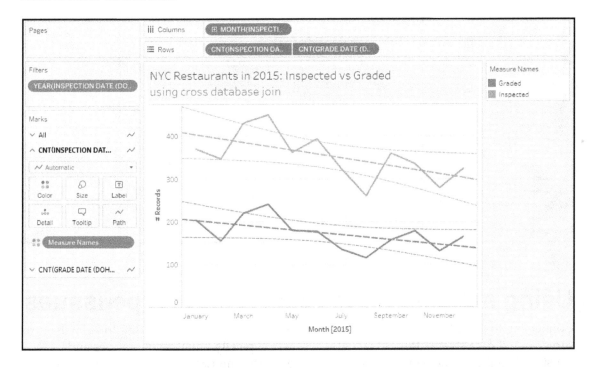

This will allow us to visualize how many restaurants were inspected and graded for a specific date:

	CUISINE DESCRIPTION	INSPECTION DATE	VIOLATION CODE	SCORE	GRADE	GRADE DATE
1	CUISINE DESCRIPTION	INSPECTION DATE	VIOLATION CODE	SCORE	GRADE	GRADE DATE
2	Indian	02-18-2016	10B	13	A	02-18-2016
3	American	05-19-2016	02G	13	A	05-19-2016
4	Chinese	04-09-2015	04L	26	B	04-09-2015
5	Tex-Mex	08-07-2014	10F	10	A	08-07-2014
6	Caribbean	12-18-2014	04L	6		
7	Japanese	07-23-2013	08A	32		
8	Bakery	01-06-2016	04N	20	B	01-06-2016
9	Bakery	05-28-2015	04L	9	A	05-28-2015
10	Russian	04-30-2015	08A	27		
11	Hotdogs	12-07-2015	08A	13		
12	Latin (Cuban, Dominican, Puerto R	06-09-2014	06C	11		
13	Chinese	05-14-2015	10F	7	A	05-14-2015
14	American	03-14-2014	10F	12	A	03-14-2014
15	Asian	01-28-2014	06E	22		
16	Seafood	12-11-2014	04H	13	A	12-11-2014
17	CafÃ©/Coffee/Tea	10-16-2015	10F	9	A	10-16-2015
18	Bakery	10-04-2014				
19	CafÃ©/Coffee/Tea	08-06-2014	10F	8	A	08-06-2014

Using schema.ini to resolve data type issues

Connecting to text files can sometimes be more challenging than connecting to a database or server-based data source. Relational databases will typically have the data types and constraints built in. Tableau can read this metadata and interpret the correct types and settings for the data set.

Text files can be tricky. We usually need to identify delimiters (that is, how is one field separated from another). If we want headers, we will need to either manually assign them from within Tableau, or override them in a configuration file.

If we connect to the file from Tableau without a configuration (or `schema.ini`) file, this is what we will get:

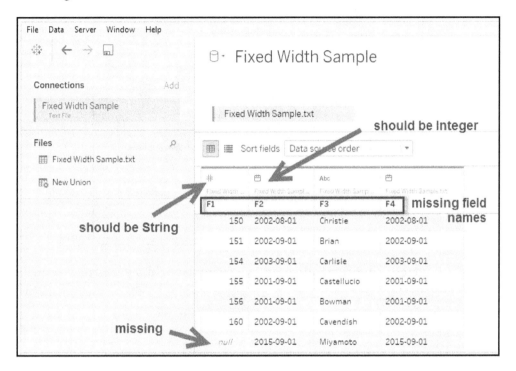

There are a few things that are incorrect or missing:

- The field names are missing.
- The first field contains a **null** value for the very last record, because Tableau assumes this field is numeric based on the first few rows. The last record has an alphanumeric value of C160, which is invalid for a numeric field. Show how to change with just default text driver properties clicking on the dropdown.
- The second field is interpreted as a date because the values, while numeric, can assume the format of *yyyymmdd*.

Tableau does allow us some flexibility when working with text files. When you click on the drop-down for the text file, there is an option for **Text File Properties**:

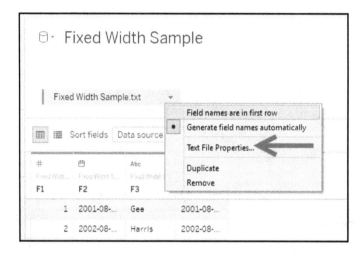

This provides another window that allows us to specify the field separators, text qualifiers (that is, character that encloses text values), character set, and locale:

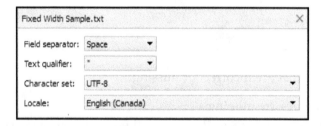

This still makes working with fixed width files without column headers a challenge. Microsoft recommends using schema.ini for all fixed length files. schema.ini provides a way to specify the data types and other configurations for the text file that Tableau can read. It does not solve all cases, but it can help with some.

 The format, supported fields, and options for schema.ini are documented in the MSDN page called Schema.ini File (Text File Driver), which can be found at http://bit.ly/msdn-schema-ini.

Tableau also has a KB article called *Resolving Incorrect Data Type Issues Related to Jet*, which can be found at the following URL: http://bit.ly/tableau-jet-engine.

What we used in this recipe is one of the simpler text files that can be cleaned up using a `schema.ini` file. In reality, there are many limitations.

If we had spaces in the third column, for example, if record #2's name is *Harris Jr*, this is what we will get in Tableau even if we specified the width of the string in the `schema.ini` file:

What if the date format was `yyyy-dd-mm` and we specified it in the `schema.ini` like this?

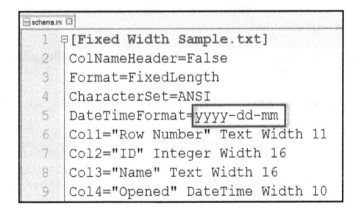

Tableau still uses the date format `yyyy-mm-dd` and ignores the specification in the `schema.ini` file:

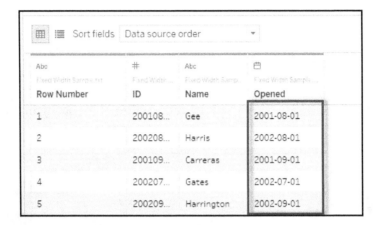

There are other variations that demonstrate the limitations of `schema.ini`. Sometimes, the best way to approach data wrangling problems is to either export to another format that Tableau can more easily read, or to resort to other tools, or even scripting. For example, Python, R, or even PowerShell are great, powerful scripting tools that can give you much more flexibility with how to shape your data.

Let's use a `schema.ini` file to resolve the data types when we connect to a fixed width text file data source with four columns.

Download this chapter's files from the Packt website and use the file called `Fixed Width Sample.txt`.

This is what the file looks like when opened in a text editor showing special characters:

95	150	20020801	Christie	2002-08-01 CRLF
96	151	20020901	Brian	2002-09-01 CRLF
97	154	20030901	Carlisle	2003-09-01 CRLF
98	155	20010901	Castellucio	2001-09-01 CRLF
99	156	20010901	Bowman	2001-09-01 CRLF
100	160	20020901	Cavendish	2002-09-01 CRLF
101	C160	20150901	Miyamoto	2015-09-01

Note that this file does not have any column headers. In addition, note the following:

- The first column should be text
- The second column should be integers
- The third column should be text
- The fourth column should be dates

1. Create a text file with the following contents:

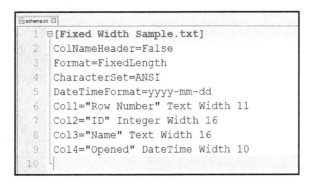

2. Save the file as `schema.ini` and save it in the same directory as the `Fixed Width Sample.txt` file.
3. Connect to the text file in Tableau:

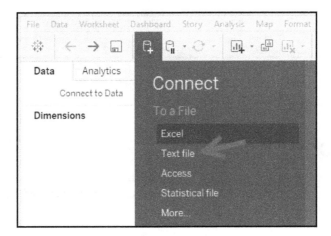

4. Confirm that there are four fields in the Tableau preview window, with the same configuration as specified in the `schema.ini` file:
   - First field is text
   - Second field is number
   - Third field is text
   - Fourth field is date:

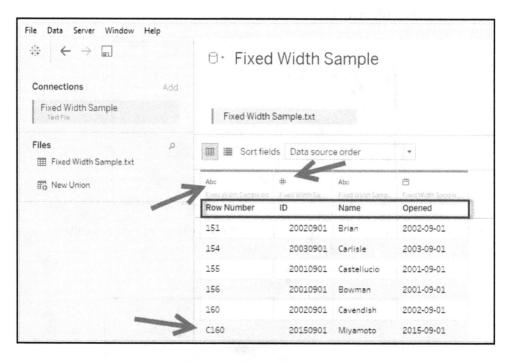

5. Add a new sheet and create your visualization using this data set.

Pivoting columns

In the file that we are using, the measure field--population--is split by age group. Each population value for an age group is provided as a column, so we end up with multiple measures:

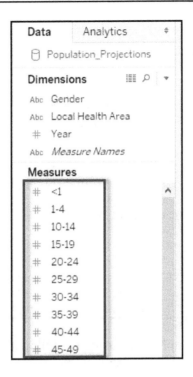

This format is hard to work with because all these measures are supposed to be a single measure. If we had a single measure for population values, and another dimension for age group, the analysis will be more flexible. We can slice and dice population by age group if we need to.

Tableau provides a way for us to shape this file by pivoting the values, using the original measure names as a dimension, and collecting all the population values into a single column. Although you may also be able to pivot at the data source level, it is great to have this capability within Tableau.

Let's prepare the data set and prepare the `.csv` file:

```
Population_Projections.csv
1  "","Local Health
   Area","Year","Gender","<1","1-4","5-9","10-14","15-19","20-24","25-29",
   "30-34","35-39","40-44","45-49","50-54","55-59","60-64","65-69","70-74"
   ,"75-79","80-84","85-89","90+","Total"
2  "0","British
   Columbia","1986","T","41594","167812","199209","196176","218240","25464
   1","273286","266181","248264","195669","156688","143634","144835","1392
   94","120433","100193","66845","40099","19669","10859","3003621"
3  "0","British
   Columbia","1987","T","42094","169356","203820","196497","217006","24578
   3","275003","270902","250563","210829","163396","144435","145743","1399
   36","126336","102649","70449","42028","20698","11128","3048651"
4  "0","British
   Columbia","1988","T","41941","172538","210669","199175","217883","23786
   5","279202","277893","257289","224097","173461","146619","147392","1418
   40","131991","103583","74296","44196","21624","11207","3114761"
```

1. Download the file from BCStats using the following URL:
   `http://www.bcstats.gov.bc.ca/StatisticsBySubject/Demography/Population`
   `Projections.aspx`

2. When you download, make the following selections and click on **Generate Output**:
   - Select **British Columbia** for **Region**
   - Select all the years
   - Select **Totals**
   - Select **5-Year Age Groups**:

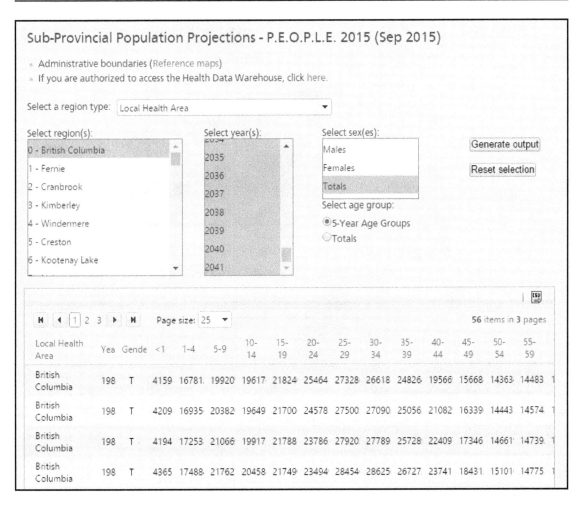

3. Beside the results pane, click on the CSV icon at the top-right corner of the results pane to download the `.csv` file. Save the file as `Population_Projections.csv`.

4. Click on the **New Data Source** icon and connect to the text file in this recipe:

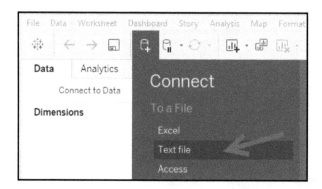

5. Select all the age groups that are presented as individual columns.
6. While all the age group columns are selected, right-click on one of the selected fields and choose **Pivot**:

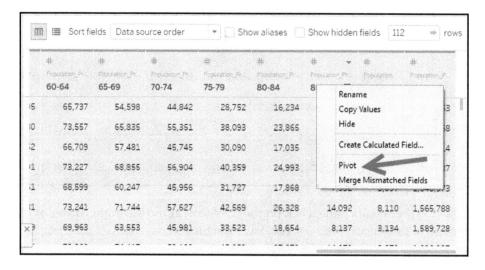

7. Right-click on the newly created **Pivot Field Names** field and choose **Rename**. Rename this field **Age Group**.

8. Right-click on the newly created **Pivot Field Values** field and choose **Rename**. Rename this field **Population**:

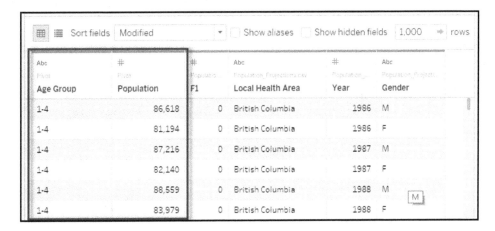

9. Under **Filters**, click on **Add**.
10. In the **Edit Data Source Filters** window, click on **Add**.
11. In the **Age Group filter** window, select the **Wildcard** tab.
12. Type `Total` under **Match value** and check the **Exclude** checkbox:

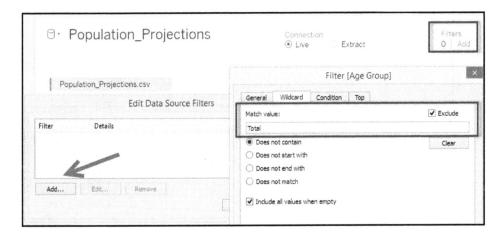

13. Click **OK** when done.
14. Add a new sheet and create your visualization using this data set.

Using unions

A union operation allows multiple sets of data to be appended to each other, that is, new records will be added to the end of the existing set of records.

Let's combine a number of **comma-separated value** (**CSV**) files into a single data set in Tableau:

1. Download the business license files from the City of Vancouver's website from `http://data.vancouver.ca/datacatalogue/businessLicence.htm`:

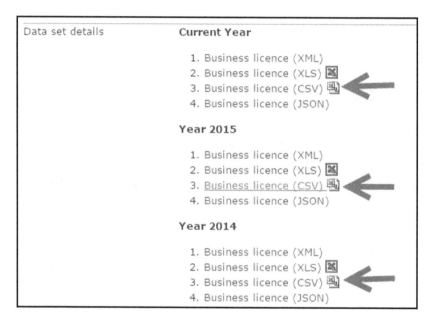

2. Download the CSV version, and save all the files in a local directory in your computer:

3. Click on the **New Data Source** icon and connect to `business_licenses.csv`, which contains the most recent year's records:

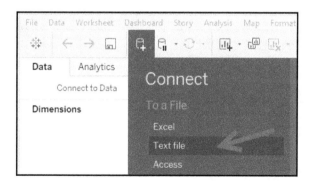

4. Drag **New Union** to just underneath `business_licenses.csv` until you see the **Drag** table to union message:

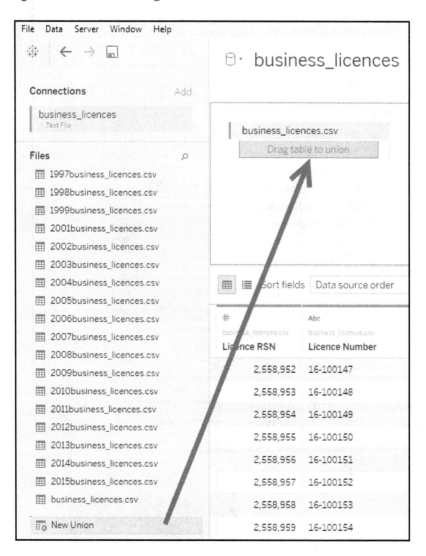

5. Select all other CSV files from the **Files** pane and drag them to the **Union** window:

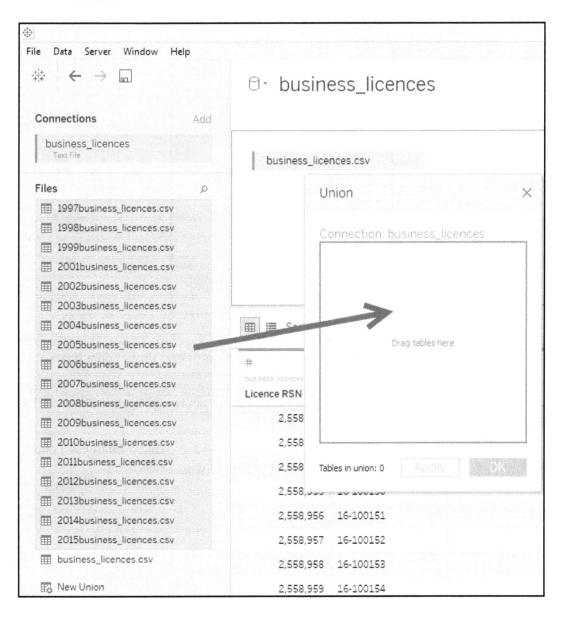

6. Click on **OK** after you confirm that all the files have been added to the **Union** window:

A union in relational databases requires what is called union compatibility. This means the two sets of records need to have the same number of columns and similar data types.

In Tableau, the union operation does not necessarily require union compatibility. If some of the incoming fields do not match the existing fields, the mismatched fields will simply have null values.

For example, if in some of our files, the **Business Name** field was called **Business Trade Name** instead, we can use Tableau's **Merge Mismatched Field** operation:

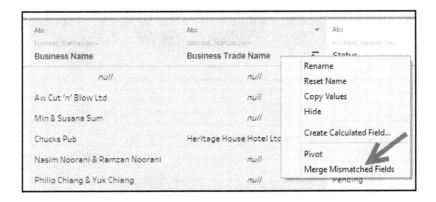

What this operation does is combine the fields into a single field in the resulting data set. It will take the first non-null value for this new combined field. Thus, we have to take care to ensure that the fields are indeed supposed to be the same but just named differently; otherwise, we risk losing information.

Should you need to undo the merge, Tableau also provides a way to remove the merge:

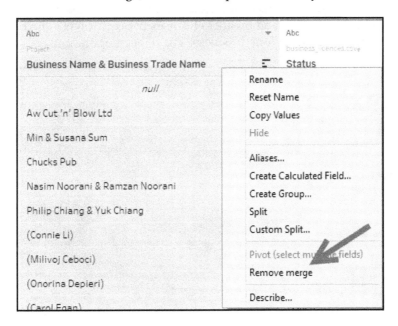

When we union files or worksheets, Tableau adds metadata fields in the resulting data set. Tableau has the **Table Name** dimension for text files, which uses the original file name as the value:

After we union our files, we can do our analysis. One possibility is a heat map. In the view below, we have a heat map of issued business licenses in downtown Vancouver. This type of visualization can indicate how long businesses have been operating:

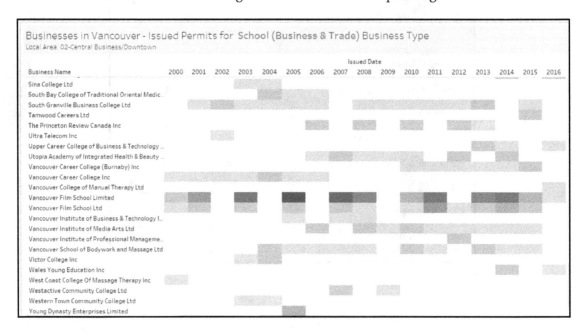

In the past, a union with multiple worksheets in the same Excel workbook could be done using a custom SQL in Excel, if using the legacy Jet connection.

In Tableau 10, the union operator is baked into the product. In this version, union works with text files (including the `.csv` and `.txt` file extensions) and multiple worksheets in Excel if saved in a single workbook. What if you need to combine multiple Excel files?

One improvement that is being promised in the future, and was showcased in the 2015 Tableau conference, is a wildcard union. This allows the union to operate on multiple files based on specific patterns on the filename. While not available in the initial release of Tableau 10, this will for sure be a much-awaited feature improvement for this operator.

A possible alternative to adding multiple Excel files is using data extracts. When you create an extract, you can append additional records from another file:

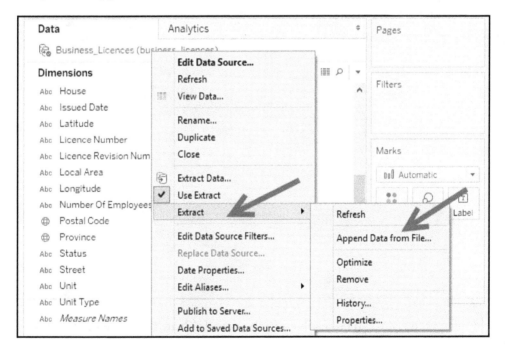

This is more restrictive than the union operator because you need to ensure the worksheet names are the same. You also need to ensure union compatibility; otherwise, you may encounter errors during the extract process. The following error is produced by the field name mismatch between the original file in the extraction and the incoming field names in the file being appended:

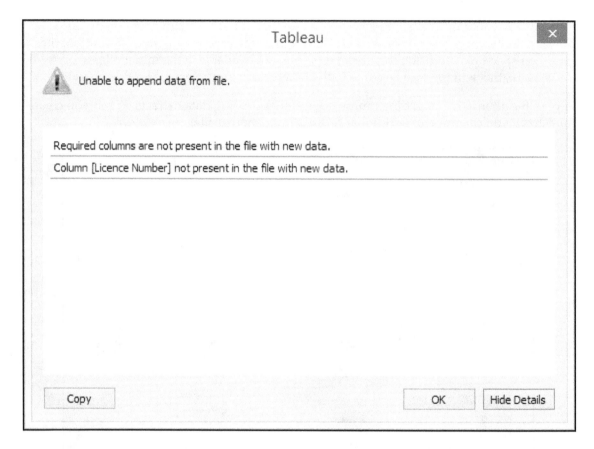

This field mismatch issue can be resolved in the new Tableau 10 Merge Mismatched Fields feature.

Learn more about the union operator from the Tableau online documentation:
`https://onlinehelp.tableau.com/current/pro/desktop/en-us/union.h tml`

Using join

A join is primarily a relational database concept that allows you to combine records from different tables using common fields. When data sets are joined, all fields are combined based on the join conditions provided.

Joins are fundamentally different from unions. In unions, the record sets are stacked on top of each other, thus producing a taller result set. A join works by combining records and fields horizontally based on common fields, thus creating wider data sets that have all the combined fields together. A join also does not require union compatibility.

Before Tableau 10, joins were limited to combining tables from the same data source, that is, the tables needed to be using a single data connection. Tableau v10 adds flexibility to the join operation by allowing cross-database joins. Tables are no longer restricted to coming from the same data source. Joins can be done on file-based data sources as well. In Excel files, each tab or worksheet acts like a table with records. If your data source is text files, each file in a folder is considered a table.

In the following example, we can see that there are two color-coded connections on the left-hand pane. One is an Excel connection, and the other is a text file connection. In the middle connection window, we can see that the join operation was allowed between the two data sources:

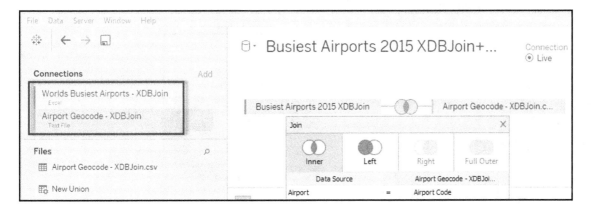

Let's combine the fields in two different Excel worksheets into one:

Download this chapter's files from the Packt website and use the file called `Worlds Busiest Airports-Join.xls`.

1. Connect to the **Excel** file in this recipe. Make sure you choose Excel from the **To a File** section:

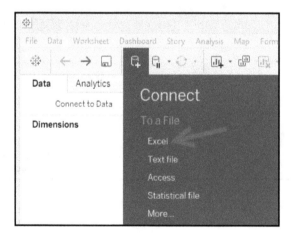

2. Drag **Busiest Airports** 2015 from the **sheets** section to the data connection window:

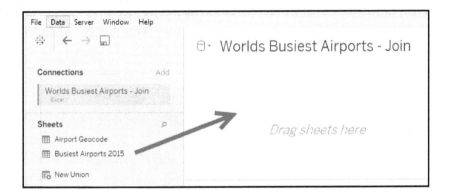

3. Drag **Airport Geocode** to the right of **Busiest Airports** 2015 in the data connection window.

4. In the **Join** window that comes up, choose **Airport** from **Busiest Airports 2015** to match up to the **Airport Code** field from the **Airport Geocode** sheet:

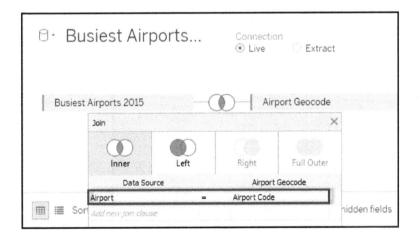

5. Add a new sheet and create your visualization using this data set.

We combined two worksheets from the same Excel workbook. Records in both worksheets will be combined only if the **Airport** field from **Busiest Airports 2015** has the same value as the **Airport Code** field in the **Airport Geocode** worksheet. This join based on the equality of values is also called an equi-join:

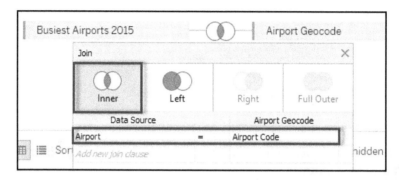

Once the fields are joined, you will find the fields from both worksheets represented in the sidebar. Fields are grouped based on their source:

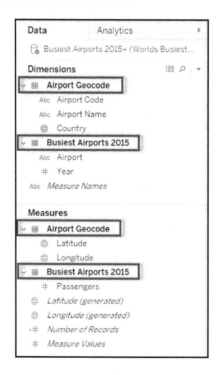

In general, we have two types of join: `inner` and `outer joins`.

`Inner joins` find matching values from both tables based on the join condition. The join condition is not always based on equality. There are cases where you may use other operators, such as greater than (>), greater than or equal to (>=), less than (<), less than or equal to (<=), or even not equal to (<>). Depending on the data source, some of these operators may not be supported.

`Outer joins`, also called preserving joins, preserve one or both sides of the tables as well as matching records. Outer joins can be further classified as `left outer`, `right outer`, and `full outer`. Some data sources do not support certain types of outer joins. Outer joins are positional; the placement of the tables relative to the JOIN operator affects the results.

A `left outer join` preserves the table to the left of the join operator and finds the matching values from the table on the right side of the operator. If a record on the left table being preserved does not have a matching value in the right table, that record is preserved but the fields from the other table will show NULL. A NULL value means the absence of value.

Here is an example of a LEFT OUTER JOIN using our worksheet in this recipe. The records in the table to the left, **Busiest Airports 2015**, are matched up to the records to the right, **Airport Geocode**, based on **Airport** and **Airport Code** fields respectively:

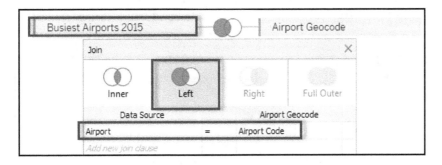

Busiest Airports 2015 has a record for **Airport** value **CDG**, but this **Airport Code** does not exist in the **Airport Geocode** worksheet. Hence, as can be seen in the following screenshot, the corresponding **Airport Geocode** fields are reporting **Null** for the **CDG** airport:

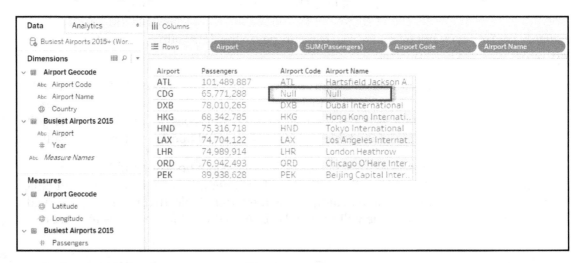

A `right outer join` is the reverse; it preserves the records from the right table and finds matching values from the left table. `Right outer joins` are not natively supported in Excel data sources. However, we could simply switch the data sources--putting **Airport Geocode** to the left and **Busiest Airports 2015** to the right --to achieve the same desired result:

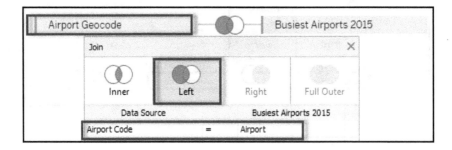

Airport Geocode has a record for **DFW**, but the **Busiest Airports 2015** worksheet does not have this. The resulting records will report **Null** for the **Busiest Airports 2015** columns for the **DFW** record:

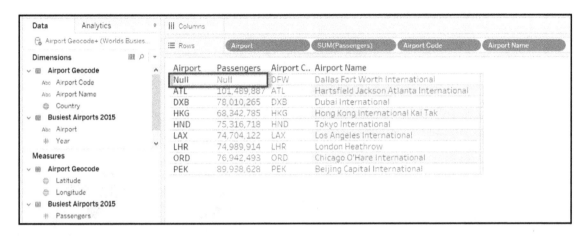

A `full outer join` preserves both tables being operated on. If the data source driver does not support this, a `full outer join` result can be derived by getting the result of the `left outer join` and appending it to the result of the `right outer join`.

There are a few other types of join--a `self-join` and a `cross join`. A `self-join` simply means that the same table is joined to itself. The actual join type can be inner or outer or even cross join. A cross join gets the cartesian product of the records in the tables being cross joined. When we get a cartesian product, we match up the records from one table to all records in the other table. If we have *m* of records in one table and *n* of records in another table, after a cartesian product, we will end up with $m \times n$ records.

Once we have combined the fields, we can start visualizing our records. Here is a possibility - creating a map that depicts the busiest airports and ranks them based on the average number of passengers:

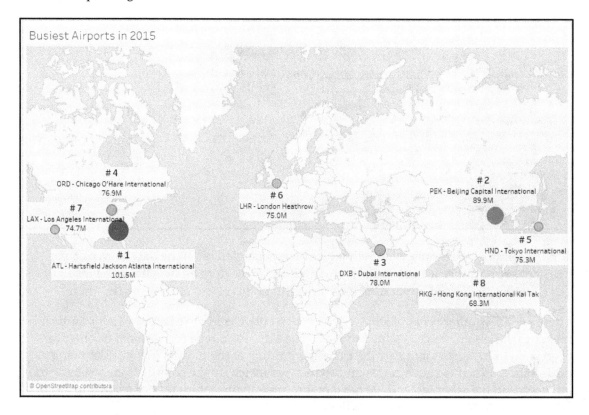

Using blends

Blends are great for data mashups. Blending in Tableau allows multiple data sources to be linked together. The data sources can be of different types - for example, one could be an Excel file while another could be a text file.

 In previous versions of Tableau, blend was the only way from within Tableau to link multiple data sources together. Starting in Tableau 10, cross-database joins are supported.

Let's combine the records from a text file and an Excel file using a blend:

1. Download this chapter's files from the Packt website and use the following files:
   - The `Airport Geocode-Blend.csv` file
   - The Worlds `Busiest Airports-Blend.xlsx` file

2. This is the content of the `Airport Geocode-Blend.csv` file:

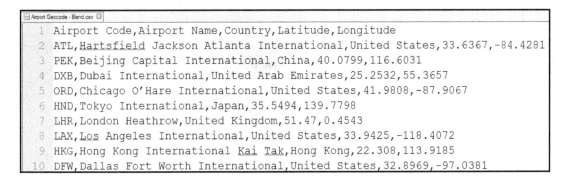

```
   ☐ Airport Geocode - Blend.csv ☒
   1  Airport Code,Airport Name,Country,Latitude,Longitude
   2  ATL,Hartsfield Jackson Atlanta International,United States,33.6367,-84.4281
   3  PEK,Beijing Capital International,China,40.0799,116.6031
   4  DXB,Dubai International,United Arab Emirates,25.2532,55.3657
   5  ORD,Chicago O'Hare International,United States,41.9808,-87.9067
   6  HND,Tokyo International,Japan,35.5494,139.7798
   7  LHR,London Heathrow,United Kingdom,51.47,0.4543
   8  LAX,Los Angeles International,United States,33.9425,-118.4072
   9  HKG,Hong Kong International Kai Tak,Hong Kong,22.308,113.9185
  10  DFW,Dallas Fort Worth International,United States,32.8969,-97.0381
```

3. These are the records in the Worlds `Busiest Airports - Blend.xlsx` file:

	A	B	C
1	Airport	Year	Passengers
2	ATL	2015	101489887
3	PEK	2015	89938628
4	DXB	2015	78010265
5	ORD	2015	76942493
6	HND	2015	75316718
7	LHR	2015	74989914
8	LAX	2015	74704122
9	HKG	2015	68342785
10	CDG	2015	65771288
11	ATL	2014	96,178,899

4. Connect to the Excel file in this recipe. Make sure you choose **Excel** from the **To a File** section:

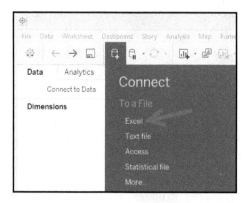

5. Go to new worksheet:

6. Click on the **New Data Source** icon, and this time connect to a **Text file**. Connect to the text file in this recipe:

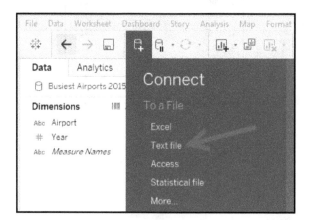

7. If you are directed back to the initial connection screen, go back to Sheet 1.

8. Under the **Data** menu, click on **Edit Relationships**:

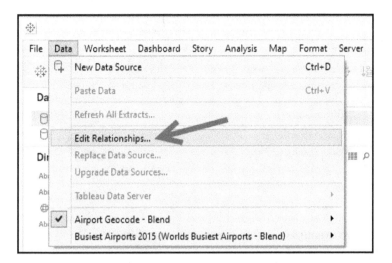

9. While **Airport Geocode-Blend** is selected as the **Primary data source**, click on **Custom** and match up **Airport Code** field to **Airport**:

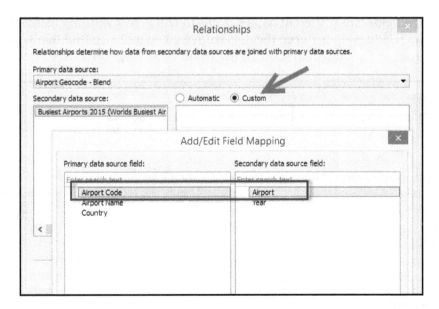

10. Click on **OK** when done.
11. While **Airport Geocode-Blend** is selected as the data source, drag Airport Code to the **Rows** shelf.

12. Switch data source to the Excel file. Notice that **Airport** now has an orange link icon beside it:

13. Continue to create your visualization using this dataset.

Note that the data sources must have some common fields before they can be blended in Tableau. By default, Tableau looks for the same field names in the data sources and links the sources together based on these fields.

However, if the fields have different names, Tableau will give a warning message indicating that there is no relationship between the data sources. You will also find that when you start using fields from one or both data sources, there will be a broken link icon:

If the field names are different, the relationship needs to be defined. To do this, we can go to the worksheet menu and select **Edit Relationships**. From there, instead of **Automatic**, **Custom** can be chosen as well as identify which fields from both sources should match up:

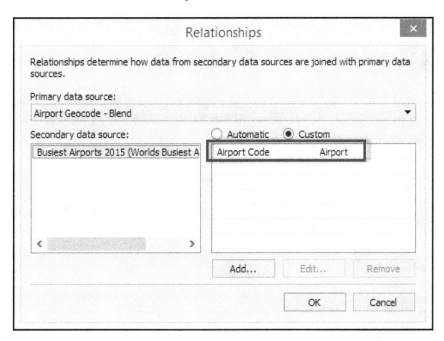

After the relationship is set, you will find that the link will be enabled. This link will only appear after you have dragged one of the blending fields in the view. If none of the blending fields are in the view, the icon will still appear as broken:

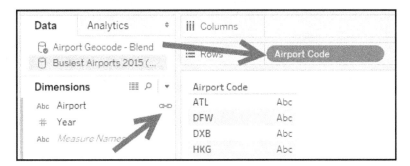

With a blend, there must be only one primary and at least one or multiple secondary data sources. The primary data source is identified by a blue check arrow icon beside it, and the secondary data sources have an orange check arrow icon:

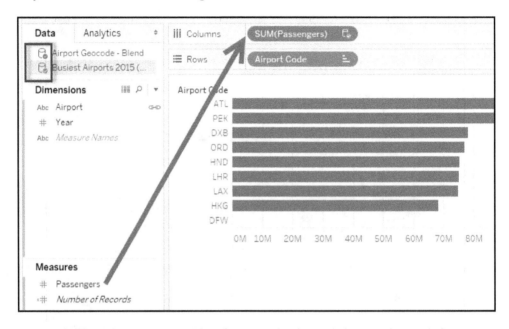

Fields from the secondary data sources will automatically be aggregated when dragged into the view or used in a calculated field. The level of aggregation follows that of the primary:

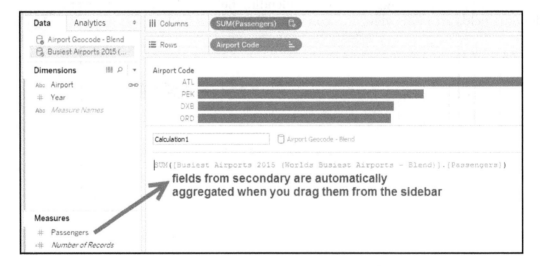

Dimension fields will also be aggregated using the **ATTR** function. If there are many related records in the secondary data source and if there are multiple values for that field, the **ATTR** function will return an asterisk (*):

This leads to a common issue faced in blends when creating calculated fields. We need to make sure that we have the primary and secondary data source fields in an aggregated format when we use them in our expressions. Otherwise, we will get the error **Cannot mix aggregate and non-aggregate arguments with this function**:

Blend settings are per worksheet. If you create a new worksheet, the data source you drag from the first will be the primary.

Now that Tableau 10 supports cross-database joins, why would we still want to consider blending data? There still some compelling reasons to go with blends. The first is, currently, the cross-database join functionality is not supported in all possible connections. Second, we may want to achieve a level of aggregation first before combining data sources .

To better illustrate this, let's consider the following two data sources:

Data Source 1 - Customer				Data Source 2 - Sales		
Customer ID	Customer Name	Credit Limit		Customer ID	Order ID	Amount
A01	John	500		A01	S01	100
B02	Miyuki	100		A01	S02	200
C03	Aisha	300		B02	S03	300

If we were to use a join operation (specifically a `left outer join`, with the customer on the left side of the join operator so it is preserved), we would get the following result. The **Credit Limit** for **Customer IDA01** is incorrect because the credit limit was doubled--$1,000 is being reported when it really is only **$500**:

This is the nature of joins, however. The join is working perfectly - it finds the matching values from the other table. Since **Customer IDA01** bought twice, **Customer ID** from the **Customer** table matched twice to the **Sales** table and, inherently, reported the credit limit twice.

If we were to blend, however, we would get the following result set, reporting some different values:

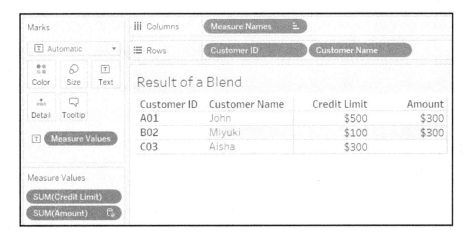

In a blend, the aggregation happens at the data source level first before the records from the two data sources are combined. Notice in the **Measure Values** card, the pill still says **SUM(Credit Limit)**--the same expression you see in the previous join operation. This time, though, the **SUM(Credit Limit)** happens at the customer data source only not at the resulting joined records. The **SUM(Credit Limit)** for **Customer IDA01** in the customer data source is still **$500** because there is only one record for that **Customer ID** in that data source.

One more important thing to know about blends is that after the records in both data sources are aggregated to the same level, the records are combined using an operation akin to a left outer join. This means that if some values in the blending field are absent in the primary, they will not be reported at all.

For example, if our primary is the **Airport Geocode**, and it does not have the airport code **CDG** which our secondary has, **CDG** will not be pulled into any view:

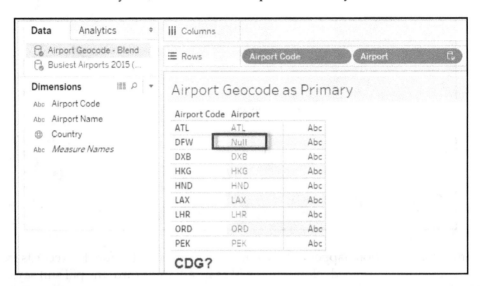

The same issue will occur even if we reverse the primary and secondary data sources, and if the new primary is missing some values that are present in the secondary. The following shows what you would see if we made **Busiest Airports 2015** the new primary data source, but it is missing the code for **DFW**:

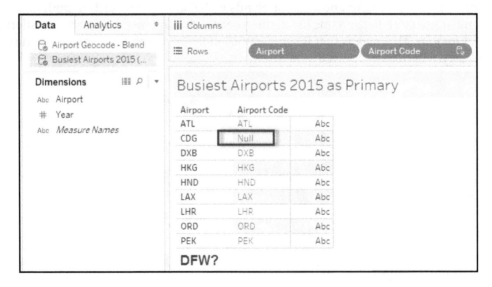

There is no magic bullet solution for this issue, however. What we need is to have another data source that has the complete set of values and make that our primary. Or, if this is a data quality issue, this is great way to illustrate why data quality is of utmost importance with data analysis. Remember--good data in, good data (analysis/visualization) out; not-so-good data in, not-so-good data (analysis/visualization) out.

Summary

In this chapter, we covered how to prepare our data for effective use in Tableau. We covered Data Interpreter and pivots to clean our data source. We then used the legacy Jet driver to shape the file and schema.ini to resolve data type issues. Next, we covered pivoting the values into a single column. We also used unions to combine different data sets, and joins to combine records from different tables using common fields. Lastly, we used blends for data mashups.

In the next chapter, we will see how calculations can be used in many ways.

6
Using Row-Level, Aggregate, and Level of Detail Calculations

One of the most incredible things about Tableau is that it is intuitive to use. Amazing discovery, analysis, and data storytelling is possible in Tableau by simply connecting to data and dragging and dropping fields. We have already seen how Tableau allows much more depth beyond simple drag and drop.

Calculations significantly extend the possibilities for analysis, design, and interactivity in Tableau. In this chapter, we'll see how calculations can be used to fix common problems with data, extend the data by adding new dimensions and measures, and provide additional flexibility in interactivity.

While calculations provide additional power and flexibility, they also introduce a level of complexity and sophistication. As you work through this chapter, try to understand the key concepts behind calculations and how they work in Tableau. Feel free to explore and experiment; the goal is not to merely have a list of calculations you can copy, but to gain knowledge of how calculations can be used to solve problems and add creative functionality to your views and dashboards.

The first half of the chapter focuses on some foundational concepts while the second half gives quite a few practical examples. The topics we'll cover include the following:

- Creating and editing calculations
- Levels of detail calculations
- Parameters
- Ad hoc calculations
- Performance considerations

We will use the following dataset in most of the examples in this chapter. It's simple and small so that we can easily see how the calculations are being done. The dataset describes six apartments, the occupants, the start and end dates of the rental period, the area (in square feet), and the monthly rental price:

Apartment	Occupant first name	Occupant last name	Start date	End date	Area	Price
A-1	Dwight	Moody	May 1	Dec 31	1,000	2,000
A-2	Mary	Slessor	Aug 1	Dec 2	800	1,600
A-3	Charles	Ryrie	Feb 16	Mar 2	1,200	800
A-4	Hudson	Taylor	May 21	June 3	1,500	1,500
B-1	Amy	Carmichael	Jan 18	Sep 18	3,000	3,000
B-2	John	Walvoord	May 1	Dec 20	800	2,400

Creating and editing calculations

A calculation is often referred to as a calculated field in Tableau because when you create a calculation, it will either show up as a new measure or a dimension in the data pane (unless it is an ad hoc calculation). Calculations consist of code that references other fields, parameters, constants, groups, or sets, and uses combinations of functions and operations to achieve a result. Sometimes this result is per row of data and sometimes it is done at an aggregate level. We'll consider the difference shortly.

There are multiple ways to create a calculated field in Tableau:

1. Select **Analysis** | **Create Calculated Field...** from the menu.
2. Use the drop-down menu next to **Dimensions** in the data pane:

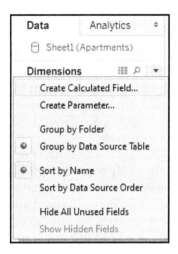

3. Right-click an empty area in the data pane and select **Create Calculated Field...**
4. Use the drop-down menu on a field, set, or parameter in the data pane and select **Create | Calculated Field...**
5. In Tableau 9.0 or later, double-click an empty area on the **Rows**, **Columns**, or **Measure Values** shelves or in the empty area on the **Marks** card to create an ad hoc calculation.

The calculated field you create will be part of the data source that is currently selected at the time you create it. You can edit an existing calculated field in the data pane by using the drop-down menu and selecting **Edit**.

When you create a calculation using the drop-down menu of an existing field or parameter, the calculation starts as a reference to that field.

The interface for creating and editing calculations looks as follows:

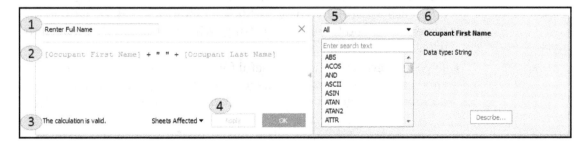

This window has several key features:

1. Once created, the calculated field (**1**) will show up as a field in the data pane with the name you enter in this text box.
2. The code editor (**2**) allows you to type in the code for the calculation. The editor includes autocomplete for recognized fields and functions. Additionally, you can drag fields, sets, and parameters from the data pane or view into the code editor to insert them into your code.

> You can also select snippets of your code in the code editor and then drag and drop the selected text into the data pane to create additional calculated fields. You may also drag and drop selected code snippets from the code window onto shelves in the view to create ad hoc calculations. This is an effective way to test portions of complex calculations.

3. An indicator at the bottom of the editor (**3**) will alert you to errors in your code.
4. Additionally, you can use the **Sheets Affected** drop-down (**4**) to see the sheets that will be affected by changes to the calculation.
5. Use the **Apply** button to save changes to the calculation and apply. Then the **OK** button will apply changes and close the editor. Changes to a calculation apply anywhere the calculation is used. Use the **X** button in the upper-right corner to close the editor without applying the changes.
6. The functions list (**5**) contains all the various functions available to be used in your code. Many of these functions will be used in examples or discussed in this chapter. Tableau defaults to showing a list of all available functions. But Tableau also groups various functions according to how they are used:

   - **Number**: Mathematical functions, such as rounding, absolute value, trig functions, square roots, exponents, and so on.
   - **String**: Functions useful for string manipulation, such as getting a sub string, finding a match within a string, replacing parts of a string, converting a string value to upper- or lowercase, and so on.
   - **Date**: Functions useful for working with dates, such as finding the difference between two dates, adding an interval to a date, getting the current date, and transforming strings with non-standard formats into dates.
   - **Type conversion**: Functions useful for converting one type of field to another, such as converting integers to a strings, floating point decimals to integers, or strings into dates, and so on.

- **Logical**: These are the decision-making functions, such as `if then else` logic or `case` statements. This category also includes functions such as `IFNULL`, `ISNULL`, and `IIF`, and some basic logical operators such as `NOT`, `AND`, `OR`, and so on.
- **Aggregate**: Functions used for aggregating, such as summing, counting, getting the minimum or maximum values, or calculating standard deviations or variances.
- **User**: Functions used to obtain usernames and check whether the current user is a member of a group. These functions are often used in combination with logical functions to customize the user's experience or to implement user-based security when publishing to Tableau Server or Tableau Online.
- **Table calculation**: These functions are different from the others. They operate on the aggregate data after it is returned from the underlying data source and just prior to the rendering of the view. These are some of the most powerful functions in Tableau. They are also some of the most complicated and misunderstood functions in Tableau.

7. Selecting a function in the list or clicking on a field, parameter, or function in the code will reveal details about the selection in the expanded space on the right (**6**). This is helpful when you are nesting other calculated fields in your code and you want to see the code for that particular calculated field or when you want to understand the syntax for a function.

Tableau supports numerous functions and operators. In addition to the functions listed on the calculation screen, Tableau supports the following operators, keywords, and syntax conventions:

- `AND`: Logical and between two Boolean (true/false) values or statements
- `OR`: Logical or between two Boolean values or statements
- `NOT`: Logical not to negate a Boolean values or statements
- `=` or `==`: Logical equals to test equality of two statements or values
- `+`: Addition of numeric or date values or concatenation of strings
- `-`: Subtraction of numeric or date values
- `*`: Multiplication of numeric values

- /: Division of numeric values
- ^: Raise to a power with numeric values
- (): Parentheses to define the order of operations
- []: Square brackets to enclose field names
- {}: Curly braces to enclose level of detail calculations
- //: Double slash to start a comment

 Field names that are a single word may optionally be enclosed in brackets when used in calculations. Field names with spaces, special characters, or from secondary data sources must be enclosed in brackets.

Level of detail calculations

Level of detail calculations (sometimes abbreviated as **LoDcalcs** or **LoD expressions**) allows you to perform aggregations at a specified level of detail, which may be different from the level of detail defined in the view, and then work with the resulting value at a row level. In this way, you can think of LoD calculations as a hybrid between aggregate calculations and row-level calculations.

Level of detail syntax

Level of detail calculations follow this basic pattern of syntax:

```
{[TYPE] [Dimension 1],[Dimension 2] : AGG([Measure])}
```

The parts of the declaration above are as follows:

- **TYPE**: This is the type of LoD calculation (FIXED, INCLUDE, or EXCLUDE); these are described in detail in the following section.
- **Dimension 1**: This is a comma-separated list of dimension fields that define the level of detail at which the calculation will be performed. You may use any number of dimensions to define the level of detail.

- **AGG**: This is the aggregate function you wish to perform (such as SUM, AVG, MIN, MAX, and so on)
- **Measure**: This is the field that will be aggregated by the aggregate function.

The types of level of detail calculations are as follows:

- **Fixed**: Aggregates at the level of detail specified by the list of dimensions in the code regardless of what dimensions are in the view. For example, the following code returns the average price per Floor:

  ```
  {FIXED [Floor] : AVG([Price])}
  ```

- Either of the following two snippets of code represent a fixed calculation of the average price for the entire data source (or the subset defined by a context filter):

  ```
  {FIXED : AVG([Price])}
  or
  {AVG([Price])}
  ```

- **Include**: Aggregates at the level of detail determined by the dimensions in the view and the dimensions listed in the code. For example, the following code calculates the average price at the level of detail defined by dimensions in the view but includes the dimension Occupant Last Name, even if Occupant Last Name is not in the view:

  ```
  {INCLUDE [Occupant Last Name] : AVG([Price])}
  ```

- **Exclude**: Aggregates at the level of detail determined by the dimensions in the view, excluding any listed in the code. For example, the following code calculates the average price at the level of detail defined in the view but does not include the Apartment dimension as a part of the level of detail, even if Apartment is in the view:

  ```
  {EXCLUDE [Apartment] : AVG([Price])}
  ```

Level of detail example

With the apartment rental data, let's say that you want to compare the area (size in square feet) of all apartments with the average size of an apartment for the building. It's fairly easy to get the area per apartment:

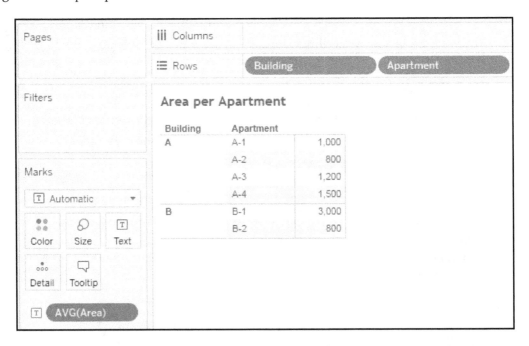

In the preceding figure, the view level of detail (level of detail defined for the view) is Building and Apartment because those are the dimensions in the view. So the average area is calculated per apartment per building.

It's also fairly easy to get the average area per building, by simply removing the apartment dimension from the view, as follows:

However, what if you want to work with both the average area per apartment and average area per building in the same view? This is where level of detail calculations come in.

There are several ways to approach the solution, but you might consider using an EXCLUDE level of detail calculation named `Average Area (exclude apartment)` with code such as the following:

```
{EXCLUDE [Apartment] : AVG(Area)}
```

When you use the calculation in a view that includes **Apartment** in the view level of detail, you get results similar to this:

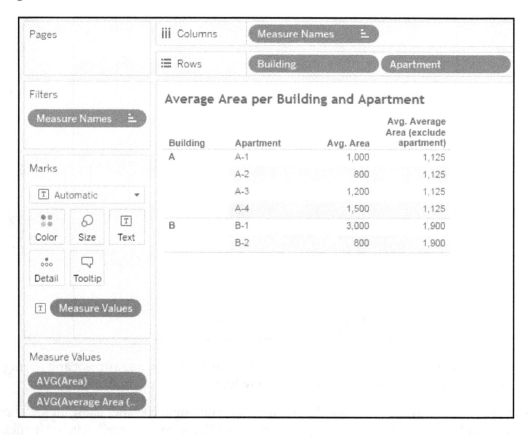

The **AVG(Area)** field on the **Measure Values** shelf is the standard aggregation of **Area** and is done at the view level of detail, so we get the average for every apartment for every building.

However, the Average Area (exclude apartment) field used on measures is calculated excluding the **Apartment** dimension, so it is calculated per building (the only other dimension in the view). The resulting value of average area per building is available for every row of data. This is why you can see the values repeated for every row, for each building in the preceding figure. (This is also why it has to be aggregated again; in this case, we used AVG, but we could have used MIN or MAX to achieve the same result.)

Additionally, we can use the value as a row-level value in addition to row-level calculations. For example, we could create a calculation to determine which apartments are higher or lower than the average for the building. Here is one such calculation, named `Above or Below Average Size?` The code for the calculation is as follows:

```
IF [Area] > [Average Area (exclude apartment)]
THEN "Above"
ELSE "Below"
END
```

When used in the view, it allows us to see which apartments are **Above or Below** the average for the building:

Parameters

Before moving to some additional examples of row- and aggregate-level calculations, let's take a little side trip to examine parameters, as they can be used in incredible ways in calculations.

A parameter in Tableau is a placeholder for a single global value, such as a number, date, or string. Parameters may be shown as controls (such as sliders, drop-down lists, or type-in textboxes) to end users of dashboards or views, giving them the ability to change the current value of the parameter. The value of a parameter is global so that if the value is changed, every view and calculation in the workbook that references the parameter will use the new value. Parameters provide another way to provide rich interactivity to end users of your dashboards and visualizations.

Parameters can be used to allow anyone interacting with your view or dashboard to dynamically do many things, including the following:

- Alter the results of a calculation
- Change the size of bins
- Change the number of top or bottom items in a **Top N Filter** or **Top N Set**
- Set the value of a reference line or band
- Change the size of bins
- Pass values to a custom SQL statement used in a data source

Since parameters can be used in calculations and since calculated fields can be used to define any aspect of visualization (from filters to colors to rows and columns), the change of a parameter value can have dramatic results.

Creating parameters

Creating a parameter is similar to creating a calculated field. There are multiple ways to create a parameter in Tableau:

- Use the drop-down menu next to **Dimensions** in the data pane
- Right-click on an empty area in the data pane and select **Create Parameter Field**
- Use the drop-down menu on a field, set, or parameter in the data pane and select **Create|Parameter...**

In the last case, Tableau will create a parameter with a list of potential values based on the domain (distinct values) of the field. For fields in the data pane that are discrete (blue) by default, Tableau will create a parameter with a list of values matching the discrete values of the field. For fields in the data pane that are continuous (green), Tableau will create a parameter with a range set to the minimum and maximum values of the field present in the data.

Parameters created from fields will only contain the values or range defined by the field at the time they are created. The list or range will not dynamically update to reflect changes in the data.

When you first create a parameter (or subsequently edit an existing parameter), Tableau will present an interface as shown:

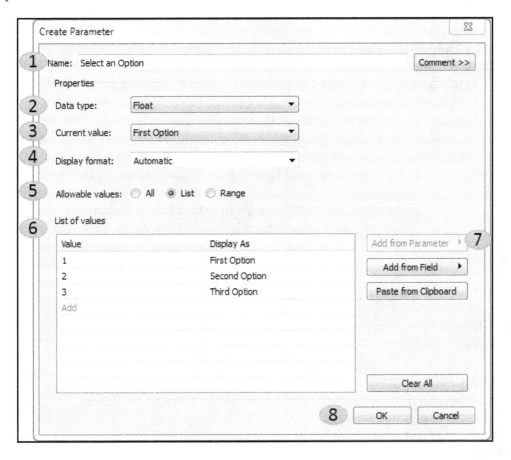

The interface contains the following features:

1. **Name** (**1**) will show as the default title for parameter controls and will also be the reference in calculations. You can also add a **Comment** to describe the use of the parameter.
2. **Data type** (**2**) defines the type of data that is allowed for the value of the parameter. The options include integer, float (floating point decimal), string, Boolean, date, or date with time.
3. **Current value** (**3**) defines what the initial default value of the parameter will be. Changing this value in this screen or on a dashboard or visualization where the parameter control is shown will change the current value.
4. **Display format** (**4**) defines how the values will be displayed. For example, you might want to show an integer value as a dollar amount, a decimal as a percentage, or display a date in a specific format.
5. The **Allowable values** option (**5**) gives us the ability to restrict the scope of values that are permissible. There are three options for **Allowable values**:
    *   **All** allows any input from the user that matches the data type of the parameter.
    *   **List** allows us to define a list of values from which the user must select a single option. The list can be entered manually, pasted from the clipboard, or loaded from a dimension of the same data type. Adding from a field is a one-time operation. If the data changes and new values are added, they will not appear automatically in the parameter list.
    *   **Range** allows us to define a range of possible values, including an optional upper and lower limit as well as a step size. This can also be set from a field or another parameter.
6. **List of values** (**6**) allows us to enter all possible values. In this example, a list of three items has been entered. Note that the value must match the data type, but the display value can be any string value. This list is static and must be manually updated. Even if you base the parameter on the values present in a field, the list will not change even if new values appear in the data. You can drag and drop values in the list to record the list.

If you are using a list of options, consider an integer data type with display values that are easily understood by your end users. The values can be easily referenced in calculations to determine what selection was made and you can easily change the display value without breaking your calculations. This can also lead to increased performance as comparisons of numeric values are more efficient than string comparisons. However, you'll want to balance the flexibility and performance of integers with readability in calculations.

7. With allowable values of **List** or **Range**, you'll get a series of buttons that allow you to obtain the list of values or range from various sources (7). **Add from Parameter** copies the list of values or range from an existing parameter; **Add from Field** copies the list of distinct values or range from a field in the data; and **Paste from Clipboard** creates the list of values from the anything you have copied to the system clipboard. **Clear All** will clear the list of values.

8. Click **OK** to save changes to the parameter or **Cancel** to revert (8).

When the parameter is created, it appears in the data pane under the **Parameters** section. The drop-down menu for a parameter reveals an option to **Show Parameter Control**, which adds the parameter control to the view. The little drop-down caret in the upper-right corner of the parameter control reveals a menu for customizing the appearance and behavior of the parameter control. Here is the parameter control, shown as a single value list, for the parameter created previously:

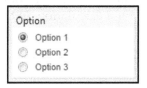

This control can be shown on any sheet or dashboard and allows the end user to select a single value. When the value is changed, any calculations, filters, sets, or bins that use the parameter will be re-evaluated and any views that are affected will be redrawn.

Ad hoc calculations

Ad hoc calculations add calculated fields to shelves in a single view without adding fields to the data pane.

Let's say that you have a simple view that shows the **Price per Renter**, as follows:

What if you want to quickly highlight any renters who had a contract of at least **$2,000**? One option would be to create an ad hoc calculation. To do so, simply double-click on an empty area of the **Columns**, **Rows**, or **Measure Values** cards or on the empty space of the **Marks** shelf and then start typing the code for a calculation. In this example, we've double-clicked on the empty space on the **Marks** shelf:

Here, we've entered code that will return `True` if the sum of **Price** is at least $2,000 and `False` otherwise. Pressing Enter or clicking outside the text box will reveal a new ad hoc field that can be dragged and dropped anywhere within the view. Here, we've added it to the **Color** shelf:

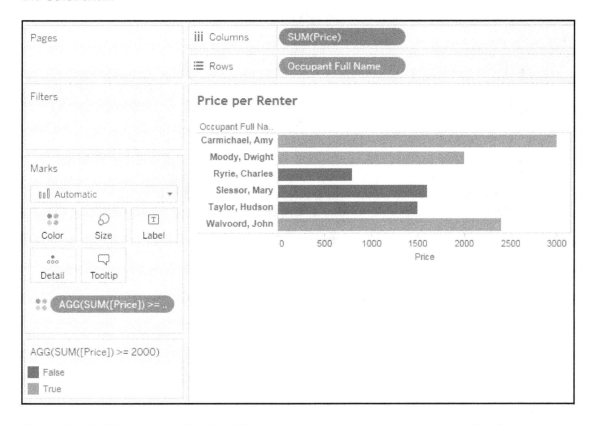

The ad hoc field is only available within the view and does not show up in the data pane. You can double-click on the field to edit the code.

> Dragging and dropping an ad hoc field into the data pane transforms it into a regular calculated field that will be available for other views using that data source.

Performance considerations

When working with a small dataset and an efficient database, you often won't notice inefficient calculations. With larger datasets, the efficiency of your calculations can start to make a fairly dramatic difference in the speed at which a view is rendered.

Here are some tips for getting the most efficiency in your calculations:

- Boolean and numeric calculations are faster than string calculations. If possible, avoid string manipulation and use aliasing or formatting to provide user friendly labels. For example, don't write this code: `IF [value] == 1 THEN "Yes"` `ELSE "No" END`. Instead, simply write `[value] == 1` and then edit the aliases of the field and set `True` to `"Yes"` and `False` to `"No"`.
- Always look for ways to increase the efficiency of a calculation. If you find yourself writing a long `IF...ELSEIF` statement with lots of conditions, see if there are one or two conditions that you can check first to eliminate checks of all the other conditions. For example, let's consider simplifying the following code:

```
IF [Type] = "Dog" AND [Age] < 1 THEN "Puppy"
ELSEIF [Type] = "Cat" AND [Age] < 1 THEN "Kitten"
END
```

- The preceding code snippet can also be written as shown:

```
IF [Age] < 1 THEN
IF [Type] = "Dog" THEN "Puppy"
ELSEIF [Type] = "Cat" THEN "Kitten"
END
END
```

- Note how the check of `Type` doesn't have to be done for any records where the age was less than 1. There can be a very high percentage of records in the dataset.
- Row-level calculations have to be performed for every row of data. Try to minimize the complexity of row-level calculations. However, if that is not possible or doesn't solve a performance issue, consider the next option.

- When you create a data extract, certain row-level calculations are materialized. This means that the calculation is performed one time, when the extract is created, and the results are then stored in the extract. This means that the data engine does not have to execute the calculation over and over. Instead, the value is simply read from the extract. Calculations which use any user functions or parameters or TODAY() or NOW() will not be materialized in an extract as the value necessarily changes according to the current user, parameter selection, and system time. Tableau's optimizer may also decide not to materialize certain calculations that are more efficiently performed in memory rather than having to read the stored value.

> When you use an extract to materialize row-level calculations, only the calculations that were created at the time of the extract are materialized. If you edit calculated fields or create new ones after creating the extract, you will need to optimize the extract (use the drop-down menu on the data source or select it from the Data menu and then select **Extract | Optimize**).

Summary

Calculations open up amazing possibilities in Tableau. You are no longer confined to the fields in the source data. With calculations, you can extend the data by adding new dimensions and measures, fix bad or poorly formatted data, enhance the user experience with parameters for user input and calculations that enhance the visualizations, and you can achieve flexibility that makes data blending work in situations where the data might have made it difficult or impossible otherwise.

The key to using calculated fields is an understanding of the three levels of calculations in Tableau. Row-level calculations are performed for every row of source data. These calculated fields can be used as dimensions or they can be further aggregated as measures. Aggregate-level calculations are performed at the level of detail defined by the dimensions present in a view. They are especially helpful, and even necessary, when you must first aggregate components of the calculation before performing additional operations.

In the next chapter, we'll explore the third main type of calculations: table calculations. These are some of the most powerful calculations in terms of their ability to solve problems and open up incredible possibilities for in-depth analysis. In practice, they range from very easy to exceptionally complex.

7
Table Calculations

Table calculations are one of the most powerful features in Tableau that enable solutions that cannot be achieved in any other way (short of writing a custom application or complex custom SQL scripts!). Table calculations make it possible to use data that isn't structured well and still get quick results without waiting for someone to fix the data at the source. They make it possible to compare and perform calculations on aggregate values across the rows of the resulting table and open incredible possibilities for analysis and creative approaches to solving problems. Table calculations can be used in any type of visualization. They range in complexity from incredibly easy to create (a couple of clicks) to extremely complex (requiring an understanding of addressing, partitioning, and data densification). We'll start off simple and move towards complexity in this chapter. The goal is to gain a solid foundation for creating and using table calculations, understanding how they work, and to see some examples of how they can be used. In this chapter, we'll consider the following topics:

- Overview of table calculations
- Quick table calculations
- Relative versus fixed
- Scope and direction
- Addressing and partitioning
- Advanced addressing and partitioning
- Custom table calculations
- Data densification

Most of the examples here will use the sample superstore data.

Overview of table calculations

Table calculations are different from all other calculations in Tableau. Row-level, aggregate calculations, and LoD expressions, which we considered in the previous chapter, are performed at the data source layer. If you were to examine the queries sent to the data source by Tableau, you'd find the code for your calculations translated into whatever flavor of SQL the data source used.

Table calculations, on the other hand, are performed after the initial query. Here's an extended diagram which shows how aggregated results are stored in Tableau's cache:

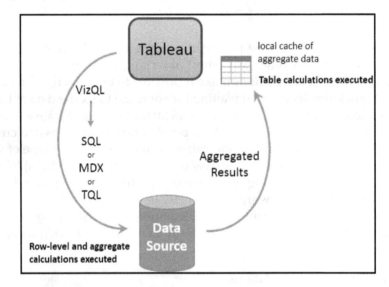

Table calculations are performed on the aggregate table of data in Tableau's cache right before the data visualization is rendered. It's very important to understand this for various reasons, including the following:

- **Aggregation**: Table calculations operate on aggregate data. You cannot reference fields in a table calculation without referencing it as an aggregate.
- **Filtering**: Regular filters will be applied prior to table calculations which means that table calculations will only be applied to data returned from the source to the cache. You'll need to determine whether you have allowed all the data necessary for table calculations to work as desired.

- **Late filtering**: Table calculations, used as filters, will be applied after the aggregate results are returned from the data source. The order becomes important. Row-level and aggregate filters are applied first, the aggregate data is returned to the cache and then the table calculation is applied as a filter that effectively hides data from the view. This allows us to take some creative approaches to solve certain kinds of problems that we'll consider in some of the examples.
- **Performance**: If you are using a live connection to connect to an enterprise database server, then row-level and aggregate-level calculations will be taking advantage of enterprise-level hardware. Table calculations are performed in the cache, which means that they will be performed on the machine that is running Tableau. You need not be concerned if your table calculations are operating on a dozen or even hundreds of rows of aggregate data. However, if you are getting back several hundred-thousand rows of aggregate data, then you'll need to consider the performance of your table calculations.

Creating and editing table calculations

There are several ways to create table calculations in Tableau:

- Using the drop-down menu for any active field, used as a numeric aggregate in the view, select **Quick Table Calculation** and then the desired calculation
- Using the drop-down menu for any active field, used as a numeric aggregate in the view, select **Add Table Calculation** and then select the calculation type and adjust the desired settings, if any
- Create a calculated field and use one or more table calculation functions to write your own custom table calculations

The first two options create a quick table calculation, which can be edited or removed using the drop-down menu on the field and selecting **Edit Table Calculation** or **Clear Table Calculation**. The third option creates a calculated field, which can be edited or deleted as any other calculated field.

A field on a shelf in the view that is using a table calculation or which is a calculated field using the table calculation function will have a delta symbol icon.

An active field is shown in the following figure:

An active field with table calculation is shown in the following figure:

Most of the examples in this chapter will show the user a text table. As the text table closely matches the actual aggregate table in the cache, this makes it easier for us to see how the table calculations are working.

When building a view that uses table calculations, especially more complex ones, try to use a table with all dimensions on the **Rows** shelf and then add table calculations as discrete values on **Rows** to the right of the dimensions. Once you have all the table calculations working as desired, you can re-arrange the fields in the view to give you the appropriate visualization.

Quick table calculations

Quick table calculations are predefined table calculations that can be applied to any field used as a measure in the view. These calculations include common and useful calculations, such as **Running Total, Difference, Percent Difference, Percent of Total, Rank, Percentile, Moving Average, YTD total, Compound Growth Rate, Year Over Year Growth**, and **YTD Growth**. You'll find applicable options on the drop-down on a field used as a measure in the view:

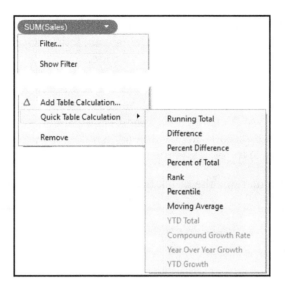

Consider the following example using the sample superstore sales data:

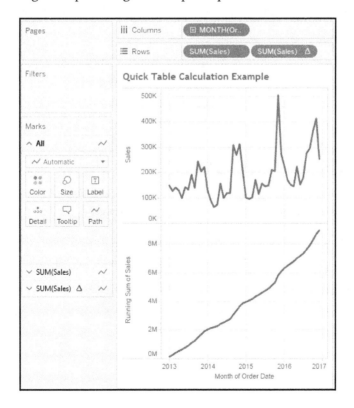

Here **Sales** over time is shown. **Sales** has been duplicated on the **Rows** shelf and another **SUM(Sales)** field has the running total quick table calculation which is applied. Using the quick table calculation, we can avoid writing any code.

You can double-click on the table calculation field in the view to actually see the code that the quick table calculations use. This turns it into an ad hoc calculation. You can also drag an active field with a quick table calculation applied to the data pane, which will turn it into a calculated field available to reuse in other views.

The following table demonstrates the quick table calculations available:

Year of Order Date	Quarter of Order ..	Sales	Running Total	Difference	% Difference	% of Total	Rank	Percentile	Moving Average	YTD	Compound Growth Rate	Year over year Growth	YTD Growth
2012	Q1	415,886	415,886			4.65%	12	31.25%	415,886	415,886	0.00%		
	Q2	352,779	768,665	-63,107	-15.17%	3.94%	13	25.00%	384,333	768,665	-15.17%		
	Q3	456,694	1,225,359	103,915	29.46%	5.10%	10	43.75%	408,453	1,225,359	4.79%		
	Q4	698,986	1,924,345	242,292	53.05%	7.81%	5	75.00%	502,820	1,924,345	18.90%		
2013	Q1	272,065	2,196,410	-426,921	-61.08%	3.04%	16	6.25%	475,915	272,065	-10.07%	-34.58%	-34.58%
	Q2	337,352	2,533,762	65,287	24.00%	3.77%	14	18.75%	438,134	609,417	-4.10%	-4.37%	-20.72%
	Q3	546,388	3,080,150	209,036	61.96%	6.10%	6	68.75%	385,268	1,155,805	4.85%	19.64%	-5.68%
	Q4	788,742	3,868,892	242,354	44.36%	8.81%	3	87.50%	557,494	1,944,547	9.57%	12.84%	1.05%
2014	Q1	294,067	4,162,959	-494,675	-62.72%	3.28%	15	12.50%	543,066	294,067	-4.24%	8.09%	8.09%
	Q2	428,267	4,591,226	134,200	45.64%	4.78%	11	37.50%	503,692	722,334	0.33%	26.95%	18.53%
	Q3	508,189	5,099,415	79,922	18.66%	5.68%	9	50.00%	410,174	1,230,523	2.02%	-6.99%	6.46%
	Q4	1,000,217	6,099,632	492,028	96.82%	11.17%	2	93.75%	645,558	2,230,740	8.30%	28.81%	14.72%
2015	Q1	536,158	6,635,790	-464,059	-46.40%	5.99%	7	62.50%	681,521	536,158	2.14%	82.33%	82.33%
	Q2	518,801	7,154,391	-17,557	-3.27%	5.79%	8	56.25%	684,992	1,054,759	1.71%	21.09%	46.02%
	Q3	722,674	7,877,065	204,073	39.35%	8.07%	4	81.25%	592,478	1,777,433	4.03%	42.21%	44.45%
	Q4	1,074,962	8,952,027	352,288	48.75%	12.01%	1	100.00%	772,079	2,852,395	6.54%	7.47%	27.87%

Relative versus fixed

Let's take a look at some of the options for table calculations. Based on the options, you can compute table calculations in one of the following two ways:

- **Relative**: The table calculation will be computed relative to the layout of the table. They might move across or down the table. As we'll see, the key for relative table calculations is scope and direction. When you set a table calculation to use a relative computation, it will continue to use the same relative scope and direction, even if you rearrange the view.

- **Fixed**: The table calculation will be computed using one or more dimensions. Rearranging those dimensions may change whether the table calculation is moving across or down the table (or even in a more complex pattern). Here the scope and direction remain fixed to one or more dimensions, no matter where they are moved within the view. When we talk about fixed table calculations, we'll focus on the concepts of partitioning and addressing.

Scope and direction

Scope and direction describe how a table calculation is computed relative to the table. When a table calculation is relative to the layout of the table, rearranging the fields in the view will not change the scope and direction:

- **Scope**: The scope defines the boundaries within which a given table calculation can reference other values
- **Direction**: The direction defines how the table calculation moves within the scope

You've already seen table calculations being calculated table (across) (that is, the running sum of sales over time) and table (down) (that is, the preceding table). In these cases, the scope was the entire table and the direction was either across or down. For example, the running total calculation ran across the entire table, adding subsequent values as it moved.

To define scope and direction for a table calculation, use the drop-down menu for the field in the view and select **Compute Using**. You will get a list of options that will vary slightly depending on the dimensions present in the view. The first few options that are listed allow you to define the scope and direction relative to the table. After the option for **Cells**, you will see a list of dimensions present in the view; we'll take a look at those in the next section.

Options for scope and direction relative to the table:

- **Scope options**: Table, Panes, and Cells
- **Direction options**: Down, across, down then across, and across then down

In order to understand these options, consider the following example:

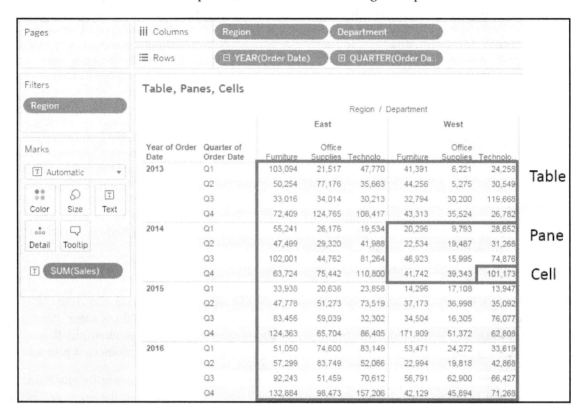

When it comes to the scope of table calculations, Tableau makes the following distinctions:

- The **Table** is the entire set of aggregate data.
- The **Pane** is defined by the next-to-last lowest level of the table (that is, the next-to-last dimension on the **Rows** and/or **Columns** shelf). In the preceding image, you can see that the intersection of **Year** on **Rows** and **Region** on **Columns** defines the panes (one is highlighted, but there are actually eight in the view).
- The cell is defined by the lowest level of the table. In this view, the intersection of one **Department** within a **Region** and one **Quarter** within a **Year** is a single cell (one is highlighted, but there are actually 96 in the view).

Working with scope and direction

Let's go through a few examples to see how scope and direction work together. You'll start by creating your own custom table calculation. Create a new calculated field named Index with the code Index().

Index:

Index is a table calculation function that starts with the value 1 and increments by one as it moves along a given direction and within a given scope. There are many practical uses for Index given how it moves for a given scope and direction.

Create the table shown previously with **YEAR(Order Date)** and **QUARTER(Order Date)** on **Rows** and **Region** and **Department** on **Columns**. Instead of placing **Sales** in the view, add the newly created Index field to the **Text** shelf. Then experiment, using the drop-down menu on the Index field and select **Compute Using** to cycle through various scope and direction combinations. In the following examples, we've only kept the **East** and **West** regions and two years:

- **Table (across)**: By default, Tableau uses table (across). In the following example, note how Index increments across the entire table:

| | | East | | | West | | |
| | | | Office | | | Office | |
		Furniture	Supplies	Technolo..	Furniture	Supplies	Technolo..
2015	Q1	1	2	3	4	5	6
	Q2	1	2	3	4	5	6
	Q3	1	2	3	4	5	6
	Q4	1	2	3	4	5	6
2016	Q1	1	2	3	4	5	6
	Q2	1	2	3	4	5	6
	Q3	1	2	3	4	5	6
	Q4	1	2	3	4	5	6

- **Table (down)**: When using table (down), Index increments down the entire table as follows:

		East			West		
			Office			Office	
		Furniture	Supplies	Technolo..	Furniture	Supplies	Technolo..
2015	Q1	1	1	1	1	1	1
	Q2	2	2	2	2	2	2
	Q3	3	3	3	3	3	3
	Q4	4	4	4	4	4	4
2016	Q1	5	5	5	5	5	5
	Q2	6	6	6	6	6	6
	Q3	7	7	7	7	7	7
	Q4	8	8	8	8	8	8

- **Table (across then down)**: This increments Index across the table, then steps down and continues to increment across and repeats for the entire table as follows:

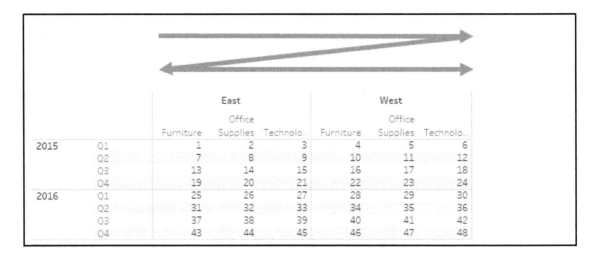

		East			West		
			Office			Office	
		Furniture	Supplies	Technolo..	Furniture	Supplies	Technolo..
2015	Q1	1	2	3	4	5	6
	Q2	7	8	9	10	11	12
	Q3	13	14	15	16	17	18
	Q4	19	20	21	22	23	24
2016	Q1	25	26	27	28	29	30
	Q2	31	32	33	34	35	36
	Q3	37	38	39	40	41	42
	Q4	43	44	45	46	47	48

- **Pane (across)**: This defines a boundary for `Index` and causes `Index` to increment across until it reaches the pane boundary, at which point the indexing restarts, as follows:

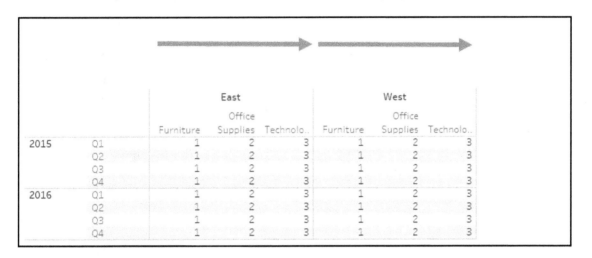

		East			West		
		Furniture	Office Supplies	Technolo..	Furniture	Office Supplies	Technolo..
2015	Q1	1	2	3	1	2	3
	Q2	1	2	3	1	2	3
	Q3	1	2	3	1	2	3
	Q4	1	2	3	1	2	3
2016	Q1	1	2	3	1	2	3
	Q2	1	2	3	1	2	3
	Q3	1	2	3	1	2	3
	Q4	1	2	3	1	2	3

- **Pane (down)**: This defines a boundary for index and causes `Index` to increment down until it reaches the pane boundary at which point the indexing restarts, as follows:

		East			West		
		Furniture	Office Supplies	Technolo..	Furniture	Office Supplies	Technolo..
2015	Q1	1	1	1	1	1	1
	Q2	2	2	2	2	2	2
	Q3	3	3	3	3	3	3
	Q4	4	4	4	4	4	4
2016	Q1	1	1	1	1	1	1
	Q2	2	2	2	2	2	2
	Q3	3	3	3	3	3	3
	Q4	4	4	4	4	4	4

- **Pane (across then down)**: This pane defines the boundary here allowing `Index` to increment across the pane and continues by stepping down:

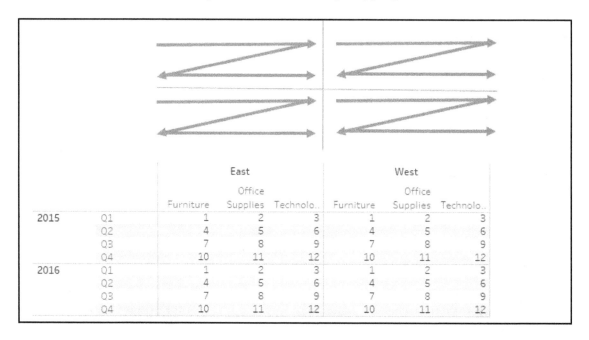

		East			West		
			Office			Office	
		Furniture	Supplies	Technolo..	Furniture	Supplies	Technolo..
2015	Q1	1	2	3	1	2	3
	Q2	4	5	6	4	5	6
	Q3	7	8	9	7	8	9
	Q4	10	11	12	10	11	12
2016	Q1	1	2	3	1	2	3
	Q2	4	5	6	4	5	6
	Q3	7	8	9	7	8	9
	Q4	10	11	12	10	11	12

You can use scope and direction with any table calculation. Consider how a running total or percent difference would be calculated using the same movement and boundaries that were shown previously.

Scope and direction work relative to the table, so you can rearrange fields and the calculation will still continue to work in the same scope and direction. For example, you could swap **Year of Order Date** with **Department** and still see `Index` calculated according to the scope and direction you defined.

Addressing and partitioning

Addressing and partitioning are very similar to scope and direction, but they are most often used to describe how table calculations are computed with absolute reference to certain fields in the view. With addressing and partitioning, you define the dimensions in the view that define the addressing (direction) and all others define the partitioning (scope).

You can get much finer control using addressing and partitioning because your table calculations are no longer relative to the table layout and you have many more options for fine-tuning the scope, direction, and order of the calculations.

To understand how this works, let's consider a simple example; using the previous view, select **Edit Table Calculation** from the drop-down menu of the `Index` field on **Text**. In the resulting dialog box, check **Department** under **Specific Dimensions**.

Here is the result of selecting **Department**:

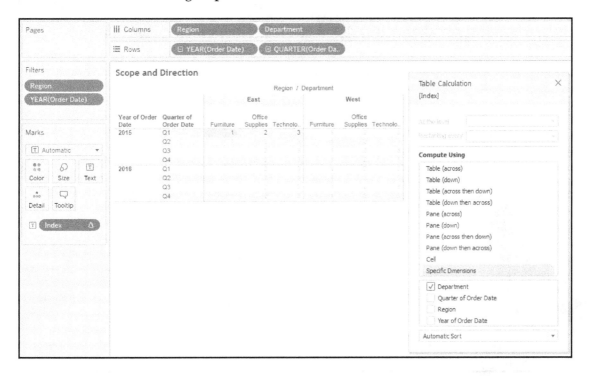

You'll notice that Tableau is computing **Index** along (in the direction of) the checked dimension, **Department**. In other words, you have used **Department** for addressing. All other unchecked dimensions in the view are implicitly used for partitioning, that is, they define the scope or boundaries at which the `Index` function must restart.

The preceding view looks identical to what you would see if you set **Index** to compute using **Pane (across)**. However, there is one major difference. When you use **Pane (across)**, Index is always computed across the pane, even if you rearrange the dimensions in the view, remove some, or add others. But when you compute using a dimension for addressing, the table calculation will always compute using that dimension. Removing that dimension will break the table calculation (the field will turn red with an exclamation mark) and you'll need to edit the table calculation via the drop-down menu to adjust the settings. If you rearrange dimensions in the view, **Index** will continue to be computed along the **Department** dimension.

The following figure is the result of clicking the **Swap Rows and Columns button** in the toolbar:

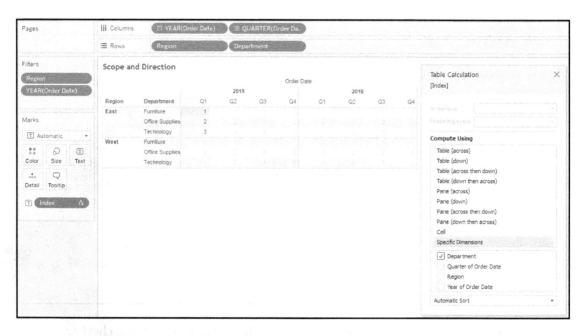

Note that Index continues to be computed along with **Department** even though the entire orientation of the table has changed. To complete the following examples, we'll undo the swap of **Rows** and **Columns** to return to the original orientation.

Advanced addressing and partitioning

Take a look at a few other examples of what happens when you add additional dimensions. For example, if you check **Quarter of Order Date**, you'll see Tableau highlight a partition defined by **Region** and **Year of Order Date** with `Index` incrementing by the addressing fields of **Quarter of Order Date** and then **Department**:

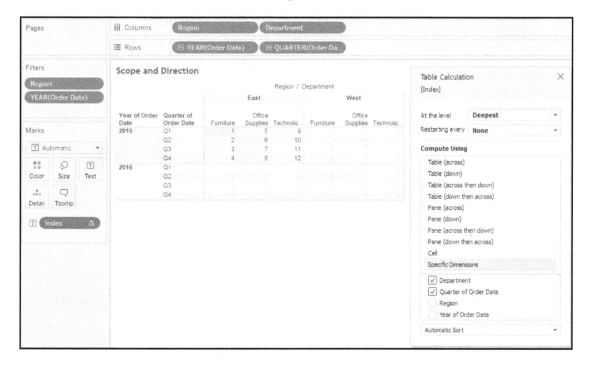

If you were to select **Department** and **Year of Order Date** as the addressing of `Index`, you'd see a single partition defined by **Region** and **Quarter**, as shown:

You'll notice in the preceding view that index increments for every combination of **Year** and **Department** within the partition of **Quarter** and **Region**.

There are a few other things to consider when working with addressing and partitioning, such as:

- You can specify the sort order. For example, if you want index to increment according to the value of the sum of **Sales**, you can use the drop-down at the bottom of the **Table Calculation** editor to define a **Custom Sort**.
- The **At the Level** option in the edit table calculation dialog box allows you to specify a level at which the table calculations are performed. Most of the time you'll leave this set at **Deepest** (which is the same as setting it to the bottommost dimension) but occasionally you might want to set it at a different level, if you need to keep certain dimensions from defining the partition but need the table calculation to be applied at a higher level. You can also reorder the dimensions by dragging and dropping within the checkbox list of **Specific Dimensions**.

- The **Restarting Every** option effectively selects the field and all the dimensions in the addressing field that is selected as a part of the partition, but allows you to maintain the fine-tuning of the ordering.
- Dimensions are the only kinds of fields that can be used in addressing the field; however, a discrete (blue) measure can be used to partition table calculations. To enable this, use the drop-down menu on the field and uncheck **Ignore in Table Calculations**.

Custom table calculations

Let's briefly consider how you can write your own table calculations instead of using a quick table calculation. You can see a list of available table calculation functions by creating a new calculation and selecting **Table Calculation** from the drop-down under **Functions**.

You can think of table calculations broken down into several categories, shown here. In each of the examples, we'll set **Compute Using | Category**, which means **Department** is the partition. The following table calculations can be combined and even nested similar to other functions:

- **Meta Table Functions**: These are the functions that give you information about the partitioning and addressing. These functions also include `Index`, `First`, `Last`, and `Size`:

Department	Category	Index	First	Last	Size
Furniture	Bookcases	1	0	3	4
	Chairs & Chairmats	2	-1	2	4
	Office Furnishings	3	-2	1	4
	Tables	4	-3	0	4
Office Supplies	Appliances	1	0	8	9
	Binders and Binder Accessori..	2	-1	7	9
	Envelopes	3	-2	6	9
	Labels	4	-3	5	9
	Paper	5	-4	4	9
	Pens & Art Supplies	6	-5	3	9
	Rubber Bands	7	-6	2	9
	Scissors, Rulers and Trimmers	8	-7	1	9
	Storage & Organization	9	-8	0	9
Technology	Computer Peripherals	1	0	3	4
	Copiers and Fax	2	-1	2	4
	Office Machines	3	-2	1	4
	Telephones and Communicati..	4	-3	0	4

`First` gives the offset from the first row in the partition. So, the first row in each partition is **0**. `Last` gives the offset to the last row in the partition. `Size` gives the size of the partition. `Index`, `First`, and `Last` are all affected by scope/partition and direction/addressing, while size will give the same result at each address of the partition no matter what direction is specified:

- **Lookup and Previous Value:** The first of these two functions give you the ability to reference values in other rows, while the second gives you the ability to carry forward values. Note that the direction is very important for these two functions:

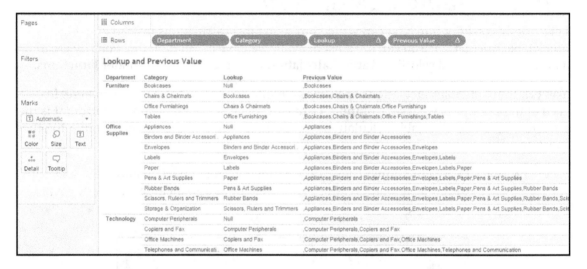

Both calculations are computed using an addressing of **Category** (so **Department** is the partition).

Here, we've used the code `Lookup(ATTR([Category]), -1)` that looks up the value of category in the row offset by −1 from the current. The first row in each partition gets a null result from the lookup (because there isn't a row before it).

For previous value, we used the following code:

```
Previous_Value("") +
"," +
ATTR([Category])
```

Note that in the first row of each partition, there is no previous value so `Previous_Value` simply returned what we specified as the default, an empty string. This was then concatenated together with a comma and the category in that row giving us the value, **Bookcases**.

In the second row, **Bookcases** is the previous value that gets concatenated with a comma and the category in that row gives us the value; **Bookcases** and **Chairs & Chairmats** become the previous value in the next row. The pattern continues throughout the partition and then restarts in the partition defined by the **Office Supplies** department:

- **Running functions**: These functions run along the direction/addressing and include `Running_Avg`, `Running_Count`, `Running_Sum`, `Running_Min`, and `Running_Max`. It is shown in the following figure:

Department	Category	Sales	Running Sum of Sales	Running Minimum of Sales
Furniture	Bookcases	507,496	507,496	507,496
	Chairs & Chairmats	1,164,586	1,672,082	507,496
	Office Furnishings	444,634	2,116,716	444,634
	Tables	1,061,922	3,178,638	444,634
Office Supplies	Appliances	456,736	456,736	456,736
	Binders and Binder Accessori..	638,583	1,095,319	456,736
	Envelopes	147,915	1,243,234	147,915
	Labels	23,446	1,266,680	23,446
	Paper	253,620	1,520,300	23,446
	Pens & Art Supplies	103,265	1,623,565	23,446
	Rubber Bands	8,670	1,632,235	8,670
	Scissors, Rulers and Trimmers	40,432	1,672,667	8,670
	Storage & Organization	585,717	2,258,384	8,670
Technology	Computer Peripherals	490,851	490,851	490,851
	Copiers and Fax	661,215	1,152,066	490,851
	Office Machines	1,218,655	2,370,721	490,851
	Telephones and Communicati..	1,144,284	3,515,005	490,851

Note that `Running_Sum(SUM[Sales]))` continues to add the sum of sales to a running total for every row in the partition. `Running_Min` keeps the value of the sum of sales if it is the smallest value it has encountered so far as it moves along the rows of the partition:

- **Window functions**: These functions operate across all rows in the partition at once and essentially aggregate the aggregates. They include `Window_Sum`, `Window_Avg`, `Window_Max`, `Window_Min`, and others:

Department	Category	Sales	Window Sum	Window Max
Furniture	Bookcases	507,496	3,178,638	1,164,586
	Chairs & Chairmats	1,164,586	3,178,638	1,164,586
	Office Furnishings	444,634	3,178,638	1,164,586
	Tables	1,061,922	3,178,638	1,164,586
Office Supplies	Appliances	456,736	2,258,384	638,583
	Binders and Binder Accessori..	638,583	2,258,384	638,583
	Envelopes	147,915	2,258,384	638,583
	Labels	23,446	2,258,384	638,583
	Paper	253,620	2,258,384	638,583
	Pens & Art Supplies	103,265	2,258,384	638,583
	Rubber Bands	8,670	2,258,384	638,583
	Scissors, Rulers and Trimmers	40,432	2,258,384	638,583
	Storage & Organization	585,717	2,258,384	638,583
Technology	Computer Peripherals	490,851	3,515,005	1,218,655
	Copiers and Fax	661,215	3,515,005	1,218,655
	Office Machines	1,218,655	3,515,005	1,218,655
	Telephones and Communicati..	1,144,284	3,515,005	1,218,655

- **Rank functions**: These functions provide various ways to rank based on aggregate values:

Department	Category	Sales	Rank of Sales
Furniture	Bookcases	507,496	3
	Chairs & Chairmats	1,164,586	1
	Office Furnishings	444,634	4
	Tables	1,061,922	2
Office Supplies	Appliances	456,736	3
	Binders and Binder Accessori..	638,583	1
	Envelopes	147,915	5
	Labels	23,446	8
	Paper	253,620	4
	Pens & Art Supplies	103,265	6
	Rubber Bands	8,670	9
	Scissors, Rulers and Trimmers	40,432	7
	Storage & Organization	585,717	2
Technology	Computer Peripherals	490,851	4
	Copiers and Fax	661,215	3
	Office Machines	1,218,655	1
	Telephones and Communicati..	1,144,284	2

- **R script functions**: These functions allow for integration with R, an analytics platform that can be used for complex scripting.
- **Total**: The `Total` function deserves its own category because it functions a little differently from the others. Unlike the other functions that work on the aggregate table in the cache. `Total` will re-query the underlying source for all the source data rows that make up a given partition. In many cases, this will yield the same result as a window function.

For example, `Total(SUM([Sales]))` gives the same result as `Window_Sum(SUM([Sales]))`, but `Total(AVG([Sales]))` will possibly give a different result from `Window_AVG(SUM([Sales]))` because the total is giving you the actual average of underlying rows while the window function is averaging the sums.

Data densification

Data densification is a broad term that indicates that missing values or records are filled in. Sometimes, specific terms, such as domain padding (filling in missing dates or bin values) or domain completion (filling in missing intersections of dimensional values), are used to specify the type of densification, but here we'll simply use the term data densification.

 Data with missing values (such as data that doesn't have a record for every single date or only contains records for products that have been ordered as opposed to all products in inventory) is referred to as sparse data.

Understanding when Tableau uses data densification and how you can turn it on or turn it off is important as you move towards mastering Tableau. There will be times when Tableau will engage data densification and you don't want it; you'll need to recognize it and understand the options to turn it off. At other times, you'll want to leverage data densification to solve certain types of problems or perform certain kinds of analysis.

When and where data densification occurs

Data densification can take place in the source if you choose to fill in missing data with certain joins, unions, or custom queries. But here we are focused on data densification that takes place in Tableau after aggregate data is returned from the source. Specifically, under certain circumstances that we'll consider as shown here, Tableau fills in missing values in the aggregate data in the cache, as seen in the following figure:

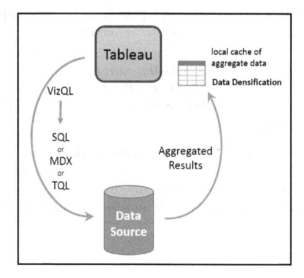

The preceding figure is very similar to the figure we examined when we started the discussion of table calculations. In fact, data densification happens at relatively the same time as table calculations and sometimes can even be triggered by table calculations. Here are some examples of times when data densification is enabled:

- When the **Show Missing Values** option is enabled for dates or bins used as headers on **Rows** or **Columns**. Here Tableau will show headers for dates or bin values (between the minimum or maximum dates/bin values), even if they don't occur in the data (or are eliminated by a filter). You can easily turn this densification on or off by selecting the desired option.

- With **Show Missing Values** enabled, certain table calculations used in the view will additionally add marks in the view for the missing headers. We'll see an example of this over here.

- Enabling the **Show Empty Rows/Columns** option (from the top menu, select **Analysis | Table Layout | Show Empty Rows/Columns**.) This causes Tableau to show all the row and column headers, even if particular values wouldn't normally be shown based on filter selections. This option is context specific, so the domain of values shown is either for the entire dataset or for the context defined by context filters. Observe the difference between the **Categories** shown with and without the option checked:

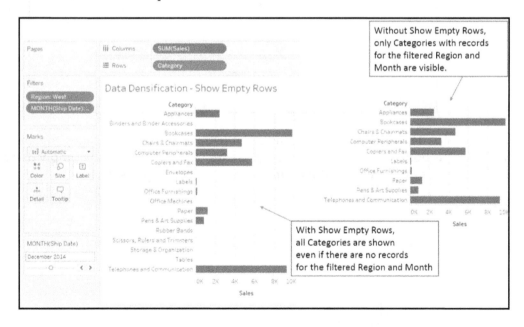

- Using certain table calculations with discrete dimensions on **Rows** and **Columns** will cause Tableau to turn on data densification. Let's take a look at an example and how to optionally turn off the resulting densification.

- Observe the difference between the following two views:

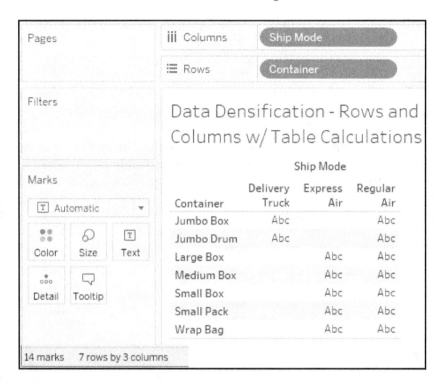

This view has **14 marks** (you can see the count in the status bar) indicating that there are 14 valid intersections of **Containers** and **Ship Modes**. Some combinations simply don't occur in the data (for example, a **Jumbo Drum** is never sent by **Express Air**).

But adding a table calculation, such as `Index()`, to the **Detail** causes Tableau to fill in the missing intersections, as shown:

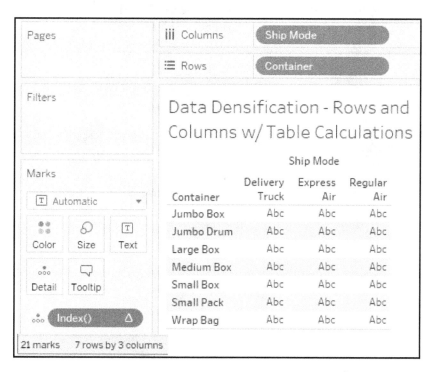

Tableau has filled in the combinations of **Containers** and **Ship Modes** and there are now **21 marks**. Sometimes this behavior might be useful (we'll see a following example), but many times you may want to avoid the densification. How can you turn it off?

Tableau has enabled the densification because of the discrete dimensions on **Rows** and **Columns**; you can rearrange the view so that only one dimension remains on **Rows** or **Columns**. This view, for example, keeps **Ship Mode** on **Detail** to keep it as a part of the view level of detail, but uses the special aggregation **ATTR** on **Columns**:

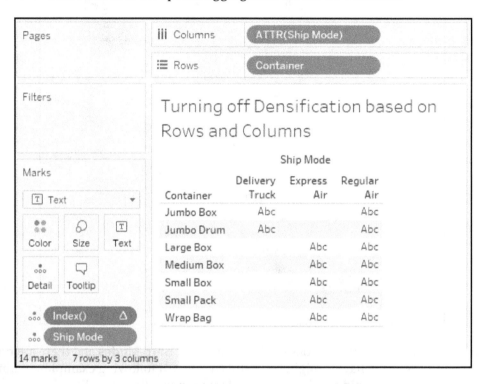

The result is a view without data densification showing only **14 marks**.

Keep an eye on the status bar and the count of marks to help you identify possible cases of data densification. You will then be able to decide when you wish to leverage densification or when it is useful to turn it off.

Leveraging data densification

As we have seen, data densification helps in showing empty rows or missing dates. However, there are cases where you can use data densification to solve problems or get around limitations of the data that would be very difficult otherwise.

Let's say that you have data that indicates dates when certain generators were turned **On** or **Off**:

Generator	Date	Action
A	Jan 13	On
B	Jan 22	On
C	Jan 25	On
D	Jan 25	On
B	Jan 27	Off
E	Jan 29	On
A	Jan 30	Off
C	Jan 30	Off

What would you do if you wanted a visualization to show how many generators were **On** for any given date? The challenge is that the dataset is sparse which means that there are only records for dates when an **On** or **Off** action occurred. This is easy to visualize in Tableau:

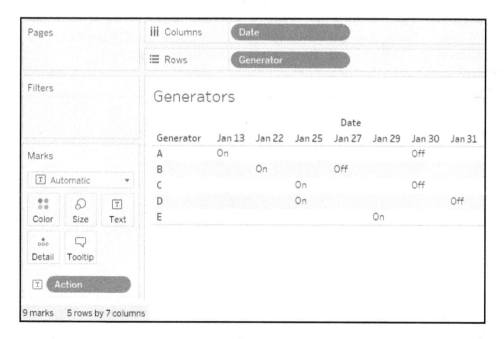

We only have **9 marks** to work with. We've already seen that Tableau can fill in missing dates and additionally, we can further force data densification using certain table calculations to fill in a value for each generator for every date.

Let's start with a calculation that takes the human friendly value of **On** or **Off** and changes it to a value we can easily add. The calculation is named `Action Value` with code:

```
IF [Action] = "On" THEN 1 ELSE 0 END
```

This will give us `1` to count the generator when it is `"On"` and `0` otherwise.

An additional calculation combined with enabling the **Show Missing Values** of the `Date` field allows us to fill in every date with a value. The new calculated field is called `Action Value for Date` and has the following code:

```
IF NOT ISNULL(MIN([Action Value]))
THEN MIN([Action Value])
ELSE ZN(PREVIOUS_VALUE(MIN([Action Value])))
END
```

This implements a table calculation that we will set to calculate across the table. If `MIN([Action Value])` is not null, then we have arrived at a date where the data gives an actual value and we'll keep that. Otherwise, we'll carry forward the `PREVIOUS_VALUE()` (a `1` if the generator was turned on or a `0` if it was turned off). The `ZN()` function will turn any null values into 0's (we'll assume the generator is off until we encounter an On). Let's move across the table, carrying forward values until we come across a value present in the data. Then we'll carry that one forward. The result is a table with all dates filled in with values, as shown:

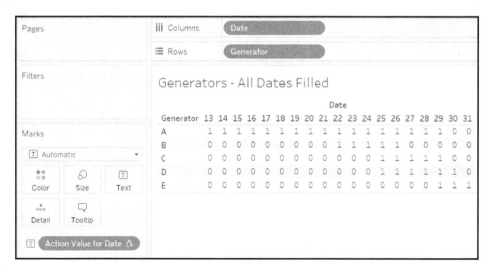

Note that every generator gets a 1 on the date it was turned on and that 1 is carried across the table until the generator is turned off, at which point we get the 0 and carry it across.

We're close, because all we have to do now is sum up the values for all generators for a given date to get the number of generators that were on; for example, on the 13th, there was only one and on the 25th, there were 4.

We can accomplish this using one more calculation that nests our existing calculation. We'll name this calculated field Generators Operating and use the following code:

```
WINDOW_SUM([Action Value for Date])
```

The key here is that we want to sum all the values down the table, but we want those values to be calculated across the table. When you use nested table calculations (table calculations referenced within the code of other table calculations), you can specify the scope/direction or addressing/partitioning for each **Nested Calculation**.

Here for example, we'll add the **Generators Operating** calculated field to **Rows** and use the drop-down menu to select the **Edit Table Calculation** option:

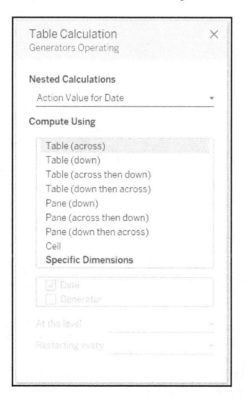

Observe that under the **Nested Calculations** heading there is a drop-down where you can change the **Compute Using** options for each nested calculation. Here, we'll set **Generators Operating** to **Table (down)** and **Action Value for Date** to **Table (across)**.

Our final view, after a bit of cleanup indicated here, will look similar to this:

The final view gives us a clear indication of how many generators were on for any given date, even though many of those dates did not exist in the data and we certainly didn't have a record for every generator for every date.

We've cleaned up the view a bit by doing the following:

- Adding a `First()` `==` 0 filter, which is computed **Table (down)** because we're getting the total sum of `Action Values for Date` for each generator and we only need to show one set of totals

- Hiding the column headers for **Generator**, because the field needs to be in the view to define the view level of detail, but does not need to be shown
- Changing **Marks** to **Area**

Would it have been easier or better to densify the data at the source by joining every generator with every date to get a record for each combination? Possibly. If it is possible, given your data source, to perform such a join, you may end up with a data set that is far easier to work with in Tableau (without having to use data densification or complex table calculations). But you'll have to evaluate the feasibility of filling in missing data at the source based on volumes of data, underlying capabilities of the database, and how quickly such transformations can be accomplished.

Summary

We've covered a lot of concepts surrounding table calculations in this chapter. You now have a solid foundation for understanding everything from quick table calculations to advanced table calculations and data densification. The practical examples we covered barely scratch the surface of what is possible, but they should give you an idea of what can be achieved. The kinds of problems that can be solved and the diversity of questions that can be answered are almost limitless!

We'll turn our attention to some lighter topics in the next couple of chapters with topics, such as formatting and design, but we'll certainly see another table calculation or two before we're finished!

8

Formatting Visualizations to Look Great and Work Well

So far you have learned how to visualize data; but have just learned that is not enough. The data needs to be presented in such a way that it makes a huge difference in the way it is received and understood. As you move beyond making great discoveries and doing great analysis, you need to look at formatting to present the story of the data. Formatting is more than just making a data visualization look good.

Tableau's formatting options give you quite a bit of flexibility. Fonts, titles, captions, colors, row and column banding, labels, shading, annotations, and much more can be customized to make your visualizations tell a story effectively.

This chapter will cover the following topics:

- Formatting considerations
- Understanding how formatting works in Tableau
- Adding value to visualizations

Formatting considerations

Tableau employs good practices for formatting and visualization from the time you start dropping fields on shelves. Tableau 10 additionally introduces a wide variety of new fonts, colors, and defaults that emphasize aesthetic appeal. You'll find that the discrete palettes use colors that are easy to distinguish, fonts, grid lines are faint where appropriate, and numbers and dates follow the default format settings defined in the metadata.

The default formatting is more than adequate for discovery and analysis. If your focus is analysis, you may not want to spend too much time fine-tuning the formatting until you have moved on in the cycle. However, when you start to consider how you will communicate the data to others, you will need to contemplate how adjustments to formatting can make a difference in how well the data story is told.

> Sometimes, you will have certain formatting preferences in mind when you start your design. In these cases, you might set formatting options in a blank workbook and save it as a template.

Here are some of the things you should consider:

- **Audience**: Who is the audience and what is the need?
- **Setting**: This is the environment in which the data story is communicated. Is it a formal business meeting where the format should reflect a high level of professionalism? Is it going to be shared on a blog to informally, or even playfully, tell a story?
- **Mode**: How will the visualizations be presented? You'll want to make sure rows, columns, fonts, and marks are large enough for a projector or compact enough for an iPad. If you are publishing to Tableau Server, Tableau Online, or Tableau Public, then did you select fonts that are safe for the web? Will you need to use the device designer to create different versions of a dashboard?
- **Mood**: Certain colors, fonts, and layouts elicit different emotional responses. Does the data tell a story that should invoke a certain response from your audience? The color red, for example, may connote danger, negative results, or indicate that an action is required. However, you'll need to be sensitive to your audience and the specific context. Colors have different meanings for different cultures and contexts. Red might not be a good choice to communicate negativity if it is also the color of the corporate logo.
- **Consistency**: Generally, use the same fonts, colors, shapes, line thickness, and row-banding throughout all visualizations. This is especially true when they will be seen together in a dashboard or even used in the same workbook. You can also consider how to remain consistent throughout the organization without being too rigid.

All of these considerations will inform your formatting decisions. Think of formatting as an iterative process. Look for feedback from your intended audience often and adjust as necessary to make sure your communication is as clear and effective as possible. The goal of formatting is to communicate the data more effectively.

Understanding how formatting works in Tableau

Tableau uses default formatting that includes default fonts, colors, shading, and alignment. Additionally, there are several levels of formatting you can customize, as shown in the following diagram:

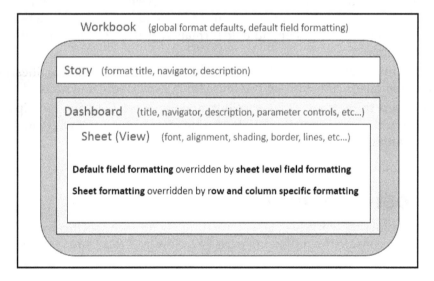

Workbook level: The following type of formatting comes under this category:

- **Workbook defaults**: From the menu bar, navigate to **Format** | **Workbook**. The ability to set certain formatting as default for the workbook is new to Tableau 10.
- **Default field formatting**: Using the drop-down menu on a field in the data pane, navigate to **Default Properties** | **Date Format** or **Default Properties** | **Number Format**. This sets the default format in Tableau's metadata and will be applied to any view where custom formatting has not been applied.

- **Story level**: Navigate to a story tab and navigate to **Format|Story** (or **Story|Format**) to edit formatting for story-specific elements. These include options for customizing shading, title, navigator, and description.
- **Dashboard level**: Dashboard-specific elements can be formatted. When viewing a dashboard, navigate to **Format|Dashboard** (or **Dashboard|Format**) to specify formatting for dashboard titles, subtitles, shading, and text objects.

Worksheet level: We'll consider the various options in the following section. The following types of formatting are available for a worksheet:

- **Sheet formatting**: This formatting includes font, alignment, shading, borders, and lines.
- **Field level formatting**: This formatting includes fonts, alignment, shading, and number and date formats. This formatting is specific to how a field is displayed in the current view. The options you set at a field level override defaults set at a worksheet level. Number and date formats will also override the default field formatting.
- **Additional formatting**: Additional formatting can be applied to titles, captions, tooltips, labels, annotations, reference lines, field labels, and more.
- **Rich text formatting**: Titles, captions, annotations, labels, and tool tips all contain text which can be formatted with varying fonts, colors, and alignment. This formatting is specific to the individual text element.

Worksheet-level formatting

Let's start by considering worksheet level formatting. Before we specifically look at how to adjust formatting, consider the following parts of a view as it relates to formatting:

Formatting: Parts of the View

Department	Category	Consumer	Corporate	Home Office	Small Business	Grand Total
Furniture	Bookcases	92,626	262,085	79,404	73,381	507,496
	Chairs & Chairmats	305,381	407,724	212,830	238,651	1,164,586
	Office Furnishings	69,528	115,506	197,188	62,412	444,634
	Tables	228,934	363,979	287,507	181,502	1,061,922
	Total	696,469	1,149,294	776,929	555,946	3,178,638
Office Supplies	Appliances	63,813	167,941	124,757	100,225	456,736
	Binders and Binder Accessor.	103,625	225,160	148,472	161,326	638,583
	Envelopes	37,643	44,462	22,577	43,233	147,915
	Labels	3,713	7,929	5,411	6,393	23,446
	Paper	53,004	89,312	61,123	50,181	253,620
	Pens & Art Supplies	24,027	36,004	21,765	21,469	103,265
	Rubber Bands	1,710	2,197	2,294	2,469	8,670
	Scissors, Rulers and Trimme.	14,628	9,625	12,947	3,232	40,432
	Storage & Organization	121,719	154,918	179,151	129,929	585,717
	Total	423,882	737,548	578,497	518,457	2,258,384
Technology	Computer Peripherals	80,805	224,142	110,840	75,064	490,851
	Copiers and Fax	148,504	205,639	174,718	132,354	661,215
	Office Machines	260,011	516,513	245,019	197,112	1,218,655
	Telephones and Communicat.	225,571	436,295	282,962	199,456	1,144,284
	Total	714,891	1,382,589	813,539	603,986	3,515,005
Grand Total		1,835,242	3,269,431	2,168,965	1,678,389	8,952,027

Customer Segment

This view consists of the following parts which can be formatted:

1. **Field labels for rows**: Field labels can be formatted from the menu (**Format|FieldLabels...**) or by right-clicking on them in the view and selecting **Format...**. Additionally, you can hide field labels from the menu (**Analysis|Table Layout)** and then uncheck the option for showing field labels or by right-clicking on them in the view and selecting the option to hide. You can use the **Analysis|Table Layout** option on the top menu to show them again if desired.
2. **Field labels for columns**: These have the same options as for rows, but may be formatted or shown/hidden independently from the row field labels.
3. **Row headers**: These will follow the formatting of headers in general, unless you specify different formatting for headers of rows only. Notice that subtotals and grand total have headers. The subtotal and grand total headers marked **a** and **b** in the preceding figure, are total row headers.
4. **Column headers**: These will follow formatting of headers in general, unless you specify different formatting for headers of columns only. Note that subtotals and grand totals have headers. The grand total header marked a column header.

5. **Pane**: Many formatting options include the ability to format the pane differently from the headers.
6. **Grand totals (column) pane**: This is the pane for grand totals that can be formatted at a sheet or column level.
7. **Grand totals (row) pane**: This is the pane for grand totals that can be formatted at a sheet or row level.

Worksheet level formatting is accomplished using the format window, which will appear on the left side, in place of the data pane. To view the format window, select **Format** from the menu and then **Font...**, **Alignment...**, **Shading...**, **Border...**, or **Lines...**:

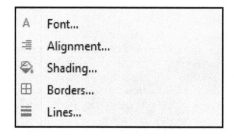

You can also right-click on nearly any element in the view and select **Format**. This will open the format window specific to the context of the element you selected. Just be certain to verify that the title of the format window matches what you expect. When you make a change, you should see the view update immediately to reflect your formatting. If you don't, you are likely working in the wrong tab of the formatting window or you may have formatted something at a lower level (for example, **Rows**) which overrides changes made at a higher level (for example, **Sheet**).

You should now see the format window on the left. It will look similar to this:

Note the following key aspects of the formatting window:

- The title of the window will give you the context for your formatting selections.
- The icons on the top match the selection options of the **Format** menu. This allows you to easily navigate through those options without returning to the menu each time.
- The three tabs, **Sheet, Rows**, and **Columns** allow you to specify options at a sheet level and then override those options and defaults at a row and column level. For example, you could make row grand totals have different pane and header fonts than column grand totals (though this specific choice would likely be jarring and is not recommended!)

- The field's dropdown in the upper-right corner allows you to fine-tune formatting at a field level.
- Any changes that you make will be previewed and result in a bold label to indicate that the formatting option has been changed from the default (notice how the font for the header under `Total` has been customized in the preceding figure, resulting in the label text of the header being shown in bold.

Clearing formatting,there are three options for clearing the format are as follows:

- **Clear single option**:In the format window, right click the label or control of any single option you have changed and select **Clear** from the pop-up menu.
- **Clear all current options**: At the bottom of the format window, click the **Clear** button to clear all visible changes. This applies only to what you are currently seeing in the format window. For example, if you are looking at **Shading** and the **Rows** tab, and then click **Clear**, only the shading options you have changed on the **Rows** tab will be cleared.
- **Clear sheet**: From the menu, navigate to **Worksheet** | **Clear**| **Formatting**. You can also use the drop-down from the Clear item on the toolbar. This clears all custom formatting on the current worksheet.

The other format options (alignment, shading, and so on) all work very similarly to the font option. There are only a few subtleties to mention:

- * **Alignment**: This includes options for horizontal and vertical alignment, text direction, and text wrapping.
- * **Shading**: This includes an option for **Row** and **Columns** banding. The banding allows for alternating patterns of shading that help to differentiate or group rows and columns. Light row banding is enabled by default for text tables, but can be useful in other visualization types such as horizontal bar charts as well. Row banding can be set to different levels which correspond to the number of discrete (blue) fields present on the **Rows** or **Columns** shelf.
- **Borders**: This refers to the borders drawn around cells, panes, and headers. It includes an option for **Row** and **Columns** dividers. You can see in the view, the dividers between the departments. By default, the level of the borders is set based on the next to last field on **Rows** or **Columns**.
- **Lines**: This refers to lines that are drawn on visualizations using an axis. This includes grid lines, reference lines, zero lines, and axis rulers. You can access a more complete set of options for reference lines and drop lines from the **Format** option on the menu.

Field-level formatting

In the upper-right corner of the **Format SUM(Sales)** window is a little drop-down labeled **Fields**. Selecting this drop-down gives you a list of fields in the current view and selecting a field updates the format window with options appropriate for the field. Here, for example, is the window as it appears for the **SUM(Sales)** field:

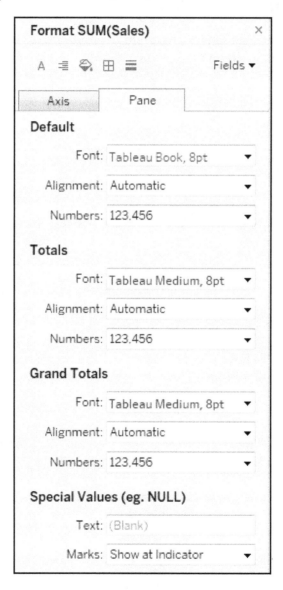

The title of the format window will alert you to the field you are formatting. The options for fields include font, alignment, shading, and number and date formats. The latter two options will over-ride any default metadata formats. Selecting an icon for **Font**, **Alignment**, and so on will switch back to the sheet level formatting. However, you can switch between the tabs: **Axis/Header** and **Pane**.

Custom number formatting:

When you alter the format of a number you can select from several standard formats as well as a custom format. The custom format allows you to enter a format string which Tableau will use to format the number. The format string allows for up to three entries, separated by semi-colons, to represent positive, negative, and zero formats. Here are some examples assuming the positive number **34,331.336000** and the negative number **-8,156.777700**:

Format string	Resulting Values
#;-#	34331 and -8157
#,###.##;(#,###.##)	34,331.34 and (8,156.78)
#,###.000000; -#,###.000000	34,331.336000 and -8,156.777700
"up "#,###;"down "#,###;"same"	up 34,331 and down 8,157

Notice how Tableau rounds the display of the number based on the format string. Always be aware that numbers you see as text, labels, or headers may have been rounded due to the format.

Also, observe how you can mix format characters such as the pound sign, commas, and decimal points with strings. The preceding example would give a label of "same" where a value of 0 would normally have been shown.

Instead of using "up" or "down" as shown in the preceding example, you could use a Unicode character, such as ▲ or ▼.

Selecting a predefined format that is close to what you want and then switching to custom, will allow you to start with a custom format string that is close.

An additional aspect of formatting a field is specially formatting NULL values. When formatting a field, select the **Pane** tab and locate the **Special Values** section, as shown in the following screenshot:

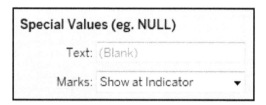

Enter any text you would like to display in the pane (in the **Text** field) when the value of the field is null. You can also choose where marks should be displayed. The **Marks** drop-down gives multiple options that define where and how the marks for null values should be drawn when an axis is being used. You have the following options:

- **Show at Indicator**: This results in a small indicator with the number of nulls in the lower right of the view. You can click the indicator for options to filter the nulls or show them at the default value. You can right-click the indicator to hide it.
- **Show at Default Value**: This option displays a mark at the default location (usually 0).
- **Hide (Connect Lines)**: This option makes sure that it does not place a mark for null values, but it does connect lines between all non-null values.
- **Hide (Break Lines)**: This causes the line to break where there are gaps created by not showing the null values.

You can see these options in the following screenshot, with the location of two null values indicated by a gray band:

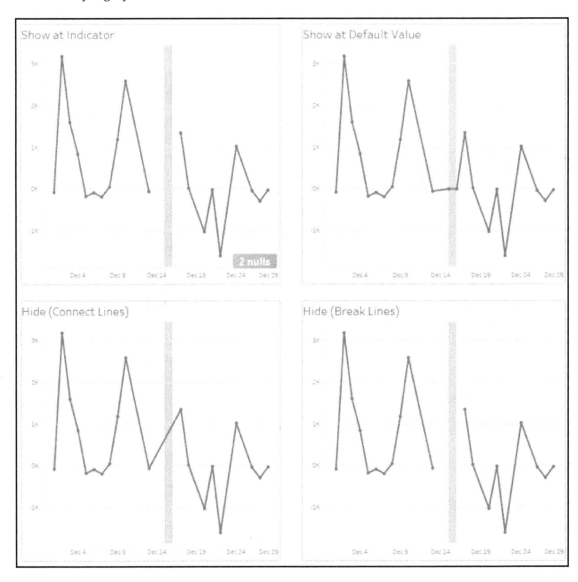

You'll notice that the preceding line charts have little circle markers at the location of each mark drawn in the view. When the mark type is a line, clicking on the **Color** shelf opens a menu that gives options for the markers. All mark types have standard options, such as color and transparency. Some mark types support additional options, such as border and/or halo, as shown here:

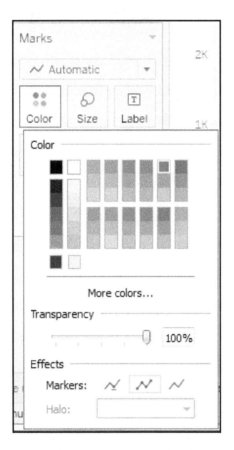

The **Hide (Break Lines)** or the **Show at Indicator** options work well in the preceding view because those two options do not obscure the null values. However, the formatting only helps with actual null values. These are the records that exist in the data, but have null, indicating no value. However, there are no records for some dates in December. In that case, the value isn't null, there isn't even a record of the data. Tableau still connects the lines across those missing days, potentially making it difficult to tell that there are gaps. In that case, consider enabling data densification (you can accomplish this by ensuring the **Show Missing Dates** option is selected from the drop-down of the **DAY(Order Date)** field on **Columns** and then adding certain table calculations such as **Index()** to the **Detail** of the view).

This causes Tableau to generate records of data for the missing dates and treat the values as null:

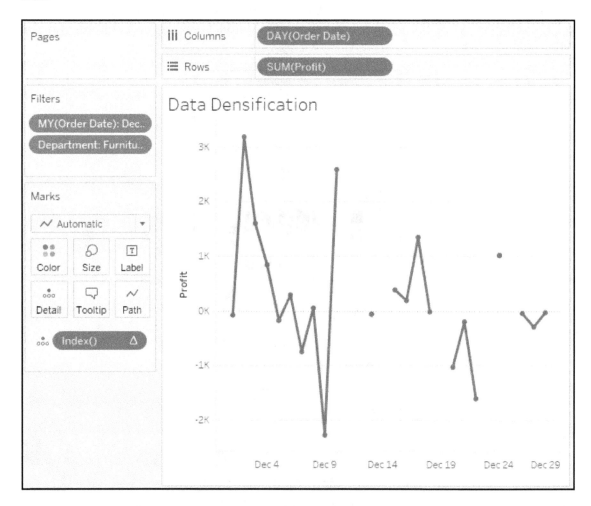

You can also use a bar chart as a visualization type that indicates the missing days more clearly:

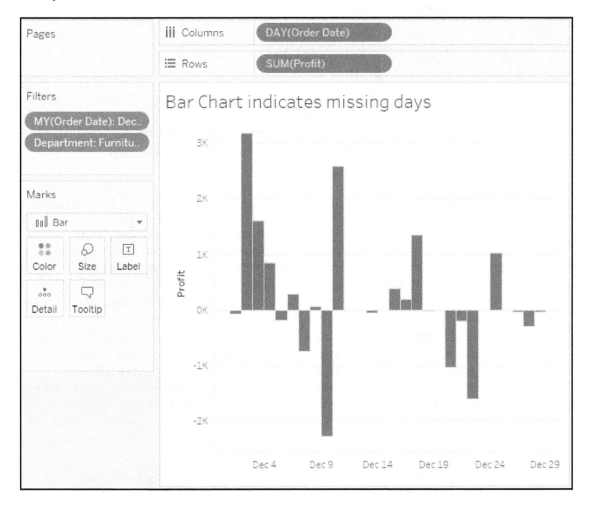

Additional formatting options

Additional formatting options can also be accessed from the formatting window. These options include:

- A myriad of options for **Reference Lines**
- Line and text options for **Drop Lines**
- Shading and border options for **Titles and Captions**
- Text, box, and line options for **Annotations**
- Font, shading, alignment, and separator options for **Field Labels**
- Title and body options for **Legends**, **Quick Filters**, and **Parameters**
- **Cell Size** and **Workbook Theme** options

You'll find most of these fairly straightforward. A few options might not be as obvious:

- **Drop Lines**: They appear as lines drawn from the mark to the axis and can be enabled by right-clicking on any blank area in the pane of the view with an axis and selecting **Drop Lines** | **Show Drop Lines**. Additional options can be accessed using the same right-click menu and selecting **Edit Drop Lines**. Drop lines are only displayed in the Tableau desktop and Reader but are not available when a view is published to the Tableau server, online, or public.
- **Titles** and **Captions** can be shown or hidden for any view by selecting Worksheet from the menu and then selecting the desired options. In addition to standard formatting, which can be applied to titles and captions, the text of a title or caption can be edited and specifically formatted by double clicking, right-clicking and selecting Edit, or by using the drop down menu for the title or caption(or the drop-down menu of the view on a dashboard). The text of titles and captions can dynamically include the values of parameters, values of any field in the view, and certain other data and worksheet-specific values.
- **Annotations** can be created by right-clicking on a mark or space in the view and selecting **Annotate** and then selecting one of the following three types of annotations:
    - **Mark** annotations are associated with a specific mark in the view. If that mark does not show (due to a filter or axis range), then neither will the annotation. Mark annotations can include a display of the values of any fields that define the mark or its location.

- **Point** annotations are anchored to a specific point in the view. If the point is not visible in the view, the annotation will disappear. Point annotations can include a display of any field values that define the location of the point (for example, the coordinates of the axis).
- **Area** annotations are contained within a rectangular area. The text of all annotations can dynamically include the values of parameters and certain other data and worksheet specific values.

You can copy formatting from one worksheet to another (within the same workbook or across workbooks) by selecting **Copy Formatting** from the **Format** menu while viewing the source worksheet (or select the **Copy Formatting** option from the right-click menu on the source worksheet tab). Then select **Paste Formatting** on the **Format** menu while viewing the target worksheet (or select the option from the right-click menu on the target worksheet tab).

This option will apply any custom formatting present on the source sheet to the target. However, specific formatting applied during the editing of the text of titles, captions, labels and tooltips is not copied to the target sheet.

Adding value to visualizations

Now that we've considered how formatting works in Tableau, let's take a look at some ways in which formatting can add value to a visualization.

Always ask yourself what the formatting adds to the understanding of the data. Is it making the visualization clearer and easier to understand? Or is it just adding clutter and noise?

In general, try a minimalistic approach. Remove everything from the visualization that isn't necessary. Emphasize important values, text, and marks while de-emphasizing those which are only providing support or context.

Consider the following visualization using all the default formatting:

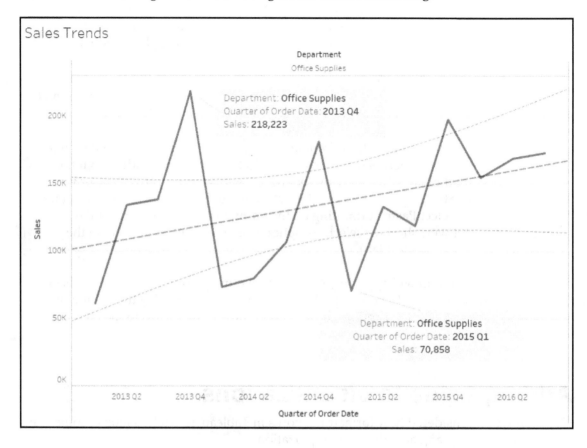

The default format works very well. But compare that with this visualization:

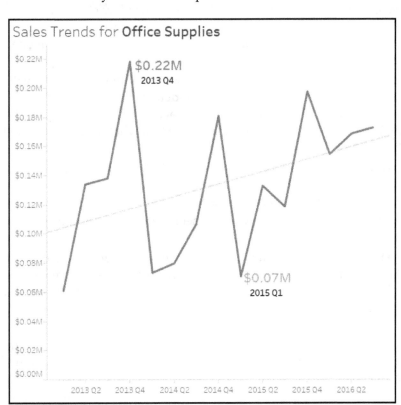

Both the preceding charts are showing sales by quarter, filtered to the office supplies department. With the exception that the top view has the department field on **Columns** in an attempt to make it clear that only office supplies sales are being shown, the field arrangement for the two views is exactly the same. The first view uses default formatting.

Consider some of the customizations in the second view:

- The **Title** has been adjusted to include the department name.
- The **Sales** field has been formatted to be shown using a custom currency with two decimal places and units of millions. This is true for the axis and the annotations. Often a high-level of precision can clutter visualization. The initial view of the data gives the trend and enough detail to understand the order of magnitude. Tooltips or additional views can be used to reveal detail and precision.

- The axis labels have been removed by right-clicking on the axis, selecting **Edit Axis**, and then clearing the text. The title of the view clearly indicates that one is looking at **Sales**. The values alone reveal the second axis to be by quarter. If there are multiple dates in the data, you might need to specify which one is in use. Depending on your goals, you might consider hiding the axes completely.

- The gridlines on **Rows** have been removed. Gridlines can add a value to a view, especially in views where being able to determine values is of high importance. However, they can also clutter and distract. You'll need to decide, based on the view itself and the story you are trying to tell, whether gridlines are helpful or not.

- The trend line has been formatted to match the color of the line. Additionally, the confidence bands have been removed. You'll have to decide whether they add context or clutter based on your needs and audience.

- The **lines**, **shading**, and **boxes** have been removed from the annotations to reduce clutter.

- The **size** and **color** of the annotations have been altered to make them stand out. If the goal had been to simply highlight the minimum and maximum values on the line, labels might have been a better choice as they can be set to display at only **Min/Max**. In this case, however, the lower number is actually the second lowest point in the view.

- Axis rulers and ticks have been emphasized and colored to match the marks and reference line (axis rulers are available under the lines option on the format window).

Formatting can also be used to dramatically alter the appearance of visualization. Consider the following chart:

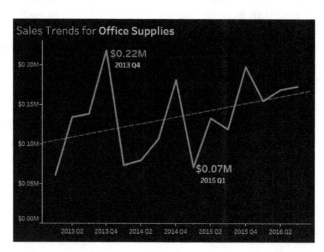

This visualization is nearly identical to the previous view with the difference of shading applied to the worksheet and the title. Additionally, fonts were lightened or darkened as needed to show up well on a black background. Some find this format more pleasing, especially on mobile devices. If the view is to be embedded in a website with a dark theme, this formatting may be very desirable. However, you may find some text more difficult to read on a dark background. You'll want to consider your audience, the setting, and mode of delivery as you consider whether such a format is the best for your situation.

 Sequential color palettes (a single color gradient based on a continuous field) should be reversed when using a black background. This is because the default of lighter (lower) to darker (higher) works well on a white background where darker colors stand out and lighter colors fade into white.

 On a black background, lighter colors stand out more and darker colors fade into black. You'll find the reverse option when you edit a color palette using the drop-down menu on the legend, double clicking the legend, or right-clicking the legend and selecting **Edit Colors...** and checking **Reversed**.

Tooltips

Tooltips add a subtle professionalism to the visualizations but are an easily overlooked aspect of visualizations as they are not always visible. Consider the following default tooltip that displays when the end user hovers over one of the marks in the preceding view:

✓ Keep Only	✕ Exclude	⊘ ▾	▦
Quarter of Order Date: **2016 Q1**			
Sales:		**$0.15M**	

Compare it to this tooltip:

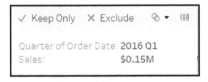

The tooltip was edited using the menu option **Worksheet | Tooltip**, which brought up an editor allowing for the rich editing of text in the tooltip:

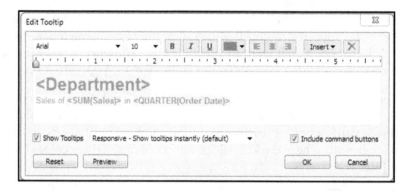

This editor is similar to those used for editing the text of labels, titles, captions, and annotations. Observe the **Insert** dropdown in the upper-right corner which allows you to insert fields, parameters, and other dynamic values. In the text, these are enclosed as a tag. You'll notice that the first tooltip included command buttons (keeping and excluding filters, creating sets, groups, and viewing the data). You'll need to decide if the command buttons add easy functionality or are distracting or confusing for your intended audience. The functionality is always available to the end user via a right-click.

 You can stop a tooltip from showing at all by unchecking the option in the editor.

Summary

With an understanding of how formatting works in Tableau, you'll have the ability to refine the visualizations you created in discovery and analysis into incredibly effective communication of your data story. Always consider the audience, setting, mode, mood, and consistency as you work through the iterative process of formatting. Look for formatting that adds value to your visualization and avoid useless clutter. Next, we'll look at how it all comes together in dashboards.

9

Advanced Visualizations, Techniques, Tips, and Tricks

With a solid understanding of the foundational principles, it is possible to push the limits with Tableau. In addition to exploring, discovering, analyzing, and communicating data, members of the Tableau community have used the software to create and do amazing things such as simulate an enigma machine, play tic-tac-toe or other games, generate fractals with only two records of data, and much more! Unlike traditional BI packages that force you through a series of wizards to create a chart based on a predefined template, Tableau really is a blank canvas and the only limits are your creativity and imagination.

In this chapter, we'll take a look at some advanced techniques in a practical context. You'll learn things such as creating advanced visualizations, dynamically swapping views on a dashboard, using custom images, and advanced geographic visualizations.

We'll take a look at the following advanced techniques in this chapter:

- Advanced visualizations
- Sheet swapping and dynamic dashboards
- Advanced mapping techniques
- Using background images
- Animation

Advanced visualizations

In Chapter 3, *Moving from Foundational to More Advanced Visualizations*, we took a look at variations of some foundational visualizations, such as bar charts, time series, distributions, and scatterplots.

Now, we'll consider some non-standard visualization types. These are merely examples of Tableau's amazing flexibility and are meant to inspire you to think through new ways of seeing, understanding, and communicating your data.

Each of the following visualizations is created using the supplied Superstore data. Instead of providing step-by-step instructions, we'll point out specific advanced techniques used to create each chart type. The goal is to leverage Tableau's features to build whatever you want.

You can find completed examples in the `Chapter 10 Complete` workbook or test your growing Tableau skills by building everything from scratch using `Chapter 10 Starter`.

Slope chart

A **slope chart** shows a change of values from one period or status to another. For example, here is a slope chart demonstrating the change in sales rank for each state in the **West Region** from **2015** to **2016**:

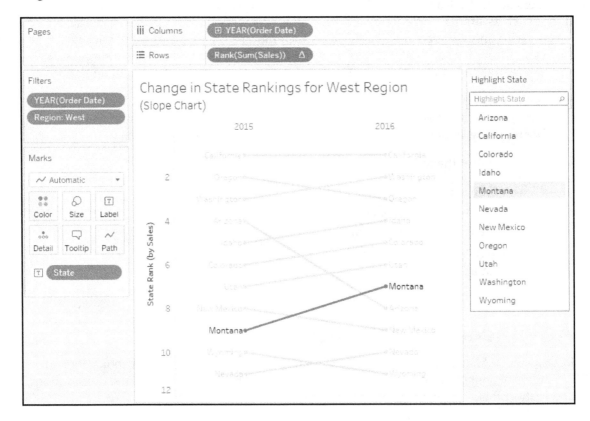

Here are some features and techniques used to create the preceding slope chart:

- The `Rank(Sum(Sales))` table calculation is computed along (addressed by) **State**. This means that each state is ranked within the partition of a single **Year**.
- **Grid Lines** for **Rows** have been set to `None`.
- The axis has been reversed (right-click on the axis and select **Edit**; then check the option to reverse).
- The label has been edited (by clicking on **Label**) to show on both ends of the line and to center vertically.
- The **Year** column headers have been moved from the bottom of the view to the top (from the top menu, go to **Analysis | Table Layout | Advanced** and uncheck the option to show the innermost level at the bottom).
- A **data highlighter** has been added (using the drop-down on the **State** field in the view, select **Show Highlighter**) to give the end user the ability to highlight one or more states.

Data highlighters are new in Tableau 10 and give the user the ability to highlight marks in a view by selecting values from the drop-down list or by typing (any match on any part of a value will highlight the mark, so for example, typing `ne` would highlight Nevada and New Mexico in the preceding view).

Data highlighters can be shown for any field you use as discrete (blue) in the view and will function across multiple views in a dashboard as long as that same field is used in those views.

Slope charts can use absolute values (for example, the actual values of **Profit**) or relative values (for example, the rank as shown in this example). If you were to show more than two years to observe the change in rankings over multiple periods of time, the resulting visualization might be called a **bump chart**, as follows:

Lollipop chart

Similar to a bar chart, a **lollipop chart** typically uses thinner lines ending in a circle allowing for some stylistic interest, as well as a place to show values or other labels. Here, for example, is a lollipop chart for sales of categories in the **Technology** department:

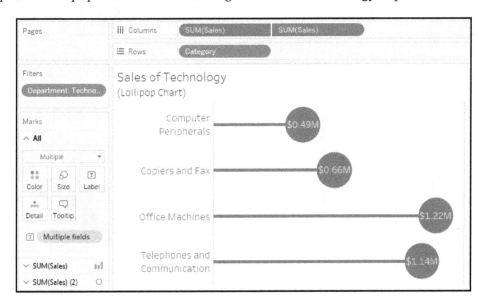

The following features and techniques are used to create this chart:

- A *synchronized* **dual axis** for **SUM(Sales)** with one mark type set to bar and sized to be very thin and the other mark type set to circle and sized to be large enough for a label
- **Sales** added to the label of the circle and formatted using a custom currency
- Axes have been hidden (right-click and uncheck **Show Header**)

Additional variations include flipping of orientation, sorting of values, and using color or highlighting to call out certain values.

Waterfall chart

A **waterfall chart** is useful when you want to show how parts successively build up to a whole. Here, for example is a waterfall chart showing how profit builds up to a grand total across **Departments** and **Categories** of products. Sometimes profit is negative, so the waterfall chart takes a dip, while positive values build up toward the total:

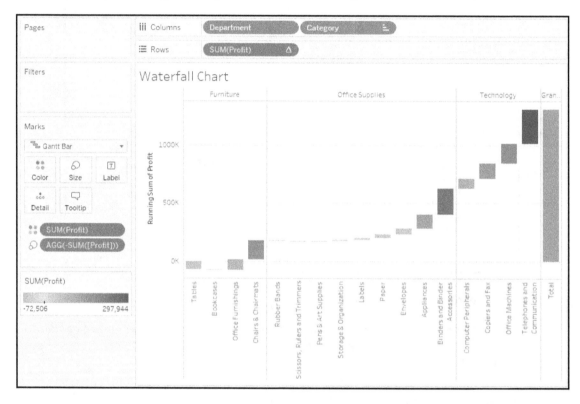

Here are the features and techniques used to build the chart:

- **Row Grand Totals** has been added to the view (dragged and dropped via the **Analytics** pane).
- The **SUM(Profit)** field on **Rows** is a running total table calculation (added using a quick table calculation) and is computed across the table.
- The mark type is set to **Gantt Bar** and an ad-hoc calculation is used with code: – SUM(Profit). This allows the Gantt bars to be drawn back down (or up for negative profit) toward the end of the previous mark.

Sparklines

Sparklines refers to a visualization that uses multiple small line graphs that are designed to be read and compared quickly. The goal of sparklines is to give a visualization that can be understood at a glance. You aren't trying to communicate exact values but rather give the audience the ability to quickly understand trends, movements, and patterns.

Among various uses of this type of visualization, you may have seen sparklines used in financial publications to compare the movement of stock prices. In Chapter 1, *Creating Your First Visualization and Dashboard*, we considered the initial start of a sparklines visualization as we looked at iterations of line charts. Here, is a far more developed example:

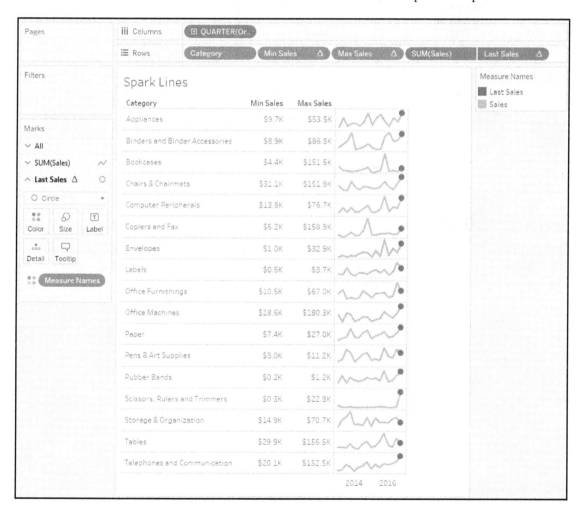

This chart was built using the following features and techniques:

- Start with a simple view of the **Sum(Sales)** by **Quarter** of **Order Date** (as a *date value*) with **Category** on **Rows**.
- Two calculated fields have been created to show the minimum and maximum quarterly sales values for each category. **Min Sales** has the code `WINDOW_MIN(SUM(Sales))` and **Max Sales** has the code `WINDOW_MAX(SUM(Sales))`. Both have been added to **Rows** as *discrete* (blue) fields.
- The **Last Sales** calculation with the code `IF LAST() == 0 THEN SUM([Sales]) END` has been placed on **Rows** and uses a *synchronized* dual axis with a circle mark type to emphasize the final value of sales for each timeline.
- The axis for **SUM(Sales)** has been edited to have **Independent axis ranges for each row or column**. And the axes have been hidden. This allows the line movement to be emphasized. Remember, the goal is not to show the exact values but rather allow your audience to see the patterns and movement.
- **Grid Lines** have been hidden for **Rows**.
- The view has been resized (horizontally compressed and set to **Fit Height**). This allows the sparklines to fit into a small space, facilitating quick understanding of patterns and movement.

Dumbbell chart

A **dumbbell chart** is a variation of the circle plot; it compares two values for each slice of data, emphasizing the distance between the two values. Here for example, is a chart showing the difference in profit between **East** and **West** regions for each category of products:

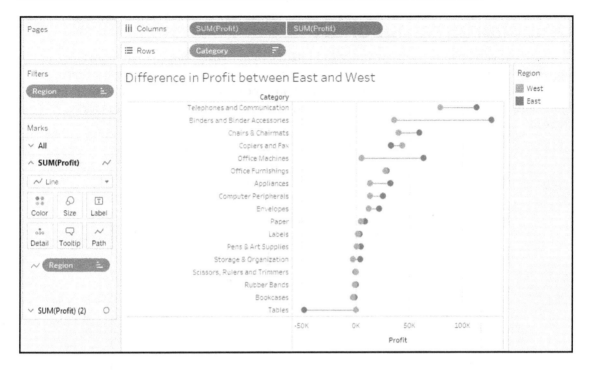

This chart was built using the following features and techniques:

- A *synchronized* dual axis of **SUM(Profit)** has been used, with one set to mark a type of **Circle** and the other set to **Line**.
- **Region** has been placed on the **Path** shelf for the line to tell Tableau to draw a line between the two regions.

> The **Path** shelf is available for **Line** and **Polygon** mark types. When you place a field on the path shelf, it tells Tableau the order to connect the points (following the sort order of the field placed on Path). Paths are often used with geographic visualizations to connect origins and destinations on routes but can also be used with other visualization types.

- **Region** is placed on **Color** for the circle mark type.

Unit chart/symbol chart

A **unit chart** can be used to show individual items, often using shapes or symbols to represent each individual. These charts can elicit a powerful emotional response, because the representations of the data are less abstract and more easily identified as something real. For example, here is a chart showing how many customers had late shipments for each region:

The view was created with the following techniques:

- The view is filtered where **Late Shipping** is true. **Late Shipping** is a calculated field that determines if it took more than 14 days to ship and order. The code is:

```
DATEDIFF('day', [Order Date], [Ship Date]) > 14
```

- **Region** has been sorted in descending order by the distinct count of **Customer ID**.
- **Customer ID** has been placed on **Detail** so that there is a mark for each distinct customer.

- The mark type has been changed to **Shape** and the shape has been changed to the included person shape in the **Gender** shape palette. To change shapes, click on the **Shape** shelf and select the desired shape(s).

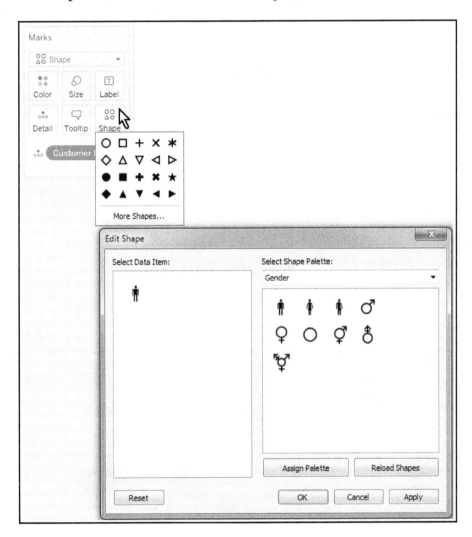

The preceding unit chart might elicit more of a response from regional managers than a standard bar chart when they are gently reminded that poor customer service impacts real people. Granted, the shapes are still abstract, but they more closely represent an actual person. You could make it more realistic by labeling the mark with the customer name or using other techniques to further engage your audience.

Normally, in Tableau, a mark is drawn for each distinct intersection of dimensional values. So, it is rather difficult to draw, for example, 10 individual shapes for a single row of data that simply contains the value 10 for a field. This means that you will need to consider the shape of your data and include enough rows to draw the units you wish to represent.

Concrete shapes, in any type of visualization, can also dramatically reduce the amount of time it takes to comprehend the data. Contrast the amount of effort required to identify the departments in these two scatter plots:

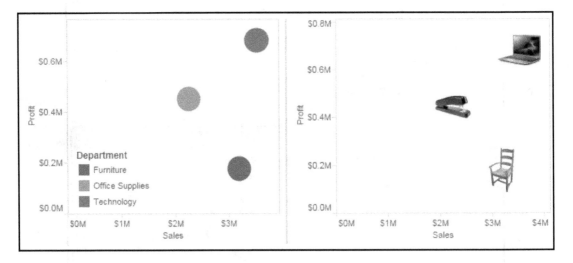

Once you know the meaning of a shape, you no longer have to reference a legend.

Placing a discrete field on the **Shape** shelf allows you to assign shapes to individual values of the field.

Shapes are images located in the `My Tableau Repository\Shapes` directory. You can include your own **custom shapes** in subfolders of that directory.

Marimekko chart

A **Marimekko chart** (sometimes also called a **Mekko chart**) is similar to a stacked bar chart, but additionally uses varying widths of the bars to communicate additional information about the data. Here, a Marimekko chart shows the breakdown of sales by region and department. The width of the bars communicates the total sales for the **Region** while the height of each segment gives you the percentage of sales for the **Department** within the **Region**:

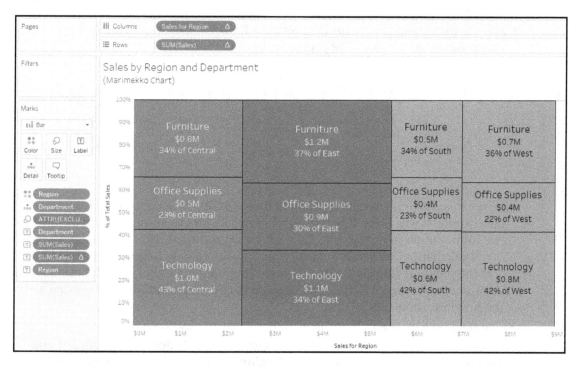

Creating Marimekko charts in Tableau leverages a feature introduced in version 10. Specifically, we leverage the ability to fix the width of bars according to axis units.

Clicking on the **Size** shelf when a continuous (green) field is on **Columns** (thus defining a horizontal axis) and the mark type is set to **Bar** reveals options for a fixed size. You can manually enter **Size** and **Alignment** or drop a field on the **Size** shelf to vary the widths of the bars.

Here are some of the details:

- The mark type has been specifically set to **Bar**.
- **Region** and **Department** have been placed on **Color** and **Detail** respectively. They are the only dimensions in the view, so they define the **view level of detail**.
- **Sales** has been placed on **Rows** and a **Percentage of Total** quick table calculation applied. The **Compute Using** (addressing) has been set to **Department** so that we get the percentage of sales for each department within the partition of the **Region**.
- The calculated field **Sales for Region** calculates the X-axis location for the right-side position of each bar. The code is as follows:

```
IF FIRST() = 0
    THEN MIN({EXCLUDE [Department] : SUM(Sales)})
ELSEIF LOOKUP(MIN([Region]), -1) <> MIN([Region])
    THEN PREVIOUS_VALUE(0) + MIN({EXCLUDE [Department] :
SUM(Sales)})
ELSE
    PREVIOUS_VALUE(0)
END
```

- While this code may seem daunting at first, it is following a logical progression. Specifically, if this is the first bar segment, we'll want to know the sum of sales for the entire region (which is why we exclude **Department** with an inline level of detail calculation). When the calculation moves to a new **Region**, we'll need to add the previous **Region** total to the new **Region** total. Otherwise, the calculation is for another segment in the same **Region**, so the **Regional** total is the same as the previous segment.
- The field on **Size** is an ad-hoc level of detail calculation with the code `{EXCLUDE [Department] : SUM(Sales)}`. As before, this excludes the department and allows us to get the sum of sales at a **Region** level. This means that each bar is sized according to total sales for the given **Region**.
- Clicking on the **Size** shelf gives the option to set the **Alignment** of the bars to **Right**. Since the preceding calculation gave the right position of the bar, we need to make certain the bars are drawn from that starting point.

- Various fields have been copied to the **Label** shelf so that each bar segment more clearly communicates the meaning to the viewer.

> To add labels to each **Region Column**, you might consider creating a second view and placing both on a dashboard. Alternatively, you might use annotations.
>
> For a more comprehensive discussion of Marimekko charts, along with approaches that work with sparse data, see Jonathan Drummey's blog post:
> `https://www.tableau.com/about/blog/2016/8/how-build-marimekko-ch`
> `art-tableau-58153`.

The ability to control the size of bars in axis units in Marimekko charts opens up all kinds of possibilities for creating additional visualizations such as cascade charts or stepped area charts. The techniques would be similar to those used here. Additionally, you can leverage the sizing feature with **continuous bins** (use the drop down menu to change a bin field in the view to continuous from discrete). This allows you to have histograms without large spaces between bars.

Sheet swapping and dynamic dashboards

Sheet swapping, sometimes also called **sheet selection**, is a technique in which views are dynamically shown and hidden on a dashboard, often with the appearance of swapping one view for another. The dynamic hiding and showing of views on a dashboard has an even broader application. When combined with floating objects and layout containers, this technique allows you to create rich and dynamic dashboards.

The basic principles are simple:

- A view *collapses* on a dashboard when at least one field is on **Rows** or **Columns** and filters are hiding or preventing any marks from being rendered
- Titles and captions do not collapse but can be hidden so that the view collapses entirely

Let's consider a view showing profit by department and category with a **Department** quick filter. The dashboard has been formatted (from the menu select **Format | Dashboard**) with a gray shading to help us see the effect:

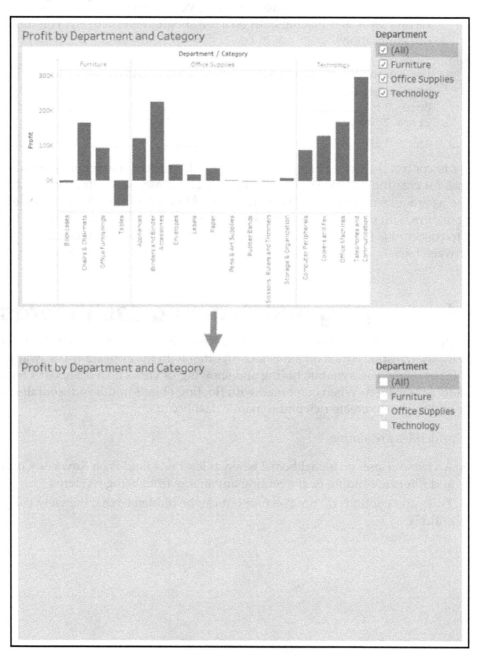

Notice how filtering out all departments results in the view collapsing. The title remains, but it could have been hidden.

In order to *swap* two different sheets, we simply take advantage of the collapsing behavior along with the properties of layout containers. We'll start by creating two different views filtered via a parameter and a calculated field. The parameter will allow us to determine which sheet is shown. Perform the following steps:

1. Create an integer parameter named `Show Sheet` with a **List** of **String** values set to `Bar Chart` and `Map`:

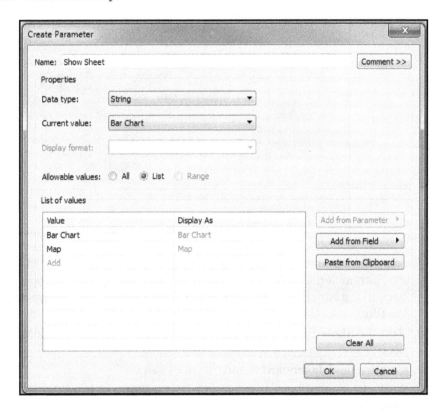

2. Since we want to filter based on the parameter selection and parameters cannot be directly added to the **Filters** shelf; instead we'll create a calculated field named `Show Sheet Filter` to return the selected value of the parameter. The code is simply `[Show Sheet]`, which is the parameter name and returns the current value of the parameter.
3. Create a new sheet named `Bar Chart` similar to the **Profit by Department** and **Category** view shown before.

4. Show the parameter control (right-click the parameter in the data window and select **Show Parameter Control**). Make sure the **Bar Chart** option is selected.

5. Add the **Show Sheet Filter** field to the **Filters** shelf and check **Bar Chart** to keep that value.

6. Create another sheet named Map that shows a filled map of states by **Profit**.

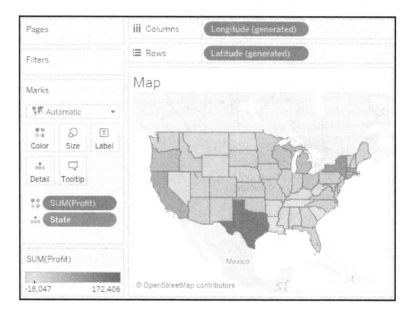

7. Show the parameter on this view and change the selection to **Map**. Remember that parameter selections are universal to the worksheet. If you were to switch back to the bar chart view, it should no longer be showing any data because of the filter.

8. Add the **Show Sheet Filter** field to the **Filters** shelf and check **Map** as the value to keep.

9. Create a new dashboard named Sheet Swap.

10. Add a horizontal layout container to the dashboard from the objects in the left window.

A vertical layout container would work just as well in this case. The key is that a layout container will allow each view inside to expand to fill the container when the view is set to fit entire view, fit width (for horizontal containers), or fit height (for vertical containers). When one view collapses, the visible view will expand to fill the rest of the container.

11. Add each sheet to the layout container in the dashboard. The parameter control should be added automatically since it was visible in each view.

12. Using the drop down menu on the **Bar Chart** view, ensure the view is set to fill the container (navigate to **Fit** | **Entire View**). You won't have to set the fill for the map as map visualizations automatically fill the container.

13. Hide the title for each view (right-click on the title and select **Hide Title**).

You now have a dashboard where changing the parameter results in one view or the other being shown. When **Map** is selected, the filter results in no data for the **Bar Chart**, so it collapses and **Map** fills the container:

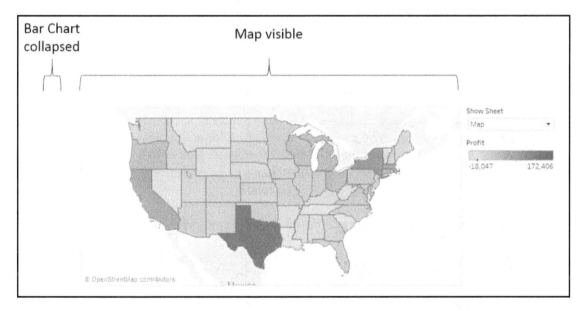

Alternately, when **Bar Chart** is selected, **Map** collapses due to the filter and the bar chart fills the container:

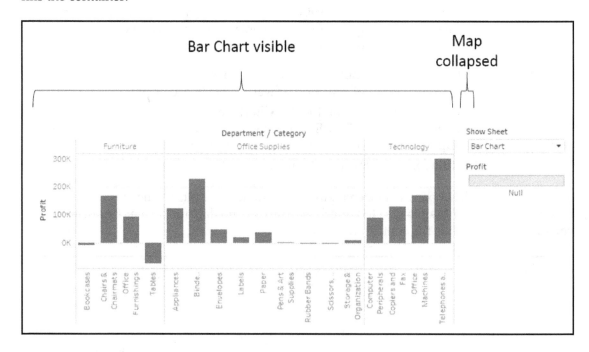

The key to collapsing a view is to have a filter or set of filters that ensures no rows of data. You can use a regular filter or action filter instead of a parameter to control the filtering. This opens up all kinds of possibilities for dynamic behavior in dashboards.

Dynamically showing and hiding other controls

Views will collapse based on filtering out all data. However, other controls such as quick filters, parameters, images, legends, and text boxes will not collapse and don't have an option to dynamically show or hide. Yet many times in a dynamic dashboard you might want to show or hide these objects. Sometimes parameters don't apply when other selections have been made. Look at the simple previous example. The **Color** legend, which was automatically added to the dashboard by Tableau, applies to the map. But when the bar chart is shown, the legend is no longer applicable.

Fortunately, we can extend the technique we used previously to expand a view to push items we want to show out from under a floating object, and then collapse the view to allow the items that we want to hide to return to a position under the floating object.

Let's extend the previous example to show how to show and hide the **Color** legend:

1. Create a new sheet named **Show/Hide Legend**. This view is only used to show and hide the **Color** legend.

2. Create an ad-hoc calculation by double-clicking on **Rows** and type the code MIN(1). We must have a field on **Rows** or **Columns** for the view to collapse, so we'll use this field to give us a single axis for **Rows** and a single axis for **Columns** without any other headers.

3. Duplicate the ad-hoc calculation on **Columns**. You should now have a simple scatter plot with one mark.

4. As this is a helper sheet and not anything we want the user to see, we don't want it to show any marks or lines. Format the view using the menu **Format | Lines** to remove **Grid Lines** from **Rows** and **Columns** along with **Axis Rulers**. Additionally, hide the axes (right-click on each axis or field and uncheck **Show Headers**). Also, set the **Color** to full transparency to hide the mark.

5. We will want this view to show when the **Map** option is selected, so show the parameter control and ensure it is set to **Map**. Then add **Show Sheet Filter** to Filters and check **Map**.

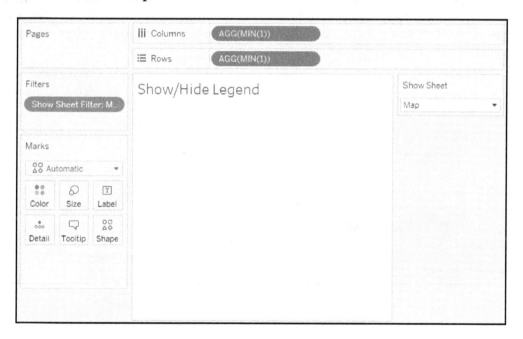

6. On the **Sheet Swap Dashboard**, add the **Show/Hide Legend** sheet to the layout container between the **Show Sheet** parameter dropdown and the **Color** legend. Hide the title for the **Show/Hide Legend** sheet.

7. Ensure that **Map** is selected. The **Color** legend should be pushed all the way to the bottom.

8. Add a **Layout Container** as a floating object. Size and position it to completely cover the area where the **Color** legend used to be. It should cover the title of the **Show/Hide Legend** sheet but not the parameter dropdown.

 Objects and sheets can be added as floating objects by holding the *Shift* key while dragging, setting the **New Objects** option to **Floating**, or using the drop-down menu on the object. You may also change the default behavior for new objects from **Tiled** to **Floating** in the dashboard pane.

9. The **Layout Container** is transparent by default, but we want it to hide what is underneath. Format the layout container using the drop-down menu and add white shading so that it is indistinguishable from the background.

At this point, you have a dynamic dashboard where the legend is shown when **Map** is shown, and it is applicable and hidden when the bar chart is visible. When **Map** is selected, the **Show/Hide Legend** sheet is shown and pushes the legend to the bottom of the layout container.

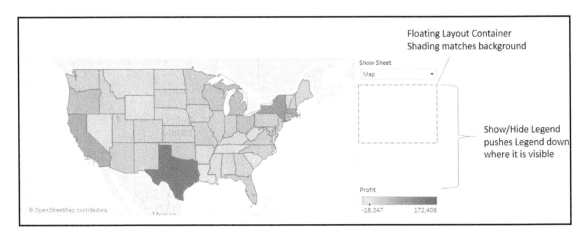

When **Bar Chart** is selected, the **Show/Hide Legend** sheet collapses and the legend, which is no longer applicable to the view, hides behind the floating layout container.

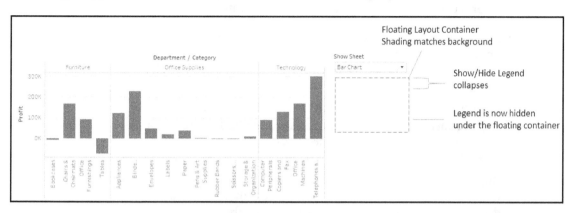

There is no limit to how many variations of this technique you can use on a dashboard. You can have as many layers as you'd like for creating a richly interactive user experience. You can even use combinations of these techniques to push views and objects on and off the dashboard.

Advanced mapping techniques

We've touched on geographic visualization throughout the book. You've seen symbol maps and filled maps. Here we'll take a look at supplying your own geocoded data along with creating custom territories.

Supplementing the standard in geographic data

In Chapter 1, *Creating Your First Visualization and Dashboard* we saw that Tableau generates **Latitude** and **Longitude** fields when the data source contains geographic fields which Tableau can match with its internal geographic database. Fields such as country, state, zip code, MSA, and congressional district are contained in Tableau's internal geography. As Tableau continues to add geographic capabilities, you'll want to consult the documentation to determine some specifics on what the internal database contains.

However, if you have latitude and longitude in your dataset or are able to supplement your data source with that data, you can create geographic visualizations with great precision. There are several options for supplying latitude and longitude for use in Tableau:

- Include latitude and longitude as fields in your data source. If possible, this option will provide the easiest approach to creating custom geographic visualizations because you can simply place **Latitude** on **Rows**, **Longitude** on **Columns** to get a geographic plot.
- Create a calculated field for latitude and another for longitude using `If...then` logic or case statements to assign latitude and longitude values based on other values in your data. This would also be tedious and difficult to maintain with many locations.
- Import a custom geographic file. From the menu, navigate to **Map | Geocoding | Import Custom Geocoding....** The import dialog contains a link to documentation describing the option in further detail.
- Connect to the data containing your latitudes and longitudes as a secondary data source and use cross database joins or data blending to achieve geographic visualization. For example, here is a visualization that has been created by joining in a file containing exact latitudes and longitudes for each address:

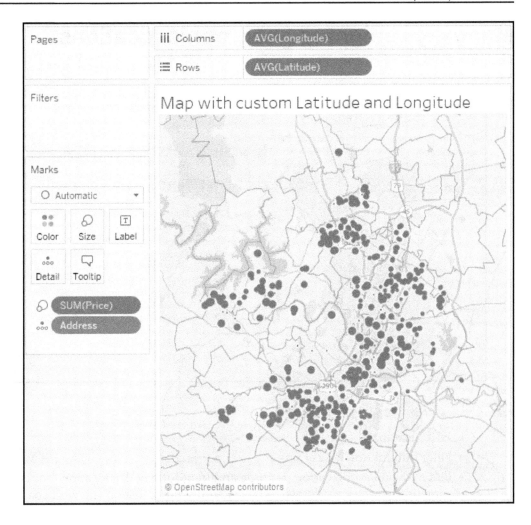

- Assign a field to a geographic role and assign unrecognized values to desired latitude and longitude locations. This option is most often used to correct unrecognized locations in standard geographic fields, such as city or zip code, but it can be used to create custom geographies as well-though this would be tedious and difficult to maintain with more than a few locations. You can assign unknown geographic locations as indicated in the following section.

Manually assigning geographic locations

Assign unknown locations by clicking on the **unknown** indicator in the lower right of a geographic visualization, as shown here:

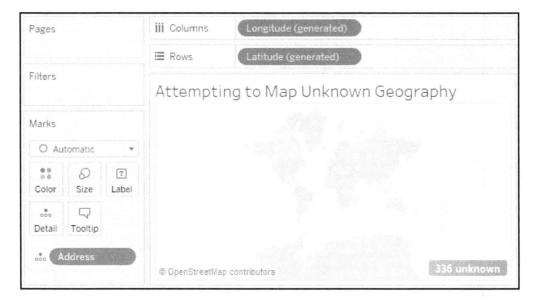

This will give you the following options:

- **Edit Locations**
- Filter out unknown locations
- Plot at the default location (latitude and longitude of 0, a location that is sometimes humorously referred to as **Null Island**, just off the west coast of Africa)

The indicator in the preceding screenshot shows **336 unknown** locations. Clicking the indicator and selecting **Edit Locations** option allows you to correct unmatched locations by selecting a known location or entering your own latitude and longitude information, as shown here:

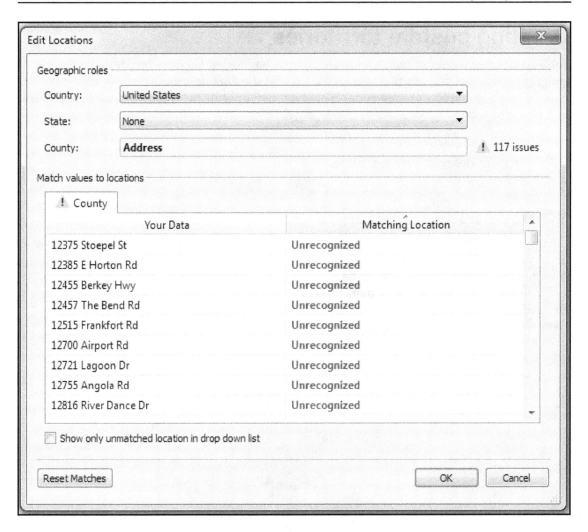

The first three options allow you to specify the geographic context by which Tableau determines the location of a field value. You may specify a **Country**, **State**, and/or **County**.

For example, Tableau may not recognize the city Mansfield until you specify the state (in the United States alone, there is a Mansfield, Texas; Mansfield, Ohio; Mansfield, Kansas; and about a dozen more!) In this example, you may specifically select a constant **State** or let Tableau know which field in the dataset defines state.

You may also set individual locations by clicking the **Unrecognized** label in the table and matching to a known location or by entering a specific latitude and longitude.

Creating custom territories

Tableau 10 introduces the ability to create custom territories. **Custom territories** are geographic areas or regions that you create (or that the data defines) as opposed to those built-in (such as country or area code). There are two options for creating custom territories in one of two ways:

- Ad-hoc custom territories
- Field-defined custom territories

Ad-hoc custom territories

Custom territories in an ad hoc way can be created by selecting and grouping marks on a map. Simply select one or more marks, hover over one, and then use the **Group** icon. Alternatively, right-click on one of the marks to find the option. You can create custom territories by grouping by any dimension if you have latitude and longitude in the data or any geographic dimension if you are using Tableau's generated latitude and longitude. Here we'll consider an example using **Zip Code**:

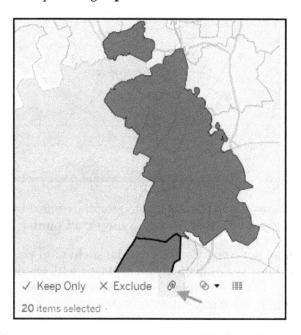

You'll notice that Tableau creates a new field, **Zip Code (group)** in this example. The new field has a paperclip and globe icon in the data pane, indicating that it is a group and a geographic field. Tableau automatically includes the group field on color.

You may continue to select and group marks until you have all the custom territories you'd like. With **Zip Code** still part of the view level of detail, you will have a mark for each zip code (and any measure will be sliced by zip code). However, when you remove **Zip Code** from the view, leaving only the **Zip Code (group)** field, Tableau will draw the marks based on the new group:

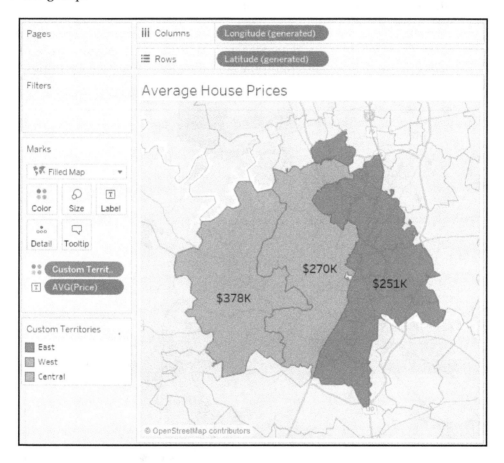

Here, the group field has been renamed to **Custom Territories** and the group names have been aliased as **East**, **West**, and **Central**.

With a filled map, Tableau will connect all contiguous areas and still include disconnected areas as part of selections and highlighting. With a symbol map, Tableau will draw the mark in the geographic center of all grouped areas.

Field-defined custom territories

Sometimes your data includes the definition of custom territories. For example, let's say your data had a field named **Region** that already grouped zip codes into various regions. That is, every zip code was contained in only one region. You might not want to take the time to select the marks and group them manually.

Instead, you can tell Tableau the relationship already exists in the data. Let's use the drop-down menu of the **Region** field in the data pane and navigate to **Geographic Role | Create From... | Zip Code. Region** is now a geographic field that defines custom territories as shown here:

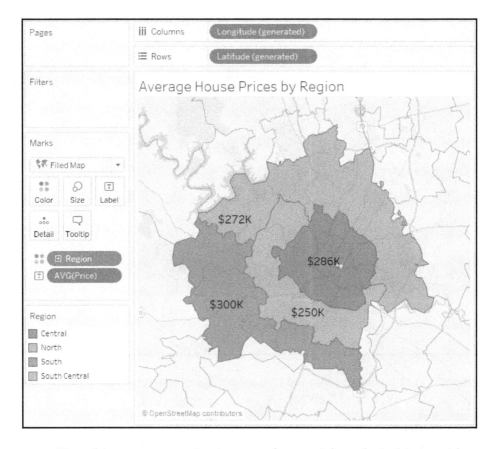

Use ad-hoc custom territories to perform quick analysis, but consider field-defined custom territories for long-term solutions because you can then redefine the territories in the data without manually editing any groups in the Tableau data source.

Some final map tips

Here are some final tips to keep in mind when creating geographic visualizations: various controls will appear when you hover over the map allowing you to search the map, zoom in and out, pin the map to the current location, and use various types of selections, as follows:

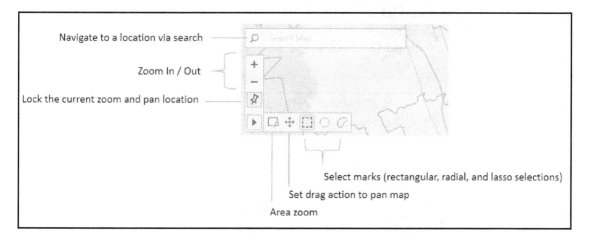

Additional options will appear when you go to **Map** | **Map Options** from the top menu:

These options give you the ability to set what map actions are allowed for the end user. Additionally, you can set the units displayed for **radial selections**. Options are **Automatic** (based on system configuration), **Metric** (meters and kilometers), and **US** (feet and miles).

There are a few other tips to consider when working with geographic visualizations:

- Use the top menu to go to **Map** | **Map Layers** for numerous options for what layers of background to show as part of the map.
- Other options for zooming include using the mouse wheel, double-clicking, *Shift + Alt + click*, and *Shift + Alt +*Ctrl+ click.
- You can click and hold for a few seconds to switch to pan mode.

- You can show or hide the zoom controls and/or map search by right-clicking the map and selecting the appropriate option.
- Zoom controls can be shown on any visualization type that uses an axis.
- The pushpin on the zoom controls alternately returns the map to the best fit of visible data or locks the current zoom and location.
- You can create a dual axis map by duplicating *(Ctrl +* drag/drop) either the **Latitude** on **Columns** or **Longitude** on **Rows** and then using the field's drop-down menu to select **Dual Axis**. You can use this technique to combine multiple mark types on a single map:

- When using filled maps, setting **Washout** to 100% in the **Map Layers** window can result in very clean-looking maps. However, only filled shapes will show, so any missing states (or counties, countries, and so on) will not be drawn.

- You can change the source of the background map image tiles using the menu and selecting **Map** | **Background Maps**. This allows you to choose between **None**, **Offline** (which is useful when you don't have an internet connection, but is limited in the detail that can be shown), or **Tableau** (the default).
- Additionally, from the same menu option, you can specify **Map Services...** to use a **WMS server** or **Mapbox**.

Using background images

Background images allow you to plot data on top of any image. You canplot ticket sales by seat on an image of a stadium, room use on the floor plan of an office building, the number of errors by piece of equipment on a network diagram, or meteor impacts on the surface of the moon. The possibilities are endless.

Let's plot the number of patients per month in various rooms in a hospital. We'll use two images of floor plans for the ground floor and second floor of the hospital. The data source is located in the Chapter 10 directory and is named Hospital.xlsx. It consists of two tabs: one for patient counts and another for room locations based on the x/y coordinates mapped to the images. We'll shortly look at how this works. You can view the completed example in the Chapter 10 Complete.twbx workbook or start from scratch using Chapter 10 Starter.twbx.

To specify a background image, use the top menu to navigate to **Map Background Images** and then click the data source for which the image applies (in this example, Hospitals). On the **Add Background Images** screen you can add one or more images.

Here, we'll start with `Hospital - Ground Floor.png`, located in the `Chapter 10` directory:

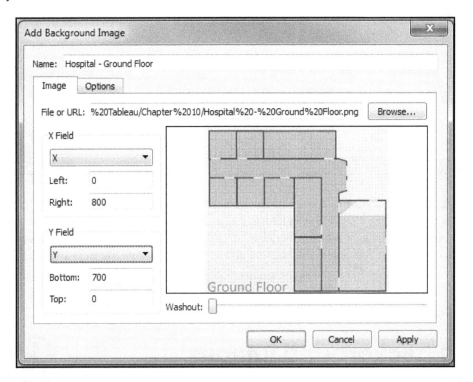

You'll notice that we mapped the fields **X** and **Y** (from the **Locations** tab) and specified the **Right** at **800** and **Bottom** at **700**. This is based on the size of the image in pixels.

You don't have to use pixels, but most of the time it makes it far easier to map the locations for the data. In this case, we have a tab of an Excel file with the locations already mapped to the X and Y coordinates on the image (in pixels). Tableau 10 offer, cross-database joins, where you can create a simple text or Excel file containing mappings for your images and join them to an existing data source. You can map points manually (using a graphics application) or use one of many free online tools that allow you to quickly map coordinates on images.

We'll only want to show this blueprint for the ground floor, so switching to the **Options** tab, we'll ensure that the condition is set based on the data. We'll also make sure to check **Always Show Entire Image**:

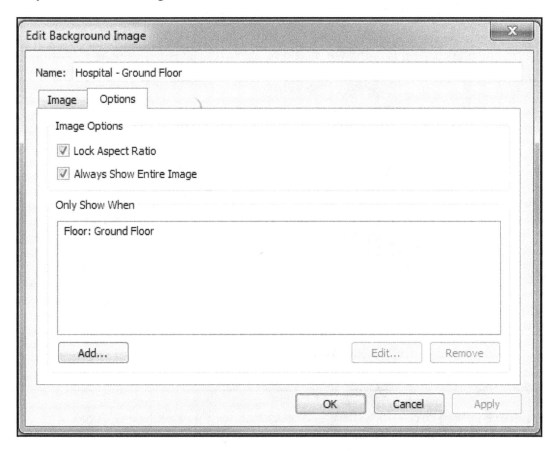

Next, repeating the previous steps we'll add the second image (Hospital - 2nd Floor.png) to the data source, ensuring it only shows for the 2nd Floor.

Once we have the images defined and mapped, we're ready to build a visualization. The basic idea is to build a scatterplot using the **X** and **Y** fields for axes. But we'll have to ensure that X and Y are not summed because if they are added together for multiple records, we'll no longer have a correct mapping to pixel locations. There are a couple of options:

- Use X and Y as continuous dimensions
- Use MIN, MAX, or AVG instead of SUM; and insure that **Location** is used to define the view level of detail.

Additionally, images are measured from 0 at the top to Y at the bottom, but scatter plots start with 0 at the bottom and values increase up. So, initially, you may see your background images appear upside down. To get around this, we'll edit the Y axis (right-click and select **Edit Axis**) and check the option for **Reversed**.

We also need to ensure that the **Floor** field is used in the view to tell Tableau which image should be displayed. At this point, we should be able to get a visualization as follows:

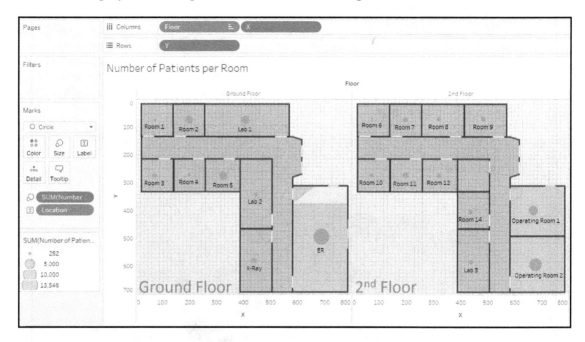

Here, we've plotted circles with size based on the number of patients in each room. We could clean up and modify the visualization in various ways:

- Hide the X and Y axes (right-click on the axis and uncheck **Show Header**)
- Hide the header for **Floor** as the image already includes the label
- Add **Floor** to the **Filter** shelf so that the end user can choose to see one floor at a time

Animation

Animated visualizations can bring data storytelling to life by revealing patterns that happen over time or emphasize dramatic events. Adding a field to the **Pages** shelf will show playback controls that allow you to *page* through each value of that field. You can do this manually, or click the play button to watch the visualization as values change automatically.

The `Chapter 10 Completed` workbook contains an example that animates the hospital floorplan shown above. You can create the same effect by adding the **Month** field to the **Pages** shelf (as a **Month date value**). Then watch as the circles change size month by month.

Experiment with the **Show History** options to see how you can view marks for previous pages.

 When you use multiple views on a dashboard, each having the same combination of fields on the **Pages** shelf, you can synchronize the playback controls (using the caret drop-down menu on the playback controls) to create a fully animated dashboard.

Animations can be shared with other users of Tableau Desktop or Tableau Reader as well. As of this writing, automatic playback controls are not available for Tableau Server, Tableau Online, or Tableau Public. However, end users can manually page through the values.

Summary

We've covered a wide variety of techniques in this chapter! We looked at advanced visualizations, sheet swapping, dynamic dashboards, some advanced mapping techniques including supplementing geographic data, custom territories, using custom background images, and animating visualizations.

There is no way to cover every possible visualization type, technique, and way of solving problems. Instead, the idea was to demonstrate some of what can be accomplished using a few advanced techniques. The examples in this chapter build on the foundations laid in the preceding chapters. From here, you will be able to creatively modify and combine techniques in new and innovative ways to solve problems and achieve incredible results! Next, we'll turn our focus on how to share those results.

10
Sharing Your Data Story

Throughout this book, we've focused on Tableau Desktop and how to visually explore and communicate data with visualizations and dashboards. Once you've made discoveries, designed insightful visualizations, and built stunning dashboards, you're ready to share your data stories.

Tableau enables you to share your work using a variety of methods. In this chapter, we'll take a look at the various ways to share visualizations and dashboards along with what to consider when deciding how you will share.

Specifically, we'll take a look at:

- Presenting, printing, and exporting
- Sharing with users of Tableau Desktop and Tableau Reader
- Sharing with users of Tableau Server, Tableau Online, and Tableau Public
- Additional distribution options with Tableau Server

Presenting, printing, and exporting

Tableau is primarily designed to build richly interactive visualizations and dashboards for consumption on a screen. However, there are good options for presenting, printing, and exporting in a variety of formats.

Presenting

Tableau Desktop and Reader features a **Presentation Mode**, which removes all authoring controls and displays only the view and navigation tabs without any toolbars, panes, or authoring objects. This mode is available in the **Window** menu or by pressing *F7* or using the option on the toolbar. Press *F7* or *Esc* to exit **Presentation Mode**.

When used with effective dashboards and stories, the **Presentation Mode** makes for an effective way to personally walk your audience through the data story.

If you save a workbook by pressing *Ctrl*+*S* while in presentation mode, the workbook will be opened in presentation mode by default.

Printing

Tableau enables printing for individual visualizations, dashboards, and stories. From the **File** menu, you can select **Print** to print the currently active sheet in the workbook to the printer, or the **Print to PDF** option to export as a PDF. Either option allows you to export the active sheet, selected sheets, or the entire workbook as a PDF. To select multiple sheets, hold the Ctrl key and click on individual tabs.

When printing, you also have the option to **Show Selections**. When this option is checked, marks that have been interactively selected or highlighted on a view or dashboard will be printed as selected. Otherwise, marks will print as though no selections have been made. The map in the following dashboard has marks for the western half of the United States selected:

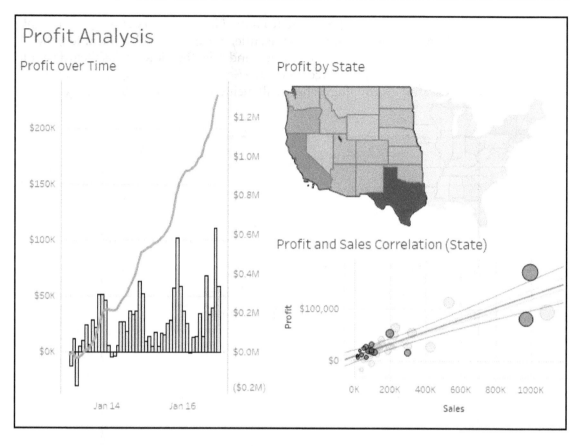

Here are some considerations, tips, and suggestions for printing:

- If a dashboard is being designed for print, select a predefined paper size as the fixed size for the dashboard or use a custom size that matches the same aspect ratio.

- Use the **Page Setup** screen (available from the **File** menu) to define specific print options, such as what elements (legends, title, or caption) will be included, the layout (including margins and centering), and how the view or dashboard should be scaled to match the paper size. The **Page Setup** options are specific to each view. Duplicating or copying a sheet will include any changes to the page setup settings:

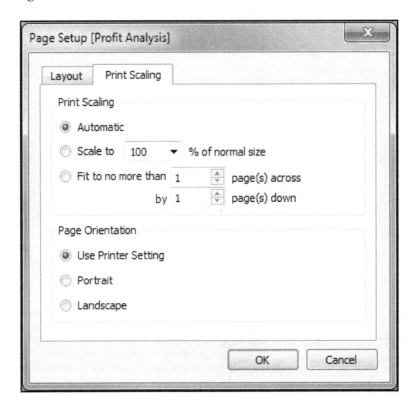

If you are designing multiple sheets or dashboards for print, consider creating one as a template, set up all the desired print settings, and then duplicate them for each new sheet.

- Fields used on the **Pages** shelf will define page breaks in printing (for individual sheets, but not dashboards or stories). The number of *pages* defined by the **Pages** shelf is not necessarily equal to the number of printed pages. This is because a single *page* defined by the **Pages** shelf might require more than one printed page.

- Each story point in a **Story** will be printed on a new page.
- Printing the entire workbook can be an effective way to generate a single PDF document for distribution. Each visible sheet will be included in the PDF in the order of the tabs, left to right. You may hide sheets to prevent inclusion in the PDF or reorder sheets to adjust the order of the resulting document. Also consider creating dashboards with images and text for title pages, tables of contents, page numbers, and commentary.
- Avoid scrollbars in dashboards as they will print as scrollbars and anything outside the visible window will not be printed.
- You can also select multiple sheets in the workbook (hold the Ctrl key while clicking on each tab) and then print only selected sheets.

Sheets may be hidden if they are views that are used in one or more dashboards or if they are dashboards used in one or more stories. To hide a view, right-click on the tab or thumbnail on the bottom strip or in the left pane of the dashboard or story workspace, and select **Hide Sheet**. To show a sheet, locate it in the left pane of the dashboard or story workspace, right-click on it, and uncheck **Hide Sheet**. You can also right-click on a dashboard or story tab and hide or show all sheets used.

If you don't see a **Hide Sheet** option, it means this sheet is not used in any dashboard and can then only be deleted.

Exporting

Tableau also makes it easy to export images of views, dashboards, and stories for use in documents, PowerPoint, and even books like this one! Images may be exported as .png, .emf, .jpg, or .bmp. You can also copy an image to the clipboard to paste into other applications. To export or copy an image, use the menu options for **Worksheet**, **Dashboard**, or **Story**.

Let's consider some of the exporting features available on Tableau Server, Tableau Online, and Tableau Public. When interacting with a view on these platforms, you will see a toolbar unless you don't have the required permissions or the toolbar has been specifically disabled by a Tableau Server administrator:

The **Download** dropdown on the toolbar allows you to download **Image**, **Data**, **Cross tab** (Excel), **PDF**, or **Tableau workbook**. Images are exported in .png format and render the dashboard in its current state. Exporting a PDF document will give the user many options, including layout, scaling, and whether to print the current dashboard, all sheets in the workbook, or all sheets in the current dashboard.

Exporting data or a crosstab will export for the *active* view in the dashboard. That is, if you click on a view in the dashboard, it becomes *active* and you can export the data or crosstab for that particular view.

Sharing with users

Let's see how to share workbooks with Tableau Desktop and Tableau Reader.

Sharing with Tableau Desktop users

Sharing a workbook with other Tableau Desktop users is fairly straightforward, but there are a few things to consider.

One of the major considerations is whether you will be sharing a packaged workbook (.twbx) or an unpackaged workbook (.twb). Packaged workbooks are single files that contain the workbook (.twb), extracts (.tde), file-based data sources that have not been extracted (.xls, .xlsx, .txt, .cub, .mdb, and so on), custom images, and various other related files.

To share with users of **Tableau Desktop**, do this:

- You may share either a packaged (.twbx) or unpackaged (.twb) workbook by simply sharing the file with another user who has the same or newer version of Tableau Desktop.

Workbook files will be updated when saved in a newer version of Tableau Desktop. You cannot open a workbook saved with a newer version of Tableau in an older version. You will be prompted about updates when you first open the workbook and again when you attempt to save it.

- If you share an unpackaged (.twb) workbook, then anyone else using it must be able to access any data sources and any referenced images must be visible to the user in the *same* directory where the original files were referenced. For example, if the workbook uses a live connection to an Excel (.xlsx) file on a network path and includes images on a dashboard located in C:\Images, then all users must be able to access the Excel file on the network path and have a local C:\Images directory with image files of the same name.

Consider using a UNC (for example, \\servername\directory\file.xlsx) path for common files if you use this approach.

Similarly, if you share a packaged workbook (.twbx) that uses live connections, anyone using the workbook must be able to access the live connection data source and have appropriate permissions.

Sharing with Tableau Reader users

Tableau Reader is a free product provided by Tableau Software that allows users to interact with visualizations, dashboards, and stories created in Tableau Desktop. All interactivity such as filtering, drill-down, actions, and highlighting is available to the end user. However, unlike Tableau Desktop, it does not allow authoring of visualizations or dashboards.

Tableau Reader is similar to many PDF readers that allow you to read and navigate the document, but do not allow for authoring or saving of changes.

To share with users of Tableau Reader, consider the following:

- Reader will only open packaged (.twbx) workbooks.
- The packaged workbook may not contain live connections to server or cloud-based data sources. Those connections must be extracted.

Be certain to take into consideration security concerns when sharing packaged workbooks (.twbx). Since packaged workbooks most often contain data, you must be certain that the data is not sensitive. Even if the data is not shown on any view or dashboard, it is still accessible in the packaged extract (.tde) or file-based data source.

Sharing with users of Tableau Server, Tableau Online, and Tableau Public

Tableau Server, **Tableau Online**, and **Tableau Public** are all variations of the same concept: hosting visualizations and dashboards on a server and allowing users to access them via a web browser.

The following table provides some of the similarities and differences between the products, but as details may change, please consult a Tableau representative prior to making any purchasing decisions:

Product	Tableau Server	Tableau Online	Tableau Public
Description	A server application installed on one or more server machines that hosts views and dashboards created with Tableau Desktop.	A cloud-based service maintained by Tableau Software that hosts views and dashboards created with Tableau Desktop.	A cloud-based service maintained by Tableau Software that hosts views and dashboards created with Tableau Desktop or the free Tableau Public client.

Licensing	Named user (set number of users) or core (unlimited users on a set number of cores).	Named user.	Free.
Administration	Fully maintained, managed, and administered by the individual or organization that purchased the license.	Managed and maintained by Tableau Software, with some options for project and user management by users.	Managed and maintained by Tableau Software.
Authoring and publishing	Users of Tableau Desktop may author and publish workbooks to Tableau Server. Web authoring gives Tableau Server users the capability to edit and create visualizations and dashboards in a web browser.	Users of Tableau Desktop may author and publish workbooks to Tableau Online. Web authoring allows Tableau Online users to edit and create visualizations and dashboards in a web browser.	Users of Tableau Desktop or the free Tableau Public client can publish workbooks to Tableau Public.
Interaction	Licensed Tableau Server users, even those without Tableau Desktop, may interact with hosted views. Views may also be embedded in intranet sites, SharePoint, and custom portals.	Licensed Tableau Online users, even those without Tableau Desktop, may interact with hosted views. Views may also be embedded in intranet sites, SharePoint, and custom portals.	Everything is public-facing. Anyone may interact with hosted views. Views may be embedded in public websites and blogs.

Limitations	None.	Most data sources must be extracted before workbooks can be published. Most non-cloud-based data sources must have extracts refreshed using Tableau Desktop on a local machine or via the Tableau Online Sync Client.	All data must be extracted and each data source is limited to 10 million rows.
Security	The Tableau Server administrator may create sites, projects, and users and adjust permissions for each. Access to the underlying data and downloading of the workbook or data can be restricted.	The Tableau Server administrator may create projects and users and adjust permissions for each. Access to the underlying data and downloading of the workbook or data can be restricted.	By default, anyone may download and view data, but access to these options may be restricted by the author.
Good uses	Internal dashboards and analytics, and/or use across departments/ divisions/clients via multi-tenant sites.	Internal dashboards and analytics. Sharing and collaboration with remote users.	Sharing visualizations and dashboards using embedded views on public-facing websites or blogs.

Publishing to Tableau Public

You may open and save workbooks to Tableau Public using either Tableau Desktop or the free Tableau Public client application. However, you need to consider the following points:

- In order to use Tableau Public, you will need to register an account
- With Tableau Desktop and the proper permissions, you may save and open workbooks to and from Tableau Public using the **Server** menu and selecting options under **Tableau Public**
- With the free Tableau Public client, you may only save workbooks to and from the Web and anyone in the world can view what you publish

- Selecting the option to **Manage Workbooks** will open a browser so that you can login to your Tableau Public account and manage all your workbooks online
- Workbooks saved to Tableau Public may contain any number of data source connections, but they must all be extracted and must not contain more than 10 million rows of extracted data each

Publishing to Tableau Server and Tableau Online

Publishing to Tableau Server and Tableau Online is a similar experience. To publish to Tableau Server or Tableau Online, from the menu,navigate to**Server**|**Publish Workbook**. If you are not signed into a server, you will be prompted to sign in:

You must have a user account with publish permissions for one or more projects. Enter the URL or IP address of the Tableau server or the Tableau online URL, your username, and password. Once signed in, you will be prompted to select a site, if you have access to more than one. Finally, you will see the publish screen:

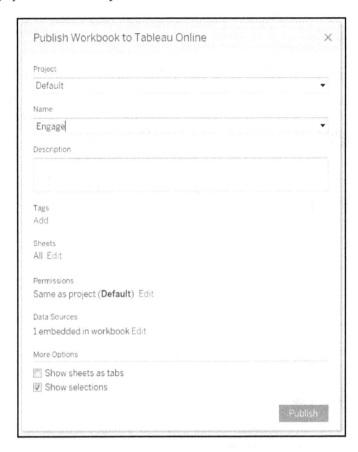

Here you will be able to select the**Project** to which you wish to publish and **Name** your workbook. If a workbook has already been published with the same name to the selected project, you will be prompted to overwrite it. You may give the workbook a **Description** and use **Add Tags** to make searching for and finding your workbook easier.

You may also specify which **Sheets** to include in the published workbook. Any sheets you check will be included; any you uncheck will not.

You may**Edit** user and group **Permissions**to define who has permissions to view, interact with and alter your workbook. By default, the project settings are used.

You also have the option to **Show Sheets as Tabs**. When checked, users on Tableau Server will be able to navigate between sheets using tabs similar to those shown at the bottom of Tableau Desktop. This option must be checked if you plan to have actions that navigate between views. **Show Selections** indicates that you wish any active selections of marks to be retained in the published views.

Editing **Data Sources** gives you options for authentication and scheduling:

- For each data connection used in the workbook, you may determine how database connections are authenticated. The options will depend on the data source as well the configuration of Tableau Server. Various options include embedding a password, impersonating a user, or prompting a Tableau Server user for credentials.
- You may specify a schedule for Tableau Server to run refreshes of any data extracts.

Any live connections or extracted connections that will be refreshed on the server must define connections that work from the server. This means that all applicable database drivers must be installed on the server; all network, Internet connections, and ports required for accessing database servers and cloud-based data must be open.

Additionally, any external files referenced by a workbook (for example, image files and non-extracted file-based data sources) that were not included when the workbook was published must be referenced using a location that is accessible by Tableau Server (for example, a network path with security settings allowing the Tableau Server process read access).

Interacting with Tableau Server

After a workbook is published to Tableau Server, other users will be able to view and interact with the visualizations and dashboards using a web browser. Once logged into Tableau Server, they will be able to browse content for which they have appropriate permissions. These users will be able to use any features built into the dashboards such as quick filters, parameters, actions, or drill-downs. Everything is rendered as HTML 5, so the only requirement for the user to view and interact with views and dashboards is a modern web browser.

The **Tableau Mobile** app, available for iOS and Android devices, can enhance the experience for mobile users as can effective use of Tableau 10's device designer.

For the most part, interacting with a workbook on Server or Online is very similar to interacting with a workbook in Tableau Desktop or Reader. Quick filters, parameters, actions, and tooltips all look and behave similarly.

You will find some additional features:

- The top menu gives you various options related to managing and navigating Tableau Server
- Below that, you'll find a breadcrumb trail informing you which workbook and view you are currently viewing
- Beneath that, you'll find a toolbar that includes several features. It is shown in the following screenshot:

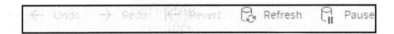

  - **Undo** and **Redo** give you the ability to step back and forward through interactions.
  - **Revert** gives you the ability to undo all changes and revert to the original dashboard.
  - **Refresh** reloads the dashboard with a refresh of the data. However, this does not refresh any extracts of the data.
  - **Pause** allows you to pause refreshing of the dashboard based on actions, filter selections, or parameter value changes until you have made all the changes you wish.
- Additional options are included to the right:

- **Original View** allows you to save the current state of the dashboard based on selections, filters, and parameter values so that you can quickly return to it at a later point. You can also find your saved views here.
- **Subscribe** allows you to schedule periodic e-mails of a screenshot of the dashboard. Tableau 10 also allows administrators to subscribe other users.
- **Edit** allows you to edit the dashboard. The interface is very similar to Tableau Desktop. Tableau 10 allows for editing individual views as well as dashboards. The Tableau Administrator can enable or disable web editing per user or group and also control permissions for saving of edited views.
- **Share** gives you options for sharing the workbook. These options include a URL you can distribute to other licensed users as well as code for embedding the dashboard in a webpage.
- The **Download** button allows you to download the data, images of the dashboard, PDF, or the workbook as described previously.

Additional distribution options using Tableau Server

Tableau Server allows for several other options for sharing your views, dashboards, and data. Along with allowing users to sign in to Tableau Server, you might consider the following options:

- Dashboards, views, and story points can be embedded in websites, portals, and SharePoint. Single sign on options exists to allow your website authentication to integrate seamlessly with Tableau Server.
- Tableau Server allows users to subscribe to views and dashboards and schedule email delivery. The email will contain an up-to-date image of the view and link to the dashboard on Tableau Server.
- The **TABCMD** utility is provided with Tableau Server and may be installed on other machines. The utility provides the ability to automate many functions of Tableau Server including export features, publishing, and user and security management. This opens up quite a few possibilities for automating delivery.
- The **REST API** allows for programmatic interaction with Tableau Server.

Summary

Tableau is an amazing platform for building useful and meaningful visualizations and dashboards based on your data. We've considered how to connect to the data, write calculated fields, and design dashboards. In this chapter, we considered how to share the results with others.

You now have a solid foundation. At its core, Tableau is intuitive, transparent, and easy to use. As you discover new ways to understand your data, solve complex problems, ask new questions, and find new answers in your data, your new Tableau skills will help you uncover new insights hidden in your data.

Index